MULTICULTURAL EDUCATION SERIES

James A. Banks, Series Editor

D1416769

Transforming the Multicultural Education of Teachers

THEORY, RESEARCH, AND PRACTICE

Michael Vavrus

Foreword by
Mary Dilworth

Teachers College
Columbia University
New York and London

Published by Teachers College Press, 1234 Amsterdam Avenue, New York, NY 10027

Author's note: The author wishes to thank the publishers below for their permission to adapt the following material:

The Evergreen State College (2000). *Student Teaching Handbook* (pp. 28, 33, 45). Olympia, WA: Author. Reprinted/adapted with permission.

J. E. Helms and D. A. Cook, *Using Race and Culture in Counseling and Psychotherapy: Theory and Process* (pp. 87–88, 90–91). Copyright © 1999 by Allyn and Bacon. Reprinted/adapted with permission.

Vavrus, M., Walton, S., Kido, J., Diffendal, E., & King, P. (1999). *Journal of Teacher Education* (vol. 50, no. 2) pp. 119–130, copyright © 1999 by American Association of Colleges for Teacher Education. Reprinted/adapted by permission of Corwin Press, Inc.

Library of Congress Cataloging-in-Publication Data

Vavrus, Michael J.
    Transforming the multicultural education of teachers : theory, research, and practice/ Michael Vavrus ; foreword by Mary Dilworth.
    p. cm. — (Multicultural education series)
    Includes bibliographical references and index.
    ISBN 0-8077-4260-0 (pbk. : alk. paper)—ISBN 0-8077-4261-9 (cloth : alk. paper)
        1. Teachers—In-service training—United States.   2. Multicultural education—United States.   I. Title.   II. Multicultural education series (New York, N.Y.)

LB1731.V38 2002
370'.71'5—dc21   2002067316

ISBN 0-8077-4260-0 (paper)
ISBN 0-8077-4261-9 (cloth)

Contents

Series Foreword

The nation's deepening ethnic texture, interracial tension and conflict, and the increasing percentage of students who speak a first language other than English make multicultural education imperative in the 21st century. The U.S. Census Bureau estimated that people of color made up 28% of the nation's population in 2000 (U.S. Census Bureau, 1998). The census predicted that their numbers would grow to 38% of the nation's population in 2025 and 47% in 2050.

American classrooms are experiencing the largest influx of immigrant students since the beginning of the 20th century. About a million immigrants are making the United States their home each year (Martin & Midgley, 1999). More than 7.5 million legal immigrants settled in the United States between 1991 and 1998, most emigrating from nations in Latin America and Asia (Riche, 2000). A large but undetermined number of undocumented immigrants also enter the United States each year. The influence of an increasingly ethnically diverse population on the nation's schools, colleges, and universities is and will continue to be enormous.

In 1998, 34.9% of the students enrolled in U.S. public schools were students of color; this percentage is increasing each year, primarily because of the growth in the percentage of Latino students (Martinez & Curry, 1999). In some of the nation's largest cities and metropolitan areas, such as Chicago, Los Angeles, Washington, D.C., New York, Seattle, and San Francisco, half or more of the public school students are students of color. During the 1998–1999 school year, students of color made up 63.1% of the student population in the public schools of California, the nation's most populous state (California State Department of Education, 2000).

Language diversity is also increasing among the nation's student population. In 1990, sixteen percent of school-age youth lived in homes in which English was not the first language (U.S. Census Bureau, 1998). Most teachers now in the classroom and in teacher education programs are likely to have students from diverse ethnic, racial, and language groups in their classrooms during their careers. This is true for both inner-city and suburban teachers.

An important goal of multicultural education is to improve race relations and to help all students acquire the knowledge, attitudes, and skills needed to participate in cross-cultural interactions and in personal, social, and civic action that will help make our nation more democratic and just. Multicultural education is consequently as important for middle-class White suburban students as it is for students of color who live in the inner-city. Multicultural education fosters the public good and the overarching goals of the commonwealth.

The major purpose of the Multicultural Education Series is to provide pre-service educators, practicing educators, graduate students, scholars, and policy-makers with an interrelated and comprehensive set of books that summarizes and analyzes important research, theory, and practice related to the education of ethnic, racial, cultural, and language groups in the United States as well as the education of mainstream students about diversity. The books in the Series provide research, theoretical, and practical knowledge about the behaviors and learning characteristics of students of color, language minority students, and low-income students. They also provide knowledge about ways to improve academic achievement and race relations in educational settings.

The definition of multicultural education in the *Handbook of Research on Multicultural Education* (Banks & Banks, 2001) is used in the Series: "Multicultural education is a field of study designed to increase educational equity for all students that incorporates, for this purpose, content, concepts, principles, theories, and paradigms from history, the social and behavioral sciences, and particularly from ethnic studies and women studies" (p. xii). In the Series, as in the *Handbook*, multicultural education is considered a "metadiscipline."

The dimensions of multicultural education, developed by Banks (2001) and described in the *Handbook of Research on Multicultural Education*, provide the conceptual framework for the development of the books in the Series. They are content integration, the knowledge construction process, prejudice reduction, an equity pedagogy, and an empowering school culture and social structure. To implement multicultural education effectively, teachers and administrators must attend to each of these five dimensions. They should use content from diverse groups when teaching concepts and skills, help students to understand how knowledge in the various disciplines is constructed, help students to develop positive intergroup attitudes and behaviors, and modify their teaching strategies so that students from different racial, cultural, language, and social-class groups will experience equal educational opportunities. The total environment and culture of the school must also be transformed so that students from diverse groups will experience equal status in the culture and life of the school.

Although the five dimensions of multicultural education are highly interrelated, each requires deliberate attention and focus. Each book in the series focuses on one or more of the dimensions, although each book deals with all of them to some extent because of the highly interrelated characteristics of the dimensions.

This informative and compassionate book is timely and significant. Research indicates that the quality of the teacher is a major factor in the academic and social achievement of students (Darling-Hammond, 1997) and that the racial, ethnic, cultural, and language gap between students and teachers in U.S.

schools is wide and increasing. In 1996, 90.7% of the nation's teachers were White, and almost three-quarters were female (National Education Association, 1997).

A number of social, political, and economic forces are having adverse effects on the preparation of effective teachers for the nation's ethnically, culturally, and linguistically diverse schools (Cochran-Smith & Fries, 2001). Among the most pernicious of these forces are the push for programs that prepare teachers quickly and the widespread high-stakes testing of teachers and students (Heubert & Hauser, 1999).

Vavrus, using critical race theory as a foundation (Ladson-Billings, 1999), describes why a narrow, technical education of teachers cannot prepare the kind of critical, reflective, and democratic teachers needed to prepare students to function as effective citizens in our diverse nation and world. He envisions and describes a liberating and transformative teacher education program that will prepare teachers who are culturally responsive, antiracist, and who can help close the achievement gap between mainstream students and students who are marginalized within U.S. schools and society.

Vavrus presents a transformative vision for teacher education that shares important characteristics with the dream of equity and social justice described by Lillian Smith (1994/1949) in her classic book *Killers of the Dream*. Smith identifies several killers of the dream, forces that prevent the realization of equity and social justice. She describes why it is easiest to identify killers of the dream who are outsiders. In the case of teacher education, proponents of testing and quick teacher education programs come easily to mind. However, as Smith perceptively points out, identifying the killers within us is a difficult and painful but liberating and transformative experience. Vavrus's book will help teacher educators to identify and disrupt the killers of the dream of equity and social justice within the teaching profession and to take thoughtful and practical action to realize this dream.

James A. Banks
Series Editor

REFERENCES

Banks, J.A. (2001). Multicultural education: Historical development, dimensions, and practice. In J.A. Banks & C.A.M. Banks (Eds.), *Handbook of research on multicultural education* (pp. 3–24). San Francisco: Jossey-Bass.

Banks, J.A., & Banks, C.A.M. (Eds.). (2001). *Handbook of research on multicultural education*. San Francisco: Jossey-Bass.

California State Department of Education. (2000). [On-line]. Available: http://data1.cde.ca.gov/dataquest

Cochran-Smith, M., & Fries, M.K. (2001). Sticks, stones, and ideology: The discourse of reform in teacher education. *Educational Researcher, 30*(8), 3–15.

Darling-Hammond, L. (1997). *The right to learn: A blueprint for creating schools that work*. San Francisco: Jossey-Bass.

Heubert, J.P., & Hauser, R.M. (Eds.). (1999). *High stakes testing for tracking, promotion and graduation*. Washington, DC: National Academy Press.

Ladson-Billings, G.J. (1999). Preparing teachers for diverse student populations: A critical race theory perspective. In A. Iran-Nejad & P.D. Pearson (Eds.), *Review of research in education* (Vol. 24, pp. 211–247). Washington, DC: American Educational Research Association.

Martin, P., & Midgley, E. (1999). Immigration to the United States. *Population Bulletin, 54*(2), 1–44. Washington, DC: Population Reference Bureau.

Martinez, G.M., & Curry, A.E. (1999, September). *Current population reports: School enrollment—social and economic characteristics of students* (update). Washington, DC: U.S. Census Bureau.

National Education Association. (1997, July). *Status of the American public school-teacher, 1995–1996*. Washington, DC: Author.

Riche, M.F. (2000). America's diversity and growth: Signposts for the 21st century. *Population Bulletin, 55*(2), 1–43. Washington, DC: Population Reference Bureau.

Smith, L. (1994). *Killers of the dream*. New York: Norton. (Original work published 1949)

U.S. Census Bureau. (1998). *Statistical abstract of the United States* (118th ed.). Washington, DC: U.S. Government Printing Office.

Foreword

This book is compelling. It leaves the reader no excuse for failing to understand the extensive and complex nature of what we call multicultural education for teachers' professional development. From the beginning, author Michael Vavrus deciphers the meanings and implications of the many terms and "isms" that are neatly situated in a host of state and national high-stakes curriculum, accreditation, and licensing standards. He presumes that the reader intends to incorporate or infuse culturally responsive practice into his or her work and lays out, in no uncertain terms, contradictions in what we say and what we do in this regard. Unlike similar volumes, Vavrus's work goes on to offer specific means and assessments for moving the agenda in teacher education and professional development closer to James Banks's highest rating of multicultural awareness and skill—transformative.

Vavrus reminds us that before schools, colleges, departments of education, and others in professional development memorize recipes for multicultural education, as well as global education, we must first consider what it is that we are trying to achieve, and then test our motives and commitments. Are we establishing course and programs in haste and without sufficient thought to comply with standards that we do not truly embrace or understand? While giving due homage to efforts of some of teacher education reform's most notable initiatives (e.g., NCATE and INTASC), the author asks, how well do we know or understand the standards and assessments to which we adhere? Do we intend to advance practice, or do we intend to perform and account for only minimal performance in this critical area of effective teaching practice?

In identifying problems with these and other policy-making authorities, though, Vavrus does not exonerate the reader from moving forward and offering new and additional information that will enhance the current system and requirements for the common good. Using the NCATE accreditation standards as a guide, he illustrates how existing rubrics can be even more powerful tools for gauging progress in the area of multicultural education than they are currently.

This volume is unique in that it documents the dire need for self-reflection and new knowledge on the part of teacher education faculty in the academy and in the field. The brief research-based vignettes and cases he offers provide sufficient evidence that you cannot teach what you do not know. Clearly, neophyte practitioners will flounder in their attempts to grasp critical cultural knowledge and skills in the absence of model teacher education faculty and school-based cooperating teachers. Therefore, it is essential that the entire learning community work to understand and provide a multicultural education.

As we proceed into this century, it appears that discussion and debate will continue regarding the merits and necessity of multicultural education as an essential component of quality teaching and learning. For those who long for greater depth and explicitness in this area this book will be an invaluable tool. For those who are incognizant this volume will be less useful, for there is little here on which to argue for the status quo.

Mary Dilworth

Preface

In the United States, thousands enroll annually in higher education teacher education programs for K–12 teacher licensure and in-service professional development. An anticipated outcome of these programs is the graduation of large numbers of teachers who are prepared to help *all* children acquire meaningful information and meet high achievement standards. State and national data, however, indicate the persistence of an achievement gap that ranks most middle-class and affluent White students over students of color and poor children (Darling-Hammond, 1997a). This racialized achievement difference continues despite teacher education programs that under state and national accreditation standards are purportedly designed to ensure the public of licensed, professionally capable K–12 teachers. Meanwhile, outside school walls, political debates about equity are often framed negatively around discriminatory racial references toward people of color, be it in regard to issues of immigration, welfare, hiring practices, housing, criminal justice, or global economics.

Within this social context, the National Council for the Accreditation of Teacher Education (NCATE, 2001b) has intensified accreditation expectations for higher education institutions. Heightened attention to internal accountability of programs mirrors 15 years of multifaceted research scholarship devoted to improving the quality of teacher preparation (see, e.g., Clifford & Guthrie, 1988; Fullan, Galluzzo, Morris, & Watson, 1998; Goodlad, 1990; Holmes Group, 1995; Johnston, Spalding, Paden, & Zifren, 1989; Soltis, 1987; Zeichner, Melnick, & Gomez, 1996). Nonetheless, John Goodlad (1999) laments that despite such studies "there is little public appreciation of or attention to the research findings that accrue from the ongoing educational inquiry" (p. 329).

Teacher education programs are often portrayed historically as the scapegoat for perceived public schooling problems, and efforts to further implicate colleges have intensified in recent years. The 21st century was initiated, for example, with the U.S. government mandating the ranking of teacher education programs primarily on the basis of standardized test scores and program completion rates by teacher candidates. The stakes are high as the government ultimately reserves the right to cut off federal financial aid to teacher education students in colleges designated by a state as "low performing" institutions (Teacher Preparation Accountability and Evaluation Commission, 2000). On another front, reported prominently on the front page of the *New York Times*, teacher preparation is enthusiastically being by-passed at the collegiate level in favor of certain local school districts offering "their own crash courses that put new teachers in the classroom after as little as three weeks" while noting that this method is superior to existing higher education models (Zernike, 2000, p. 1). An additional attack on higher education comes from those who believe that a multicultural curricular focus in teacher education programs erodes the academic quality of the elementary and secondary school curriculum (cf. Stotsky, 1999). All of these examples reflect a reductionist approach to teacher education that suggests teachers should focus on "basic skills" teaching that is undergirded by linear, one-dimensional classroom pedagogical techniques.

This book goes against the grain of calls to limit the education of teachers to a repertoire of technical approaches executed in a presumed color-blind cultural vacuum. Instead, this book recognizes the important role teacher education programs can play in providing culturally responsive teachers for 21st-century public school classrooms. Culturally competent teachers hold the promise of improving the achievement levels of students from poor neighborhoods and children of color. An equitable formal education for all students is unlikely to be accomplished by graduates from fast-track teacher education programs (see, e.g., Darling-Hammond, 1994; Popkewitz, 1998). Nevertheless, as the research in this book indicates, higher education and school district in-service programs need to dramatically accelerate the incorporation of transformative multicultural education into their institutional approaches to teacher education curriculum, pedagogy, and evaluation.

The primary purpose of this book is to provide a range of transformative perspectives on the multicultural education of teachers for educational analysts, policymakers, and faculty and administrators in K–12 settings and higher education who are responsible for preservice and in-service teacher education. The overriding motivation and goal for this book is systemic institutional improvement that can benefit all children and youth in our schools. Woven throughout each chapter are program design considerations in the context of multicultural dimensions (see Banks, 1993d, 2001b; Zeichner et al., 1998). This book can also be helpful for individual preservice teachers, licensed teachers and administrators, education graduate students, and teacher educators who are interested in learning more about multicultural education as they examine their own beliefs and practices. Accordingly, this book can be read as a text both to assist institutional reform and to enhance an individual educator's multicultural understandings and actions.

Chapter 1 serves to frame a transformative imperative by examining a range of multicultural education conceptions. Fundamental challenges for transformative teacher education are described in the context of this book's conceptual and historical research orientation. To maintain a focus on the learning of all students, especially those historically marginalized from White norms of achievement, I prioritize issues of race, racism, and culturally responsive teaching through analyses of and recommendations for institutional transformation. Articulated by law faculty of color, critical race theory (CRT) is an important influence on my research approach. The introductory first chapter places CRT as a legitimate perspective for understanding the multicultural education of teachers.

Interwoven with transformative theory and research is teacher education practice. Chapter 2 reviews the current status of multicultural education reform in teacher education, whereas Chapter 3 examines ways to incorporate multicultural reform into a teacher education program. Examples of assessment rubrics are provided to capture (a) teacher reflection on cultural encapsulation for multicultural, antibias teaching goals, (b) teacher actions resulting from reflection on multicultural advocacy for all students, (c) teacher knowledge of multicultural, antibias curriculum planning, and (d) democratic classroom management that honors cultural diversity.

Chapter 4 analyzes the multicultural effectiveness of teacher education standards from NCATE (2001b) and the Interstate New Teacher Assessment and Support Consortium (INTASC, 1992). The chapter addresses what is absent from these highly influential standards for the incorporation of a transformative multicultural perspective into a teacher education program. Proposed as additional performance-based assessment rubrics to NCATE standards are elements derived from transformative multicultural education. Program assessments include (a) multicultural historical foundations, (b) contemporary multicultural knowledge and skills, (c) multicultural dispositions, (d) multicultural curriculum, (e) multicultural practices, (f) institutional multicultural leadership, and (g) multicultural resources.

Chapter 5 examines theoretical and practical considerations for a teacher education program to respond pragmatically to racism. Key concepts and definitions pertaining to racism are presented. Issues surrounding teacher racial identity formation are considered as a means to help teachers be culturally responsive. Antiracist teacher education practices are juxtaposed to restraining influences of calls for tolerance and status quo managed expressions of antiracism. The chapter provides an overview of curricular efforts by college faculty who address racism in their teaching.

Chapter 6 examines globalization as a multicultural concept. In explaining historical links between globalization and colonialism, emphasis is placed upon Eurocentric concepts of progress, development, civilization, and 21st-century expressions of manifest destiny. Global economic effects on education are described to explain how school–business alliances contribute to student reconstitution as forms of human capital rather than participant-citizens in a culturally diverse society. The undermining impact of global economic ideologies on multicultural education is presented with particular attention to the foundation of INTASC (1992). The chapter includes globalization's implications for the multicultural education of teachers.

Chapter 7 describes how one teacher education program approaches and acts on democracy in a multicultural context. Because democracy is often applied unreflectively in teacher education programs, the chapter is organized around "provocative declaratives," statements purposely formulated to elicit reactions to held values and beliefs. The chapter outlines how developmentally appropriate teaching and learning is inseparable from issues of democracy and diversity and how this sensibility can be carried into student-teaching internships. Presented are cooperating teacher and teacher candidate perspectives about incorporating a democratic multicultural orientation into K–12 teaching and learning.

Chapter 8 concludes the book by proposing learning communities as an effective structural and conceptual approach for organizing interdisciplinary aspects of a teacher education program. I describe advantages of a learning community model for including multicultural knowledge bases, controversial issues, and transformative practices. An underlying argument is that a carefully constructed learning community can reduce teacher avoidance and resistance toward multicultural concepts. A discussion of who might constitute the membership of a learning community is taken up along with pragmatic and ethical considerations as to where and with whom a teacher education program should initiate a learning community.

Although I assume final responsibility for the content of this book, it was not written without the inspiration of many. This book could not have been conceived without the depth of research and commitment by a long line of multicultural scholars over the past quarter century. The opening chapter's attention to multicultural education conceptions and dimensions reflects my conversations with many thoughtful educators who fear *multicultural education* has become an empty and co-opted phrase. The voices of those educators who are professionally committed to social justice goals stimulated me to articulate a transformative approach as to how an institution can become a culturally competent force for K–12 children through multicultural education. Experiences that reinforced the importance of having an institutional focus include the opportunities I have had working directly with professionally reflective institutional representatives of teacher education programs.

I wish to acknowledge a number of individuals who have directly affected my approach to this book through collaborations, deliberations, and engaging conversations. They include Mustafa Ozcan; members of the American Association of Colleges for Teacher Education's Committee on Multicultural Education (1996–1999), under the leadership of Jacqueline Jordan Irvine, David Whitehorse, and Mary Dilworth; Sue Feldman; Lori Blewett; and the following members of The Evergreen State College: Peter Bohmer, Emily Decker, Betsy Diffendal, Peter Dorman, Terry Ford, George Freeman, Angela Gilliam, Jeanne Hahn, Jan Kido, Stephanie Kozick, Dan Leahy, Larry Mosqueda, Raul Nakasone, Yvonne Peterson, Ratna Roy, David Rutledge, Sarah Ryan, Zahid Shariff, Masao Sugiyama, and Sherry Walton. I want to thank Dan Leahy and British Columbia Teachers' Federation researcher Larry Kuehn for their perceptive comments on a draft of Chapter 6. Emily Decker was invaluable in providing me critical feedback and insights regarding the conceptualization and logistics of higher education learning communities that are described in Chapter 8. I also appreciate suggestions received from supportive reviewers for Teachers College Press.

Olivia Archibald, my colleague and partner for the past 20 years, has been a faithful supporter and provider of constructive ideas to all phases of my research on multicultural education. I am grateful to Olivia for her patience in offering helpful critiques of early drafts of this work.

Jim Banks's professional support and thoughtful editorship were invaluable throughout the writing of this book. Without his belief in the importance of a book focused on the institutional responsibility of higher education for the multicultural education of teachers, this book would not have been possible.

Transforming
the
Multicultural Education
of Teachers

CHAPTER 1

Multicultural Teacher Education: Transformative Conceptions and Dimensions

This book is a study of teacher education at an institutional level of higher education and K–12 in-service programs. Individual faculty and administrators unequivocally make necessary and important contributions to the multicultural education of teachers. Nonetheless, sustained multicultural education requires a transformative institutional commitment to prepare culturally responsive teachers.

Multicultural education is *"a total school reform effort designed to increase educational equity for a range of cultural, ethnic, and economic groups"* (Banks, 1993c, p. 6, emphasis in original). Multicultural education goals are multidimensional. Dimensions include content integration for an inclusive elementary and secondary school curriculum, multicultural knowledge construction processes, prejudicial discrimination reduction, an equity pedagogy, and an empowering school culture and social structure for all children and youth (Banks, 1993d, 2001b). Multicultural education can help teachers acquire knowledge, skills, and dispositions that serve all children and youth, especially students whose interests have been historically marginalized by institutions and people in privileged positions. To attain this purpose, culturally responsive and relevant teachers need professional development from institutions committed to multicultural education reform (Gay, 2000; Irvine, 1992, 2001; Ladson-Billings, 1995b).

Teacher education programs have generally perceived multicultural education as a possible elective or singular addition within a Eurocentric core curriculum that is supported by conventional pedagogies and systems of evaluation. Since the late 1970s, state and national teacher education requirements have produced institutional inclusions of multicultural education in various forms. A variety of teacher education emphases have created a contested terrain as to what constitutes multicultural education conceptually and pragmatically.

This introductory chapter examines a range of multicultural education conceptions. Distilled from various theories recognized by leading multicultural scholars, the chapter articulates why a transformative approach to teacher education is necessary. Examined is how transformation—a concept drawn from critical theory—can incorporate issues of knowledge, power, and social change into the multicultural education of teachers. Fundamental challenges for transformative teacher education are described in the context of this book's conceptual and historical research orientation.

Given contemporary multicultural education's roots in the civil rights movement, this book incorporates issues of race, racism, and antiracism as a major organizing principle. The chapter discusses the value in using *critical race theory* to orient preservice and in-service teacher education around the centrality of race and transformative multicultural education.

CONCEPTIONS OF MULTICULTURAL EDUCATION

During the past decade multicultural scholars have sought to differentiate and clarify multicultural education conceptions. This section briefly summarizes prominent theories under headings based on four categories advanced by Cameron McCarthy and Arlette Ingram Willis (1995) as ranges of "discourses on racial inequality" (p. 69) in their essay "The Politics of Culture." Their multicultural classifications include (a) cultural understanding, (b) cultural competence, (c) cultural emancipation, and (d) critical emancipatory multiculturalism. Within these theoretically distinctive categories, transformative potential is often eroded by assimilationist accommodations. McCarthy and Willis's categorizations suggest the complexities surrounding "cultural" in multiculturalism (see Jeevanantham, 2001). Linked under each heading are theoretical conceptions by James Banks (1993a, 1993b, 1993d, 2001b), Stephan May (1999), Peter McLaren (1994), and Christine Sleeter and Carl Grant (1999).

Cultural Understanding

McCarthy and Willis's (1995) "discourses of cultural understanding . . . promote the idea of pride in one's ancestry and cultural heritage and seek to reduce prejudice and stereotypes by fostering intercultural exchanges" (pp. 69–70). Parallels exist with Sleeter and Grant's (1999) identification of approaches that emphasize "teaching the exceptional and culturally different" and "human relations." The former approach seeks to ameliorate perceived knowledge and behavioral deficits while striving to assimilate "culturally different" populations into mainstream society. A human relations orientation highlights commonalities among all people through tolerance and social acceptance in conventional ways. Aspects of Banks's (1993d, 2001b) prejudice reduction dimension through curricular interventions are congruent with cultural understanding.

A cultural understanding conception is also similar to Banks's (1993a, 2001b) typology classifications of "contributions" and "additive" approaches to multicultural knowledge in a school's curriculum. To meet cultural understanding aims, contributions of culturally relevant events and role models are thematically added to a standard school curriculum. McLaren (1994) categorizes cultural understanding from the perspective of an undisturbed Eurocentric monoculturalism as "conservative multiculturalism." When cultural understanding fosters a sense of sameness rather than cultural difference, McLaren labels this approach "liberal multiculturalism." May (1999) observes that both conservative and liberal commentaries on multiculturalism support cultural understanding if perceived as stabilizing national identity and unity based on a common culture.

Although purportedly promoting cultural understanding, significant aspects of different cultural perspectives are minimized. Furthermore, when differences are presented, they are cast as if unequal power relationships do not exist. Tacitly assumed as normal is the necessity of stable White-dominated social institutions that foster asymmetrical distributions of wealth and power. When advocates of cultural understanding truncate Banks's (1993d, 2001b) dimension of prejudice reduction, they imagine that just with "understanding" racial discrimination will be eliminated. Because a conception of cultural understanding constructs multicultural education as a means to correct "problems" of difference, assimilation to a dominant cultural ideology is inherent for this approach. Although cultural understanding can serve as a fundamental prerequisite for the creation of an equitable society, alone it works primarily to preserve the status quo.

Cultural Competence

McCarthy and Willis (1995) conceive "cultural competence" as a condition in which "values of cultural pluralism should have a central place in the school curriculum" (p. 70). In some instances cultural competence is analogous to Sleeter and Grant's (1999) notion of "single-group studies" with its emphasis on bilingualism and ethnic studies. Cultural competence is congruent with Banks's (1993a, 2001b) typology category "transformational" approach to mainstream curriculum. Similarly, Sleeter and Grant's (1999) "multicultural education" concept promotes a transformation of educational processes to reflect democratic goals in a culturally diverse society. Like Banks's (1993d, 2001b) prejudice reduction dimension, cultural competence is committed to cross-cultural interactions supportive of antiracism (see McAllister & Irvine, 2000). Cultural competence strives toward Banks's (1993d, 2001b) concept of an equity pedagogy designed to empower historically marginalized school populations.

Unlike cultural understanding, cultural competence challenges assimilationist normalizing of Eurocentric teaching and learning. Cultural competence is a fundamental step toward the development of equitable schooling environments. A singular focus on cultural competence without consideration of broader social justice goals can, however, limit transformative possibilities for multicultural education.

Cultural Emancipation

McCarthy and Willis's (1995) third conception of multicultural education is based on "models of cultural emancipation." Cultural emancipation approaches advocate a "reformist multicultural curriculum [that] can boost school success and economic futures . . . in the job market and in society" for youth of color (pp. 71–72). McLaren (1994) suggests that this approach can be understood as "liberal multiculturalism" when it overlooks the challenges people of color face in competing equally with Whites in a capitalist society. Liberal multiculturalism assumes that schooling alone and without corresponding societal changes can beneficially change conditions for oppressed populations.

The concept of cultural emancipation captures a social change element present in Grant and Sleeter's (1999) analysis of approaches that are single-group studies, multicultural education, and "social reconstruction." Social reconstruction not only focuses on conditions of oppression and discrimination, but also includes citizen involvement to create a more politically and economically equitable society (see Grant & Secada, 1990; Watkins, 1991; Zeichner, 1992). Also congruent with cultural emancipation are Banks's (1993a, 2001b) transformational and "social action" approaches. Like cultural emancipation, Banks's social action approach aims to empower marginalized young people to participate in decisions about important social issues that can transform presumed predetermined life choices and opportunities.

A "left-liberal multiculturalism," according to McLaren (1994), casts cultural emancipation and differences as cultural essentialism in search of an authentic Other. This perspective of left-liberal multiculturalism retains a Eurocentric orientation in which cultural "meaning production," that is to say, who articulates and disseminates knowledge about *the Other*, remains unquestioned (p. 52). Cultural identity is reduced to a personal pursuit that is independent of history and social relations. May (1999) cautions that some leftist conceptions of cultural emancipation, while outwardly advocating antiracism, can fail to adequately "conceptualize and address the increasing articulation of new 'cultural racisms' where 'race' as a signifier is transmuted into the seemingly more acceptable discourse of 'cultural differences'" (p. 12). Thus race and racism can become muted topics under a cultural emancipation conception of multicultural education.

Cultural emancipation adds to a conception of cultural competence by placing multicultural education in a socio-economic context. Cultural emancipation embraces not only affirmative action in life opportunities for youth of color but also can be used to analyze the importance of a more socially just distribution of personal wealth as a democratic bedrock of equality. As McLaren (1994) and May (1999) caution, cultural emancipation has a tendency to assume fixed racial and ethnic identities when focusing on cultural differences that can blur the complexities of racism. Although cultural emancipation is generally located outside assimilationist conceptions of multiculturalism, Eurocentric hegemony over school and, hence, societal knowledge construction and production is not necessarily brought to the forefront of analysis.

Critical Emancipatory Multiculturalism

To analyze shortcomings of the three multicultural education categories cited above and to present alternatives, McCarthy and Willis (1995) offer a "critical emancipatory multiculturalism" conception. Critical emancipatory multiculturalism provides a critique of Eurocentrism "that is ascendant in curriculum and pedagogical practices in education" as opposed to just articulating "a language of inclusion" (p. 74). Active citizen participation in public life through democratic processes enables this conception of multicultural education.

Like Banks's (1993d, 2001b) dimension of knowledge production and McLaren's (1994) category "critical and resistance multiculturalism," critical emancipatory multiculturalism challenges the premises of Eurocentric canons. By offering alternatives to Eurocentrism, this concept questions exclusionary outcomes present in White-privileged interpretations of a common culture. Critical emancipatory multiculturalism stresses how cultural and racial hierarchies emerge from historically constructed knowledge through unequal power relations. Within this historical commentary, critical emancipatory multiculturalism acknowledges the social construction of cultural and racial identities. Similar to May's (1999) discussion of "critical multiculturalism," McCarthy and Willis's (1995) work indicates that by taking an approach cognizant of an instability and wide diversity among racial identities, the result can be "a more complex understanding of the educational and political behavior of different communities of color" (p. 78). Subsequently, the intricacies of racism and an antiracist advocacy are conceptualized under critical emancipatory multiculturalism.

The sociopolitical aspect of this approach recognizes the need to have a concurrent transformation of school and society. The goals of Sleeter and Grant's (1999) categories of multicultural education and social reconstruction can be more fully realized within critical emancipatory multiculturalism. Banks's (1993a, 1993d, 2001b) transformed school curriculum that incorporates social action for equity is congruent with critical emancipatory multiculturalism. McLaren (1994) explains that critical and resistance multiculturalism advances "a transformative political agenda" to avert multicultural education serving as a "form of accommodation to the larger social order" (p. 53). Hence critical cultural emancipation abandons assimilationist and Eurocentric pretenses.

A TRANSFORMATIVE CONCEPTION OF
MULTICULTURAL EDUCATION

Conceptions of multicultural education are overlapping rather than independent, an observation similar to what Banks (1993a, 2001b) notes regarding his typology of curricular approaches. Cultural understanding, cultural competence, and cultural emancipation are multicultural education classifications that each contain elements that are worthy of emulation. To varying degrees, each multicultural representation encourages some form of transformation. For example, to have transformative teaching occur, cultural competence is a necessary prerequisite skill and disposition (McAllister & Irvine, 2000). Transformation is also embedded in cultural emancipation's recognition that children of color and the poor need improved opportunities to succeed in schools and in their chosen occupations. However, approaches grouped under cultural understanding and human relations tend to focus on transforming individuals who deviate from dominant social norms so that they can assimilate into existing social structures. Sleeter and Grant (1999) note that an assimilationist approach is how the majority teaching population of Whites perceive the role of multicultural education.

Alternatively, the consensus among Banks (1993a, 1993b, 1993d, 2001b), McLaren (1994), Sleeter and Grant (1999), and May (1999) is for a critical emancipatory multiculturalism conception of multicultural education as the best possibility to transform social relations and institutions to overcome discriminatory schooling and societal conditions. Banks (1993d, 2001b), for example, presents his five multicultural education dimensions—content integration, knowledge construction processes, prejudice reduction, an equity pedagogy, an empowering school culture and social structure—not linearly but as interactive factors synergistically necessary for transformation. Multicultural scholars are in agreement that multicultural education is multidimensional and should provide poor students and populations of color with schooling perspectives and social prospects not predicated on Eurocentric preeminence and inequitable wealth distributions.

Transformation and Critical Theory

On one level multicultural education is unopposed to cultural understanding when it can lead to transformative knowledge and actions supportive of cultural differences. This book, however, departs from a human relations cultural understanding conception of transformation by using the signifying descriptor *transformative multicultural education*. Here transformation comes from a critical theory tradition. Transformation is not bound to a human relations notion of cultural deficits and cultural understanding, where expected behaviors of marginalized populations are externally directed.

In critical theory transformation "problematizes the structures of history that embody who we are and have become" (Popkewitz, 1999, p. 3). By making conventional views of U.S. history and educational practices problematic, transformation resists White assimilationist conceptions of social change in favor of concern over social justice and equity. The urgency for a critically based transformative concept of multicultural education is underscored by the thousands of teachers who are exposed to teacher education and "profess to understand [multicultural education], even if they know little or nothing about it, because policy mandates require the inclusion of multicultural content in their courses" (Sleeter & Grant, 1999, p. 152). Such knowledge gaps suggest that a teacher education program can play a significant role in expanding preservice and in-service teachers' conceptions of multicultural education.

Transformation, the Status Quo, and Power

Transformative multicultural education does not assume that transformed knowledge and approaches can readily substitute for canonized structures and processes. When transformative academic knowledge is introduced, it generally coexists uneasily in practice with mainstream, status quo knowledge (Banks, 1993b). Transformative multicultural education pragmatically recognizes and engages this tension as an inherent aspect of meeting multicultural education goals.

For most of the 20th century the social sciences presented knowledge and interpretations of social experiences as politically neutral. This social science paradigm both (a) privileged status quo psychological interpretations of individuals and social groups along a normal/abnormal continuum and (b) emphasized Eurocentric mainstream grand theories of history. Since the mid-1970s this social science model has experienced a gradual but consistent shift. This paradigm change incorporates unequal power relations between politically dominant and historically subordinated groups within and across national borders. Social variables such as race, class, and gender are now rarely validated within a White privileged political and economic framework. In the opening decade of the 21st century the dynamics of these variables are legitimately studied in order to reduce discrimination and oppression so that the human condition can be improved (see Oshinsky, 2000; Popkewitz, 1999; Wallerstein, 1999).

Transformative multicultural education reflects this paradigm shift. Transformative multicultural education counters neutral, isolated images of educational policies and practices by bringing to the forefront critical theory's unifying concept of power relationships. Whereas educational psychology prefers models of individual behavior as separate from inferred stable social contexts, power actively places the individual within a dynamic sociopolitical context. For example, by studying power within schooling processes, teachers can come to understand "the actors who control and in whose benefit existing arrangements work" (Popkewitz, 1999, p. 5). By incorporating a critical orientation toward power and transformation, a teacher education program can create conditions for its own faculty and K–12 teachers to analyze institutions for both their emancipatory and oppressive capacities.

Transformation and Teacher Agency

A transformative approach envisions teachers holding agency, that is to say, the capacity to challenge and resist unjust schooling arrangements through localized forms of social action in order to benefit historically marginalized children and youth. This possibility for social change by teachers is anchored in an acceptance that "the relations between knowledge, power, and social change continually need to be interrogated" (Popkewitz, 1999, p. 8). Equally important, teacher agency is tempered by and connected to historical possibilities. Thus teacher actions are simultaneously constrained and enabled by degrees of knowledge and understandings of the sociohistorical context in which a teacher acts.

A teacher's agency and subjective identity are not assumed to be transcendent of dominant power relations. Indeed, the notion of teacher "voice" can actually be domesticated by existing social structures and dominant ideologies that work against multicultural education goals (see Althusser, 1971; Fendler, 1999). Nevertheless, historical arrangements of teaching, learning, and schooling are never fixed and inevitable. Emancipatory opportunities exist because teacher agency holds the potential for transformative multicultural expression.

Dominant ideologies as pervasive belief systems and knowledge bases affect the knowledge, skills, and dispositions of teachers. Popkewitz (1994) explains that "professional knowledges are not only knowledges that describe the world but are systems of ideas and practices that authorize how people find out who they are and what they are in society" (p. 7). In a transformative framework, professional practices as presumed models of "excellence" become inseparable from ideologies as to how teachers should mediate multicultural knowledge to their pupils (see Goldberg, 1993, chap. 2). To realize teacher agency, transformative multicultural education sees the development of teacher critical reflection and practice as a strategic responsibility for a teacher education program.

Anyon (1994) and Banks (2001b) observe that some scholars operating in a tradition of critical theory discount the potential of teacher agency for transformation. This assumption concludes that because schools are located within a larger political setting, it is unrealistic to expect teachers to make social changes for multicultural education goals in schools. External social forces obviously govern and set expectations for schools and limit the influence of multicultural education (deMarrais & LeCompte, 1995; Olneck, 2000). Nonetheless, Paulo

Freire (1998) aptly explained, "It is true that education is not the ultimate lever for social transformation, but without it transformation cannot occur" (p. 37). McLaren (1994) points out that multicultural education ought not simply be about protesting unjust social conditions but should be actively involved in transforming those situations. Transformative multicultural education rejects fatalistic assumptions about social change by advancing emancipatory possibilities supported by teacher agency to transform oppressive schooling conditions.

RESEARCH FOCUS

In "The New Scholarship of Teacher Education" Kenneth Zeichner (1999) outlines some major research categories. This book falls within his strand of "conceptual and historical research" (pp. 10–11). Other research dimensions identified by Zeichner—such as survey research, case studies, learning to teach research, impact of various teacher education activities—help to inform this book's research focus. "Self-study" (p. 11), an emerging research strand, contributed to positions developed throughout this book.

My own venture into professional self-study, with a personal essayist concerned with author(ity) positions, centered on my role and perspective as a faculty-administrator institutionally accountable for two distinctly different teacher education programs (Vavrus & Archibald, 1998). During more than 15 years as a faculty-administrator of teacher programs, I came to understand institutional and professional obstacles that individual teacher educators can face in developing a holistic picture of teacher preparation. Through a self-study analysis of social justice perspective in these two programs along with national and international teacher education experiences, I became convinced of the importance of a teacher education program faculty that can grapple and act *collectively* and *institutionally* on the importance of multicultural integrity in the education of teachers.

By working within a conceptual and historical research framework, this book is interdisciplinary in its transformative perspective. Sources are drawn from teacher education studies and related educational literature in addition to legal studies, economics, social philosophy, history, and contemporary news accounts. Because multicultural education is an interdisciplinary field that combines theory and practice, the breadth of these sources is employed to extend current multicultural conversations in teacher education.

Historical Challenges for Transformative Teacher Education

This book maintains that a teacher education program is capable of transforming its curriculum, pedagogy, and evaluation approaches in order to respond to multicultural commitments. The active creation of possibilities and actions for social justice, however, rubs against a historical grain of teacher education program "reform." Zeichner (1999) writes,

> Program development has often been a reaction to the mandates of state departments [of education] and legislatures more than it has been a thoughtful, analytic, and forward-looking process based on the attempt to implement a set of coherent, well thought out principles and ideas about what teachers need to know and need to be able to do. (p. 12)

Corollary to this reactive condition is that few faculty are systematically introduced to and prepared for a broad understanding of preservice and in-service teacher education (Koster & Korthagen, 2001).

Besides facing a conserving stance toward teacher education program design, a transformative approach is confounded by ambiguous institutional commitments to multicultural education. This uncertain multicultural resolution can negatively affect the knowledge base and subsequent practices of teachers (Melnick & Zeichner, 1997). While serving as principal investigator for a study about a school district's efforts to respond to state findings of multicultural noncompliance (Vavrus & Determan, 1996; Vavrus, Ozcan, Determan, & Steele, 1996), I became further convinced of the necessity of having a sustained institutional commitment to the multicultural education of teachers.

A primary task for this particular school district was both institutional development and teacher professional development. Staff development approaches focusing on just implementation of mandates tend not to have a lasting impact (Bradley, 1995; Fullan, 1990). Because successful staff development hinges on the social climate of a school district (Joyce, 1990), Fullan (1990) urges a shift from staff development to "institutional development [so that] changes in schools as institutions . . . increase their capacity and performance for continuous improvement" (p. 11). Institutional development and commitment are necessary to meet the equity goals of transformative multicultural education.

This book recognizes the challenge teacher education programs face in light of historical expectations to produce teachers who enable the status quo (Spring, 2001). As described within this book and observed through national educational expressions, the decades of the 1990s and 2000s evidence burgeoning attention to transformative possibilities for multicultural education in teacher education and K–12 classrooms. This relatively new and expanding critical chink in a dominant wall of educational discourses and practices has allowed a transformative light to recapture some of the significant historical purposes of multicultural education (see, e.g., Banks, 1996, 1998, 2001b; Sleeter & Grant, 1999; Watkins, 1994).

Race and Multicultural Education

Mindful of the origins of multicultural education, this book prioritizes the concept of race. Bringing race to the forefront of teacher education is a fundamental concern for transformative multicultural education (Cochran-Smith, 1995a, 1995b; King & Castenell, 2001a, 2001b; Sleeter, 1994, 1995a, 1995b; G.P. Smith, 1998a, 1998b). Avoiding the interplay between race and power can undermine the effective development of culturally responsive teachers. Using critical race theory (CRT) is one way for a teacher education program to reconceptualize issues of race in its curriculum, pedagogy, and evaluations.

A Critical Race Theory Perspective. CRT has its roots in multicultural legal studies (Brooks & Newborn, 1994). By extending critical theory and critical legal studies, faculty of color in U.S. law schools created CRT to draw attention to the limitations of equality based on a legal system conceived under White privilege (Brooks & Newborn, 1994; Crenshaw, Gotanda, Peller, & Thomas, 1995a; Delgado, 1995a; Harris, 1994). CRT offers an alternative approach to dominant practices of White silencing of racial discrimination in institutional policies and practices by putting "race at the center of critical analysis" (Roithmayr, 1999, p. 1). Like multicultural education, CRT is an interdisciplinary field. CRT draws from the scholarship of postcolonialism and racial and ethnic identity formation and is transdisciplinary in its perspective-taking (Tate, 1997).

Two common interests unify CRT. First is an effort to understand how White privilege or supremacy has been able to subordinate people of color while maintaining a legal system that purports to provide equal protection under the law. Second, echoing critical theory's concept of transformation, CRT strives to change racially oppressive conditions under "an ethical commitment to human liberation" (Crenshaw, Gotanda, Peller, & Thomas, 1995b, p. xiii). Cornell West (1995) asserts that CRT "compels us to confront critically the most explosive issue in American civilization: the historical centrality and complicity of law in upholding white supremacy (and concomitant hierarchies of gender, class, and sexual orientation)" (p. xi).

CRT begins with the premise that "racism is normal, not aberrant, in American society" (Delgado, 1995b, p. xiv). White privileged notions of racial equality contend that institutional racism does not exist or appears only as a deviation from the norms of a presumed fair society. CRT theory and historical research counter this master metanarrative or dominant socio-political chronicle to describe how Whites tend to tolerate antiracism when White interests are benefited or at least not threatened (Bell, 1995a, 1995b). CRT exposes claims of a neutral "color-blind" meritocratic foundation of public policy by detailing the role of White legal bias in the continuing legitimatization of racism (Crenshaw, 1995,

1997, 1998; Flagg, 1998; Gotanda, 1995; Harris, 1993; Kousser, 1999). Applicable to a study of transformative multicultural education, CRT finds that "no scholarly perch [exists] outside the social dynamics of racial power from which merely to observe and analyze" (Crenshaw et al., 1995b, p. xiii). CRT understands race and racism as central and intersectional to all public policy analyses and actions.

Critical theorists have also provided sympathetic critiques to shortcomings of CRT claims at its present stage of development. CRT's original "Black/White paradigm" continues to need expansion to be more inclusive of racialized perspectives from Native Americans, Latinos, and Asian Americans (Alfieri, 1997, p. 1649). A major CRT issue is how disparate interests of groups can converge into a collective and pragmatic antiracist plan, especially if White antiracist narratives and propositions are incorporated into a CRT perspective (E. Taylor, 2000). Critical race theorists have also been encouraged to be mindful of the importance of translating marginalized perspectives into an advocacy that can be realized through practice (Alfieri, 1997; Esposito & Murphy, 2000). Likewise, CRT has been challenged to more clearly articulate alternative standards of practice that multiple forms of affirmative action can take (Brooks & Newborn, 1994). These critiques are not dissimilar to the challenges that exist for transformative multicultural education.

Critical Race Theory and Education.   Analyses of educational practices that use CRT seek to demystify color blindness and its subsequent oppressive outcome on the lives of children and youth of color (Ladson-Billings, 1999a, 1999b; Ladson-Billings & Tate, 1995; Lynn, 1999; Roithmayr, 1999; Solórzano, 1997; Solórzano & Villapano, 1998; Tate, 1997; E. Taylor, 1999a, 1999b, 2000; Villenas, Deyhle, & Parker, 1999). Law professor Daria Roithmayr (1999) notes that CRT provides a way to understand how presupposed neutral educational concepts such as "knowledge, truth, merit, objectivity, and 'good education' are in fact ways of forming and policing the racial boundaries of white supremacy and racism" (p. 4). Presumably neutral educational standards—even those ostensibly intended to support multicultural education—can be analyzed for Eurocentric biases. CRT can help teachers look at their own social and professional positions in relationship to the perspectives and knowledge of families and children of color. CRT can lend authority to historically marginalized voices.

CRT explains how civil rights laws "to remedy racial inequality are often undermined" (Tate, 1997, p. 234) prior to and during implementation in a manner that rarely threatens the legal foundation of White property rights and citizenship (Harris, 1993; Ladson-Billings, 1999a). One example is the historic 1954 U.S. Supreme Court case of *Brown vs. Board of Education.* Although the outcome of this case attended to some of the worst conditions of racial exclusion, discriminatory systems of ability tracking based on race continue inside "integrated" U.S. schools today (Banks, 2000; Green, 1999; Oakes, Garmoran, & Page, 1992; Welner & Oakes, 1997). By assuming that racial integration was the solution, the Court avoided the topic of a racialized hierarchy that negatively skews educational resource allocations and opportunities for people of color, leaving the issue lingering into the 21st century (Harris, 1993). Although rarely recalled, a court-argued rationale for *Brown vs. Board of Education* was to better position a White U.S. government against charges of racial apartheid by communist nations. *Brown vs. Board of Education* also converged with White southern business profit interests that were threatened nationally and internationally by state-sanctioned racial segregation (Bell, 1995a).

CRT can provide a teacher education program a transformational perspective to examine contemporary civil rights policies for their strengths and weaknesses in serving marginalized students of color. CRT can assist educators to develop programs that transform civil rights orientations to more thoroughly benefit families and children of color. As part of this process, CRT places race, racism, and educational equity in a historical and legal context. Although issues of socioeconomic class and gender discrimination obviously deserve transformative analyses and multicultural education solutions, CRT points out their singular perspective "shortcomings vis-à-vis race" (Ladson-Billings & Tate, 1995, p. 49). CRT analyses can contribute to a more profound grasp of how U.S. capitalism negatively skews life opportunities for people of color and individuals born into poverty, disproportionately to the rest of the population.

Ladson-Billings (1999b) draws together examples of CRT practice in teacher education. Highlighted is Jacqueline Jordan Irvine's work at Emory University to help teachers negotiate professional challenges in under-resourced urban schools. She guides teachers in an effort to overcome detrimental gaps between urban schooling environments and interests of African-American children and their families. Irvine's culturally responsive sensibilities contrast with urban education orientations that attempt to "rescue" populations of color for assimilationist goals. Boston College's Marilyn Cochran-Smith uses a CRT approach of story-telling to help teachers construct their own narratives of race and racism. She uses these teacher-generated texts to critically analyze teaching from a transformative perspective. At Santa Clara University, the University of New Orleans, and now as provost at Spelman College, Joyce King incorporates a CRT orientation to deconstruct the premises of liberalism so that teachers understand how incremental notions of progress and social change can make "marginalized groups appear to be impatient malcontents rather than citizens demanding legitimate citizen rights" (Ladson-Billings, 1999b, p. 232).

CRT makes imperative the necessity for sweeping changes to school and community-based racism. Exclusionary practices require transformative alternatives. CRT can complement analyses and goals of transformative multicultural education. Ladson-Billings (1999a) contends that curriculum, instruction, assessment, school funding, and desegregation should be analyzed by using race, racism, and White privilege as centrally defining variables. CRT adds to an understanding of how institutional racism perpetuates schooling inequities within a White-dominated metanarrative about educational purposes and practices. Ladson-Billings writes, "Adopting and adapting CRT as a framework for educational equity means that we will have to expose racism in education *and* propose radical solutions for addressing it" (p. 27). This book represents a modest contribution toward that goal.

CHAPTER 2

Multicultural Education Reform: The Status of Teacher Education

Teacher education programs are a critical link for the development of teachers who hold a culturally responsive, multicultural view of teaching and schooling. Teacher education can be central to helping teachers enhance the academic achievement and future life opportunities for all children and youth. The educational reform report of the National Commission on Teaching and America's Future called attention to the importance of having teachers who can positively affect the schooling outcomes of children and youth rather than replicate situations where social class and ethnicity are the primary determinants of achievement (Darling-Hammond, 1997a). The need for multicultural reform is evidenced by beginning teachers who continue to "feel inadequately prepared and seldom choose to teach in multicultural schools, especially those with high rates of poverty" (Valli & Rennert-Ariev, 2000, p. 15).

Teachers well-qualified in traditional teaching skills may not necessarily possess the multicultural knowledge, dispositions, and skills to meet the needs of culturally diverse student populations. As Sleeter (1992) discovered in her study of staff development on multicultural education, most experienced classroom teachers believe in a pulling-oneself-up-by-the-bootstraps ideology that can thwart multicultural reform efforts. That is to say, many teachers assume individual merit and perseverance alone form the key to academic success. An example of this is a White central Los Angeles teacher, documented in the film *Fear and Learning at Hoover Elementary* (Simon, 1997), who had a master's degree in curriculum development, held high expectations for her students, and was able to teach many of her young Spanish-speaking children to read English. Nevertheless, she remained chillingly detached from and unsympathetic about the living conditions of her struggling, impoverished Mexican immigrant students and their families, factors that inhibited student attendance and academic achievement. She viewed students through a White lens of her grandparents' European immigration history and equated assimilation with being an American. Using herself as an example, she attributed the success and failure of students simply to how hard they worked. Like many White teachers, she acknowledged that she had never experienced discrimination, was "very spoiled as a child" growing up in New York, and in a color-blind breath contended that she had "never judged people on what they looked like on the outside" and had "never been a racist." Despite her professing a total commitment to her students, this elementary teacher with a master's degree chose to quit her job at the end of the school year. This teacher's apparent absence of cultural competence blocked her from understanding the social realities of immigrants of color who live in poverty and how those conditions can hinder the attainment of even minimum academic achievement targets (see, e.g., Suárez-Orozco & Suárez-Orozco, 2001). Thus even teachers with recognized teaching credentials and advanced degrees may lack the multicultural repertoires and sensibilities appropriate for providing the kind of academic and social help their students need under conditions of racial discrimination and poverty.

This chapter provides an overview of the goals of multicultural education reform and the status of multicultural education in teacher education programs. One of the primary goals of multicultural teacher education is to incorporate transformative academic multicultural knowledge and approaches throughout the curriculum in order to displace traditional orientations that marginalize or ignore multicultural education. Based on an analysis of the research literature on multicultural content integration reform in teacher education programs, the chapter emphasizes a methodology that concentrates upon the interpretations and implementation strategies used by both preservice and experienced teachers. Content integration is presented as an accessible means to start gauging the extent to which internal transformative multicultural reform is occurring at the institutional level for teacher education programs. Sources of the limitations on content integration for multicultural reform are presented and include the influence of K–12 cooperating teachers on preservice teachers' notions of multicultural practice. By problematizing the current status of multicultural teacher education activities, the chapter contextualizes subsequent topics in this book.

REFORM WITH A MULTICULTURAL PERSPECTIVE

Multicultural education is a reform effort that strives to create conditions within public schools for fostering equality and equity for all students. Unlike dominant reform strands that focus mainly on student and teacher testing as the primary objective to increase student achievement, multicultural education interrogates political conditions of educational practices that obstruct the goals of equity and equality. As Banks (1993d) explains, the fundamental goal of multicultural education "is to reform the school and other educational institutions so that students from diverse racial, ethnic, and social-class groups will experience educational equality" (p. 3). An underlying assumption of multicultural education reform is the recognition that hegemonic racial, ethnic, and social-class interpretations favor the schooling opportunities for students from privileged backgrounds. Hegemony exists when dominant groups block or undermine the legitimacy of alternative perceptions and explanations from historically subordinated groups (deMarrais & LeCompt, 1995). Multicultural reform speaks to the problem of a dominant social consensus that creates silences around the educational needs and aspirations of underrepresented groups of children and youth and their families. Multicultural education reform considers factors that contribute to student underachievement within broader school reform efforts and, as Nieto (1997) notes, permits

> educators to explore alternatives to systemic problems that lead to academic failure for many students . . . [multicultural education] fosters the design and implementation of productive learning environments, diverse instructional strategies, and a deeper awareness of how cultural and language differences can influence learning. School reform with a multicultural perspective thus needs to begin with an understanding of multicultural education with a *sociopolitical context.* (p. 389)

The sociopolitical context of teaching and learning is precisely what is left out of most dominant reform initiatives, but is integral to multicultural education.

Additionally, gender equity and social justice claims of the disabled are important human rights categories that are often placed in the multicultural camp. Multicultural reform here, however, is devoted to gender and disabilities when intersecting with race, ethnicity, and social class. Gender and disabilities are appropriate multicultural topics when included comprehensively within the entire range of multicultural education issues rather than as isolated units. Exclusive attention in teacher education programs to either gender or disabilities is one limitation uncovered by Sleeter and Grant (1999) in their examination of single-group studies. Sleeter and Grant are clear that when they speak about transformative multicultural education reform, they are focusing on differences defined "by unequal positions of power" and include "gender, disability, and sexual orientation" along with "race, language, and social class" (p. viii). Many educators continue to assert that they are multicultural in their approaches when they choose to focus on gender and disabilities in the absence of attention to race, ethnicity, and social class. Gender and disabilities rights justify study and reform on their own merits. However, to use gender and/or disabilities rights studies exclusively as examples of multicultural education misrepresents the totality of multicultural reform and tacitly sanctions the avoidance of thorny issues connected with race and class (Vavrus, 1998).

The reform movement of multicultural education provides a socially conscious antidote to reforms narrowly conceived around mainstream standards and assessments. Over the past 20 years multicultural education supported reforms have provided a deeper understanding into the prospects for transforming the traditional school into one with a democratic, inclusive, and civic face. Multicultural education is a site where attention is given to conceptions of democracy in a culturally pluralistic society. Nationally, multicultural educators have continually stressed the need for teachers to gain familiarity with and competence in becoming multicultural in their attitudes, knowledge base, and performance skills. Imbedded within this expectation is the desire to have a teaching force with a deeper understanding of the relationship of the school curriculum to a pluralistic society (Tyson, 1994; Zimpher & Ashburn, 1992). The need has increased for teachers to understand and interact effectively with diverse cultural groups outside the standard school boundaries and provide curricular opportunities reflective of this diversity. To meet this multicultural goal, teachers should hold a knowledge base that is responsive to the conditions of people historically placed on the margins of society's political and economic activities (Collins, 1993; Gay, 2000).

Multicultural education is a reform movement that is developing a significant knowledge base. Throughout the 1990s much was learned and shared about the complexity of multicultural education theory and practice. The multicultural literature in the United States during this era was enriched by dozens of scholarly books and reference guides for practice. Collectively these resources offer a wealth of reform insights that can help guide teacher education reform.[1] James Banks's ascendancy to the presidency of the American Educational Research Association (AERA) in the late 1990s marked a multicultural coming of age for the largest professional research association in the world. Among neoconservative monoculturalist adversaries of multicultural education, his presidency and influence were a cause of alarm (see Stotsky, 1999). Just 20 years previously, AERA marginalized social institutional perspectives in favor of quantifiable psychological and experimentally designed studies in controlled settings where social variables generally went unacknowledged. Now multicultural education theorists and researchers find themselves a more integrated part of the AERA community. Through their work with the National Association of Multicultural Education (NAME) in the 1990s, Carl Grant and Donna Gollnick were instrumental in creating annual professional conferences and a viable journal on practices and resources best devoted to multicultural education reform. With the advancement of NAME, multicultural education reform has a recognized national home. The growth in multicultural education scholarship, international recognition of the value of multicultural education in the educational research community, and a separate professional organization devoted to multicultural education are all indicators of the robustness of multicultural reform at the dawn of the 21st century.

STATUS OF MULTICULTURAL EDUCATION IN TEACHER EDUCATION

Notwithstanding institutional pockets of promising practices, most teacher education programs are hesitant when it comes to incorporating multicultural reforms with depth and fidelity. While seeking to increase the number of faculty and students of color, many programs have rhetorically embraced multicultural education but seem unable to make necessary multicultural across-the-curriculum changes despite the growing literature in the field during the 1990s. The major changes observed in teacher education in the past decade included an increase in the use of information technologies and more attention to a variety of fundamental knowledge bases (Imig & Switzer, 1996), but not in multicultural education reform. Even given the efforts by the National Council for the Accreditation of Teacher Education (NCATE) to require teacher preparation programs to have coherent conceptual frameworks that inform the entire curriculum—a goal reinforced by the National Commission on Teaching and America's Future (Darling-Hammond, 1997a) and the American Council on Education (1999)—fragmentation of courses remains the norm (Wisniewski, 1999). NCATE accreditation, despite state rankings weighted on this criteria (Quality Counts 2000, 2000), does not guarantee that teacher education programs will hold a social consciousness toward meeting the learning needs of politically marginalized students. Wisniewski's (1999) critique of a random sample of institutional reports of NCATE-approved colleges reveals a "tenuous" link at best to any kind of mainstream or multicultural education reform (p. 17). Apparently there is a "lack of persuasive evidence that institutions perceive themselves to be part of a reform movement beyond doing what is required by the accreditation process" (Wisniewski, 1999, p. 32). Compounding this entire dilemma for multicultural education reform is the continuing dominance of a Eurocentric orientation toward schooling that either excludes or places on the curricular margins multicultural content (Banks, 1993b, 1994; Collins, 1993; Estrada & McLaren, 1993; Gollnick, 1992b; Irvine, 1992; Kincheloe & Steinberg, 1998; Martin, 1991; McCarthy, 1994; Watkins, 1994).

Condition of Culturally Responsive Teacher Education

Contemporary applications of the phrase *culturally responsive teaching* clearly differ from historic practices of schools exclusively attending to and privileging middle-class and Eurocentric values. In contrast to assimilationist teaching, culturally responsive pedagogy values and appropriately incorporates a student's culture into instruction (Irvine, 2001). Multicultural teacher education and staff development is a place where teachers can learn to become culturally responsive practitioners. As Ladson-Billings (1995a) explains, "Multicultural teacher education occupies a critical position between multicultural theory and multicultural practice" (p. 756).

Yet reaching this multicultural goal of a culturally responsive teaching force through teacher education remains difficult and elusive. For more than a decade researchers within the field have been in agreement that multicultural education concepts should be infused throughout the teacher preparation curriculum. This practice is inconsistent with presenting only isolated units within the curriculum (Gollnick & Chinn, 1994). For prospective teachers to gain cultur-ally-responsive pedagogical skills (Gay, 2000; Irvine, 1992; Irvine et al., 2001; Ladson-Billings, 1995b), research verifies that an introductory experience through one multicultural education course in the teacher preparation curriculum is inadequate (Bennett, 1989; Bliss, 1990; Ladson-Billings, 1995a; Larkin, 1995; McDiarmid & Price, 1990; Vavrus, 1994; Vavrus & Ozcan, 1998). Even when multicultural information that reduces the stereotyping attitudes of preservice teachers is included in the teacher preparation curriculum, both student teachers and practitioners generally do not demonstrate competence in applying a curric-ular knowledge base with multiple perspectives about the interconnectedness of various cultures and histories (Banks, 1993b, 1994; Garcia & Pugh, 1992; Tran, Young, & DiLella, 1994).

Condition of Multicultural Teaching Internships

Research is inconclusive on the added value of multicultural education when teaching experiences with culturally diverse student populations are taken into account. In a study of 16 urban teachers in culturally diverse settings, Rios (1991) found that teachers were generally disengaged from multicultural educa-tion. Nearly all the teachers considered themselves color-blind or, at best, hold-ing a human relations perspective on cultural understanding. These urban teach-ers tended to consider as primary those teaching practices informed by a "principle of student control" (p. 175). They perceived student learning prob-lems as emanating from individual and cultural deficiencies. The one exception was a teacher who held a social reconstructionist orientation and viewed student behavior and achievement as the result of complex interactions between (a) an individual and an individual's culture and (b) an "incompatibility" with a school's culture and teacher characteristics (p. 187). These results led Rios to conclude that "simply putting teachers in multicultural contexts is not going to guarantee more sophisticated thinking about multicultural education" (pp. 194–195; also see Rushton, 2001).

   Although Grant and Secada (1990) report that "experiences with represen-tatives from diverse populations are worthwhile for teachers," they also caution that any positive gain seems "predicated on the student [teachers] and teachers having support mechanisms . . . [and] some external motivation for their efforts" (p. 418). Brown and Kysilka (1994) reinforce this argument with their critique of a student teacher intern who failed to make important connections with her unit on Mexico and the Mexican heritage of some of her students: "This student teacher most likely saw multicultural and global applications as a technical de-mand of the curriculum, not as an extension of pupils' learning or a celebration of an individual's background and culture" (p. 314). These insights support what an earlier study of cross-cultural understandings noted about additional knowledge of other people not necessarily leading to "increased respect, understanding, or acceptance" (Simpson, 1972, p. 222). On the other hand, we are continually faced with the experiential knowledge that has shown the advantages of immersion in cultural perspectives unlike one's own when handled in a culturally appropriate manner. Sleeter (1995a, 2001) finds that teacher candidates who intern for social service agencies staffed preferably by people of color show gains in their expressions of cultural competence. *Guided* immersion field experiences, a topic examined further in Chapters 3 and 5, can help teachers to examine their own social positions in order to better understand the perspective of individuals from culturally different backgrounds.

By the early 1990s teacher education programs offered only a few documented studies and reviews that analyzed the multicultural education pedagogy of teacher preparation programs (Gollnick, 1992a; Grant & Secada, 1990; Mason, 1987; Ramsey, Vold, & Williams, 1989; Spears, Oliver, & Maes, 1990). Studies revealed that during the student teaching experience, often considered by teachers the most important component of their preservice education, the attitudes of cooperating teachers toward multicultural education were a key variable that influenced the context in which student teachers must enact lessons with multicultural content (Garcia & Pugh, 1992; Nel, 1992). More current research documents the inability of teacher candidates to make positive multicultural changes in the final phase of their preparation programs (Goodwin, 1997; Grant & Zozakiewicz, 1995; Luft, 1997; Vavrus, 1994). Although research data are limited on how K–12 cooperating teachers interpret the infusion of multicultural content into the school curriculum by student teachers, Haberman and Post (1990) documented how the multicultural orientations of cooperating teachers are skewed toward individualistic, psychological models rather than to group or societal perspectives. The negative impact of uninformed cooperating teachers on student teacher multicultural knowledge inclusion is also described in contemporary research (Gormley, 1995; Moore, 1996; Vavrus & Ozcan, 1998).

GAUGING MULTICULTURAL TEACHER EDUCATION CURRICULUM REFORM

Content integration is one area that can be an accessible starting point for multicultural education reform within higher education and K-12 staff development programs. Content integration, according to Banks (1993d), considers the degree "to which teachers use examples, data, and information from a variety of cultures and groups to illustrate key concepts, principles, generalizations, and theories in their subject area or discipline" (p. 5). Multicultural content integration is a reform area in which all programs can engage without demonstrative resource shifts. Content integration measures can serve as a gauge for assessing the extent to which multicultural education reform is a priority within programs for higher education teacher preparation and K-12 staff development. For example, if an analysis of the teacher education curriculum were to indicate that content integration rests on perfunctory acknowledgement of cultural heroes rather than evidence of multiculturally reconstructing the curriculum, a program can next begin to pinpoint curricular areas needing correction. Data collected on multicultural content integration during actual teacher performance can reveal the extent to which a program is effectively transforming its professional education curriculum. This information base becomes imperative because if the professional education curriculum is not multiculturally transformed teachers will continue to experience difficulty in delivering a meaningful multicultural-based curriculum.

The challenge to transform the conventional curriculum of either a teacher education program or a public school is considerable. By simply adding multicultural information to the standard curriculum, teachers have generally failed to include multiple perspectives and to interconnect the histories of various cultures and groups (Banks, 1993b, 1994; Cochran-Smith, 2000; Lynch, 1986). To counter an additive content integration curriculum strategy, Banks (1993b) calls for the incorporation of transformative academic knowledge that

> consists of concepts, paradigms, themes, and explanations that challenge mainstream academic knowledge and that expand the historical and literary canon . . . [under the recognition] that knowledge is not neutral but is influenced by human interests, that all knowledge reflects the power and social relationships within society, and that an important purpose of knowledge construction is to help people improve society. (p. 9)

Transforming the curriculum multiculturally is not just a technical exercise. Rather, transformation is a complex curricular endeavor charged with social and political aspects.

Determining preservice and experienced teacher approaches and dispositions toward multicultural curriculum infusion during the student teaching internship phase can serve as indicators of (a) a teacher education program's effectiveness and (b) the ability of future teachers to teach from a multicultural orientation. A program striving to graduate teacher candidates who are knowledgeable in multicultural curriculum transformation, for example, may wish to reassess the teacher education curriculum to determine if teacher candidates are capable of taking at best an additive approach toward multicultural education in student teaching. In this instance faculty may need to revise foundations courses so that they are more explicit about the political dynamics surrounding the school curriculum and multicultural content integration. Instructional methodology courses would require explicit skill development for broadening conventional curriculum for multicultural inclusion. Student teaching expectations would need to reflect program goals for antibias and multicultural curriculum transformation (Adams, Bell, & Griffin, 1997; Derman-Sparks & Phillips, 1997; Gillborn, 1995; Kivel, 1996).

How Banks's (1993a) "Levels of Integration of Multicultural Content" can be helpful is seen in three studies. These studies in the 1990s used Banks's taxonomy to determine the range and depth of multicultural education lessons presented and developed by student teachers. Beginning with contributions and additive levels and then moving to transformational and social action approaches, Banks (1993a) offers a taxonomy for categorizing multicultural content integration. Both conventional and critical stances toward a multicultural curricular incorporation may be analyzed with Banks's schema.

The central aspect of each of the three studies asked teacher candidates and cooperating teachers to note which of the following approaches they used and to provide rationales and examples:[2]

(1) The Contributions Approach: focuses on heroes, holidays, and individual cultural events.
(2) The Additive Approach: adds content, concepts, themes, and perspectives to the curriculum without changing its structure.
(3) The Transformational Approach: changes the structure of the curriculum to enable students to view concepts, issues, events, and themes from the perspective of diverse ethnic and cultural groups.
(4) The Social Action Approach: enables students to make decisions on important social issues and take actions to solve them. (Banks, 1993a)

The highest level in Banks's model, social action, requires the implementation of the theory of social reconstructionism in the context of multicultural education (Grant & Secada, 1990; Zeichner, 1993).

One study analyzed teacher candidates' multicultural content integration (Vavrus, 1994), whereas another examined global education content infusion from a multicultural perspective (Vavrus & Ozcan, 1996). A third study considered K–12 cooperating teacher approaches with student teacher interns for implementing multicultural content into the curriculum (Vavrus & Ozcan, 1998). Located in a state noted nationally for consistently high rankings on ACT and SAT scores, the settings for the three studies were three undergraduate liberal arts colleges situated in the same region in the Midwest with predominantly White preservice teachers. Approximately 115 teacher candidates and cooperating teachers, respectively, participated in each of the three studies. The teacher education faculty from the three colleges had made a commitment to incorporate a multicultural perspective across the curriculum by articulating a critical social perspective within their program-wide conceptual framework (Vavrus, 1994). Global education themes have not experienced the same scrutiny and research in schemata development that multicultural education has (Johnson & Ochoa, 1993) and did not provide an accessible framework for content analysis (cf. Merryfield, Jarchow, & Pickert, 1997; Merryfield, 1996). Therefore, for the global education study (Vavrus & Ozcan, 1996) student teacher responses were also compared to Banks's (1993a) approaches to multicultural education.

Contributions and Additive Approaches to Multicultural Reform

The vast majority of those studied—70% of the preservice teachers and 82% of the cooperating teachers—gave their exclusive attention to content inclusion consistent with the contributions and additive approaches (Vavrus, 1994; Vavrus & Ozcan, 1996; Vavrus & Ozcan, 1998). Teacher education students and their cooperating teachers operating at the contributions and additive levels were generally unable to articulate how the inclusion of certain cultural elements contributed to the development of positive images of a particular ethnic group. The apparent assumption by many teachers was that by sampling Mexican food, for example, their students would gain a positive appreciation of people of Mexican heritage (Vavrus, 1994).

Student teacher interns who used these approaches were apparently trying to focus on a human relations dimension where the commonality of humankind is emphasized. Human relations approaches that use cultural understanding (see Chapter 1) may not necessarily be an inappropriate *beginning* activity because "multicultural education is first a *people-oriented* study" (Spears et al., 1990, p. 61). For student teachers of younger children a human relations emphasis was a common strategy because, as one intern put it, "First grade is a difficult grade to really get into racism and sexism. It is even difficult to get into differences due to cultures" (Vavrus, 1994, p. 50). A fourth-grade student teacher thought her students in a study of Mexico "discovered that, although it is a different culture, there are many similarities" (p. 50). Second-grade pupils, according to a student teacher, learned "that no matter what a person looks like (e.g., color of skin, shape of face, height, etc.), we do not treat them any differently than the way that we want to be treated" (p. 50). Using a human relations approach to avoid discussions of racism overlooks, however, the fact that young children already come to school with preconceived notions of the Other (see Carter & Goodwin, 1994). By the end of the 1990s kindergarten teacher Segura-Mora (1998/1999), for example, continued to find it necessary to devote extensive curricular time with children of color who believe only "White" skin or straight hair is beautiful.

In other instances teacher candidates objectified cultural events and populations of color. Their tendency was to mythologize certain groups, especially

Native Americans, and disconnect their histories from contemporary realities. As the age of pupils increased, student teachers appeared more cognizant of the need to make their inclusions historically accurate and current. Nevertheless, references to Latino cultures, for example, were almost exclusively devoted to Mexico, with no connections reported to the rapidly increasing Latino populations within the United States and with just one biographical inclusion of a successful Latino American (Vavrus, 1994).

For preservice teachers, global education implied teaching about the natural world, other cultures, and the world in general. Some emphasized environmental issues. Others noted the interconnection between people and the natural world. Some stressed the importance of learning about other people and cultures. All of these responses, however, gave an impression of accepting the global status quo, perceiving the primary curricular goal as "learning about the world" (Vavrus & Ozcan, 1996, p. 7).

The most common explanation, reported by K–12 cooperating teachers for favoring the contributions and additive levels, was based on the ease of application within their previously designed curriculum plans. The next most frequent reason pertained to the belief in the appropriateness of multicultural content for the pupils of cooperating teachers. That is to say, teachers added multicultural content to the curriculum on the basis of idiosyncratic understandings as to what is suitable multicultural content to teach their students. These understandings appear to be based more on personal interpretations of multicultural suitability than on informed professional reflections. The least common rationale was their concern with the limited time for student teaching and the perceived competence of student teacher interns (Vavrus & Ozcan, 1998). In summary, teachers based their multicultural content integration criteria on classroom efficiency and as a result screened pupils from complex multicultural knowledge. The student teaching internship was not a limitation in and of itself.

Transformational and Social Action Approaches to Multicultural Reform

Unlike teachers who favored a contributions and additive approach, cooperating teachers tended to give reasons for selecting the transformational and social action levels that cited neither ease of application nor the competency of student teachers. The one common refrain was that these levels were best for their pupils (Vavrus & Ozcan, 1998) although, as the following section illustrates, misconceptions confounded this result. Approximately 30% of the teacher candidates, having been exposed to teacher education program curricular attempts to integrate multicultural education content, were mindful of and sympathetic to the importance of transformational and social action approaches. However, not all student teachers who saw the need for using a transformational approach were successful. One explained that the senior high school English cooperating teacher did not allow deviation from the "predetermined curriculum" and that he "encountered a desire from his students to continue with the way schools have been done" (Vavrus, 1994, p. 50).

Another secondary English student teacher noted resistance to moving beyond the additive level due to "firmly entrenched bigotry, ignorance, and provinciality" (Vavrus, 1994, p. 50). A teacher candidate interning in a high school biology classroom complained that restrictions on transformation in the sciences stem from the perception that multicultural education is "only for social studies" (p. 50). A student teacher of fourth graders in a school and community that was almost exclusively White noted that a difficulty for her content integration was "the lack of a multicultural environment. The students just have no chance to experience other cultures and people of different races and backgrounds" (p. 50). In order to make their multicultural topics more meaningful to their students, a third of the student teachers used some form of active visual media or invited guest speakers to represent multicultural themes. Although 10% of the student teachers reported they were using a social action approach, only 4% actually attempted to engage themselves at this level. Within that latter group half believed that they were involved in social action solely by discussing current multicultural issues of community and national concern. A hunger march and a response to neighborhood racism were two positive examples of social action content integration organized by student teachers. An exceptional case was a student teacher who was able to incorporate the racial turmoil of the local community directly into her existing multicultural lesson plans on prejudice and the history of the civil rights movement.

As the previous narrative portends, preservice teachers who approach global education from the vantage of being concerned about human inequities and environmental problems appeared to have acquired a somewhat different interpretation of global education from that of their peers. The differentiation stems from an awareness of world problems and the need to find solutions. Teacher candidates in this category emphasized the interaction among nations where national decisions may negatively impact other countries or may create social problems of global dimensions. Problem-solving approaches to issues in which U.S. dominant financial interests create negative environmental and human living conditions is a way in which students were able to begin transforming the existing curriculum (Vavrus & Ozcan, 1996).

Factors Limiting Content Integration for Multicultural Reform

Through data analysis of studies on multicultural content integration, program faculty can identify gaps in the effectiveness of their multicultural teacher education curriculum. The origins of multicultural curricular fissures and shortcomings can be brought to the forefront of faculty deliberations on multicultural reform. In the preceding studies that analyzed multicultural approaches, comments from preservice and cooperating teachers revealed three specific factors that limited content integration during the student teaching internship: *inadequacy of preparation*, *resistance and avoidance*, and *misconceptions*. Pervading and potentially confounding teacher candidate implementation of multicultural curricular concepts is a fourth factor, *the influence of the cooperating teacher*.

Inadequacy of Preparation.   Regardless of the multicultural content integration approach used, nearly half of the cooperating teachers reported that student teachers had experienced difficulty in knowing how to alter the curriculum to incorporate multicultural perspectives (Vavrus & Ozcan, 1998). Some teacher education students striving to meet transformational and social action levels found themselves struggling against an inadequate knowledge base. As part of a United Nations activity, one preservice teacher reflected on her limited social science background: "I was learning about the cultures at the same time as my students and they would ask me questions that I was unable to answer" (Vavrus, 1994, p. 51). Student teacher interns who addressed regional racial problems tended to acknowledge the topic only after being thrust into the position of having to respond to concerns coming from their pupils. One student teacher explained that local racism was awkward for him: "I was hesitant before starting. I thought some students or their parents might have different views about the racial issues and that it may pose a problem" (p. 51).

On the whole, preservice teachers confronted with issues of racial conflict lacked preparation in pedagogical skills to respond to their pupils through systematic curriculum transformation or social action. The inability to respond from a multicultural orientation to social controversies is a formidable problem, especially when it results from racism. We will return in Chapter 5 to the subsequent responsibility of teacher education programs in helping teachers at all stages of their work develop pedagogically based antiracist repertoires.

Resistance and Avoidance.   Avoidance of higher multicultural content integration approaches was often confounded by resistance to these perspectives. Over four fifths of the cooperating teachers reported the transformational or social action approach as inappropriate for future teachers (Vavrus & Ozcan, 1998). In other cases an insufficient knowledge base resulted in student and teacher avoidance in attempting transformational and social action approaches. Reflecting a conserving orientation toward knowledge construction, a music student teacher stated that the contributions and additive approaches were sufficient because the purpose of the curriculum was "not to transform the past" (Vavrus, 1994, p. 51).

Limitations on the possibilities for multicultural content integration are further confounded by cooperating teachers who view multicultural education as "not applicable" and feel "too pressed for time to just 'change' the curriculum" to include multicultural education (Vavrus & Ozcan, 1998, p. 104). As one stated, "Our students are starting to feel 'stuffed' with multicultural education; we can't do anymore without facing a backlash!" (p. 104). A secondary teacher said, "College professors ought to spend a few weeks in our junior high and high schools to get a feel for what real problems we as teachers face and I think you'll find multiculturalism way down the list" (p. 104). By marginalizing multicultural education reform, mainstream reforms—intentionally or not—may be having the effect of reinforcing this kind of multicultural negativism.

When analyzing multicultural content integration from a global education perspective, state and scholarly guidelines for teacher educators and K–12 schools (see Iowa Department of Education, 1989; Merryfield, 1996, 1997; Pickert, 1997) often lack overt attention to curriculum transformation that prioritizes an examination of (a) the distribution of natural and political resources, (b) the source of problems associated with natural and social systems, (c) global power structures, and (d) the possibilities for making a better world for all people. In its social studies standards for all high school students, Oregon, for example, does not have any examination items that assess student knowledge about "the lives of people around the world or environmental conditions" (Bigelow, 1999, p. 7). If a social reconstructionist approach were applied to transforming the global aspect of a multicultural education curriculum, teacher education students and their cooperating teachers as representatives of the dominant culture (see Althusser, 1971) would need to learn how to become "capable of examining why their group exclusively enjoys the social and financial rewards" of a global society (Grant & Sleeter, 1993, p. 56). Chapter 6 investigates this issue further from the perspective of global economic constructs that distort the goals of multicultural education reform.

Misconceptions.   Some teacher candidates were unaware of the degree of their own cultural encapsulation and the skewed effect this can have for creating multicultural content integration. Not understanding the dynamics of cultural encapsulation led some to assert a value neutrality toward multicultural concepts. Apparently unaware of the raging debate in academia and state governments over the role of history teaching in multicultural education, a high school history teacher candidate intern claimed that he was "neutral as a teacher" and was able to give "both positive and negative aspects of all peoples" (Vavrus, 1994, p. 51). His comments suggest that he, along with other teachers, might misconceive multicultural education by mistakenly considering himself and his texts free from political and social values.

The largest subset of cooperating teachers who favored the social action approach perceived it as one that student teachers can accomplish. Unfortunately, most responses were unique and vague. That is to say, the rationales generally given by the cooperating teachers for selecting either the transformational and social action approaches were not similar to or consistent with the descriptions given by Banks (1993a) for these levels. One fifth of the cooperating teachers responded that "any" or "all" of the approaches were fitting for student teacher interns to use. These responses appear to stem from cooperating teachers confusing Banks's (1993a) curriculum approaches with either learning styles, such as a teacher reasoning that pupils "need various ways to learn" (Vavrus & Ozcan, 1998, p. 101), or teaching styles as evidenced by another teacher explaining that multicultural approaches ought to be determined by "whatever student teachers feel the most comfortable with and feel they are able to teach successfully" (p. 101).

Overall cooperating teachers' reasoning for selecting the transformational and social action levels suggests that they might not understand the conceptual constructs involved in transforming the curriculum. Most failed to grasp what social action actually means for the classroom curriculum. Although cooperating teachers cite the appropriateness of the social action approach, research showed that only in rare instances were social action activities as defined by Banks (1993a) and others (Grant & Secada, 1990; Zeichner, 1993) actually being planned and enacted by student teacher interns (Vavrus, 1994; Vavrus & Ozcan, 1996; Vavrus & Ozcan, 1998). Misconceiving and, therefore, discounting the value of transformational and social action approaches may be a function of societal expectations that have historically called on teacher education to socialize teachers away from being the kind of moral voices that might result in public conflicts. School systems may be furthering this status quo expectation as a means to garner public and governmental financial support for public education. Transformational and social action multicultural education curriculum goals may ultimately be perceived by teachers under current tacit school system restraints as too politically volatile to pursue.

Influence of K–12 Teachers on Preservice Teachers.   Studies on student teaching interns and K–12 cooperating teachers collectively imply some potential shortcomings relevant to the multicultural education knowledge base held by cooperating teachers as conveyed to future classroom teachers. Cooperating teachers appear more comfortable with contributions and additive approaches. The degree of ease teachers feel with these levels may mirror the extent of their knowledge base in multicultural education. Cooperating teachers also tend to lack consistent criteria in choosing approaches for integrating multicultural content into the curriculum. The most common rationale for selecting the levels of multicultural content integration appears to have less to do with curricular effectiveness and appropriateness for their pupils and more to do with issues of classroom efficiency such as ease of application by the cooperating teacher and the student teacher intern. The nature of the contributions and additive approaches lend themselves to the least amount of curricular modification and may also account for cooperating teachers' choice of these two approaches. For instance, one teacher favored the additive approach because it "does not cause large disruptions to existing curriculum" (Vavrus & Ozcan, 1998, p. 104). This implies that, in comparison to Banks's (1993a) typology, cooperating teachers generally hold low expectations of future teachers' ability to integrate multicultural content into the curriculum.

Cooperating teacher multicultural content integration decisions could also be a function of the condition where an inadequate subject knowledge base, such as in multicultural education, results in inflexible curriculum implementation by teachers (Walker, 1990). An insufficient multicultural knowledge base may end in classroom teachers holding "a basic skills orientation to teaching that seems to render multicultural concerns superfluous" (Grant & Secada, 1990, p. 418). Thus, for some K–12 teachers under whom future teachers must learn, multicultural education is interpreted as an excessive instructional activity. For many teachers multicultural education stands outside what is understood as the school's "official knowledge" and curricular goals, belying the actual political struggle over school curricula, policies, and teaching approaches (see Apple, 1993).

K–12 cooperating teachers' attitudes toward multicultural education, coupled with studies of student teachers' multicultural content infusion, suggest that regardless of their previous knowledge preservice teachers tend to use the approach considered most important and practical by their cooperating teachers and are generally discouraged from attempting the deeper multicultural levels of transformation and social action (Garcia & Pugh, 1992; Goodwin, 1997; Grant & Zozakiewicz, 1995; Haberman & Post, 1990; Moore, 1996; Vavrus, 1994; Vavrus & Ozcan, 1998). Minimizing multicultural content integration was the case even when student teachers had been previously exposed to Banks's typology for moving to the transformational and social action levels (Vavrus, 1994; Vavrus & Ozcan, 1996; Vavrus & Ozcan, 1998). These factors may be attributed to cooperating teachers who impose their ideas of multicultural education on student teachers and/or to student teachers who look up to cooperating teachers as significant models of teaching. Either way, the beliefs of cooperating teachers about multicultural education appear as an influential variable on the teaching expectations and behaviors of future teachers.

CONCLUSION

Multicultural education aims to reform the practices of teaching and schooling in order to benefit the achievement and life opportunities of all children and youth. Yet during the past 20 years dominant reform efforts have tended to diminish multicultural education concerns for equity (Carlson, 1997). Current dominant reforms generally emphasize measurable outcomes that prioritize test scores for the individual child in reading and mathematics over nearly any other curricular considerations or corollary reform initiatives (Hirsch, Koppich, & Knapp, 1998). While advocating for academic achievement gains for young people primarily from marginalized racial groups and social classes, multicultural education reform strives to overcome the negative effects of discrimination against children and youth from these groups. Dominant educational reforms structured around a model of meritocracy treat the individual as removed from the social forces of race and class, concepts central to multicultural education. Given the focus on individualism, issues that affect group identity and cultural differences are either downplayed or ignored. Under dominant reform models the individual is constituted as holding the reasoning capacity to either rise or fall within a society on the basis of one's own merit independent of social, political, and economic constraints. Transformative multicultural education reform challenges the assumptions of meritocratic reforms in a society where people of color and those in or near poverty regularly face bigotry and discrimination. A teacher education program curriculum that strives to become multicultural in outlook and practices should grapple with notions of individualism and meritocracy where dominant groups hinder the learning opportunities of students from socially marginalized groups.

How teacher candidates and their cooperating K–12 teacher-mentors interpret multicultural education implementation in the classroom is an important beginning data point for teacher educators to determine the status of their internal multicultural education reform efforts. Rather than assuming that multicultural information in the curriculum is having a transformative impact on teachers, teacher education programs can systematically assess the extent of multicultural transformation. A preferable location to gather data is when preservice teachers are in the field working in classrooms, ideally during the student teaching internship. Full-time student teaching provides adequate time for a teacher candidate to develop and implement lessons with multicultural content. Banks's (1993a) "Levels of Integration of Multicultural Content" is an accessible typology for conducting internal program analyses to determine the kind of content integration that both teacher candidates and cooperating teachers tend to favor.

The information from program-conducted research offers a means to compare program goals for multicultural content integration by teachers to actual practice. Even when program faculty and administrators state that they strive to develop within teachers the dispositions and skills to make socially critical curricular changes to support the goals of multicultural education, they may find through this methodology that significant gaps exist between program aspirations and practices. Specifically, revelations of a predominant inclination toward an additive approach to multiculturalism can suggest that a program's curricular goals for multicultural education reform are falling short of expectations. Teacher candidates and cooperating teachers who envision contributions and additive approaches to content integration as constituting the whole of multicultural education appear to hold an inadequate understanding of the transformative dimension and imperative of multicultural education reform.

Teachers who use an additive approach exclusively seem inclined to view populations of color as remote, deficient, or exotic (Vavrus, 1994; Vavrus, 1998; Vavrus & Ozcan, 1998). Teacher educators may also discover in their data factors that limit multicultural content integration by their graduating teacher candidates. Identifying sources that hinder content integration can provide program faculty with information for program improvement. Such factors might include inadequacy of preparation in a preservice teacher's content area and instructional methodologies, ideological resistance, the counterproductive influence of some cooperating teachers, and general misconceptions about the origins and purposes of multicultural education. Results from such studies can be more broadly shared with the education community so that teacher educators can consider this knowledge as part of programmatic efforts to make teaching multicultural. Without this kind of information, program self-assertion and isolated success stories may serve as substitutes for meaningful multicultural education reform within teacher education.

CHAPTER 3

Incorporating Multicultural Reform
Into the Teacher Education Curriculum

Multicultural reform goals are advanced when institutions make changes that enhance the multicultural education of teachers. While multicultural reform recognizes the importance for a White-majority teaching population to have the skills necessary for working with culturally diverse student populations, Valli and Rennert-Ariev (2000) found that most contemporary reform efforts[1] are far from agreement on making structural changes for multicultural education that "are likely to have mission and resource-related implications for institutions" (p. 12). A teacher education program's mission or conceptual orientation, however, is what can drive the structure and content of the preparation curriculum and determine resource allocation. When faculty collectively consider the interrelationship between mission and curriculum from a multicultural reform perspective, the possibilities are heightened for incorporating multicultural values, content, and skills throughout the teacher education curriculum.

In this chapter, we examine four interrelated solutions for creating a multicultural teacher education curriculum. First, teacher education faculty are encouraged to begin by revisiting program conceptual frameworks in order to address the depth of multicultural commitment based on what is currently known about multicultural education in the field of teacher education. Second, as part of this process, conceptual frameworks designed as models of teacher reflection are reconsidered in the context of ideologies that work for transformative multicultural reflection. Third, how programs can conduct internal analyses is described with an eye toward systematically incorporating multicultural education content across the entire teacher preparation curriculum. Finally, teacher education programs with clear understandings of their multicultural mission and procedures can begin the task of collaborating with K–12 school personnel so that multicultural connections can increase in the education of all teachers.

CREATING A MULTICULTURAL TEACHER
EDUCATION CONCEPTUAL FRAMEWORK

The obstacles are considerable for the conceptual rethinking required for the transformation of significant numbers of teacher education programs nationally depicted as "woefully traditional and almost 100% Eurocentric in perspective" (Boyer, 1990, p. 244). Immediate steps are available, though, for any teacher education program to undertake actions for becoming thoroughly engaged in multicultural reform. To discount the value of mission reconceptualization may result in the perpetuation of programs enabling "countless incidents of indifference and neglect on the part of individuals who have it in their power to make a difference" (Goodlad, 1990, p. 67) and providing "shoddy preparation that angers and embarrasses those who care deeply about the minds and welfare of America's young" (Holmes Group, 1995, p. 1). In other words, for programs to be comprehensively infused with multicultural concepts, they need to collectively conceptualize multicultural education as "more than an ethnic additive single course on multicultural education or human relations" (Talbert-Johnson & Tillman, 1999, p. 205). A program's conceptual framework is the place for faculty to start.

Purpose and Process

Because of accreditation requirements for the National Council for the Accreditation of Teacher Education (NCATE) and an increasing number of states with NCATE partnerships, most teacher education programs are required to articulate program-wide conceptual frameworks. Understood to be backed by a supporting knowledge base rationale, the conceptual framework is intended to inform all aspects of the teacher education curriculum (NCATE, 2001b). The conceptual framework is the primary collective place for program faculty to philosophically commit to multicultural education reform. As NCATE (2001b) standards explain, the conceptual framework "establishes the shared vision" for teacher education institutional "efforts" (p. 10) to prepare future teachers for work with school children and youth. Inherently, faculty deliberations for agreeing upon a program-wide conceptual framework are filled with ideological tensions (Gideonse, 1989), and historically programs have delegated multicultural conceptual accountability to just a few interested faculty, usually faculty of color (see Gollnick, Osayande, & Levy, 1980; Raines, 1998). Nevertheless, when David Imig, president of the American Association of Colleges for Teacher Education, and education dean Tom Switzer (1996) consider the future of teacher education, they are adamant on the need for faculty deliberations on formidable social issues affecting teaching and learning. They write:

> Until faculty are afforded the time to step back from the daily routines and to engage in a moral conversation about *their responsibilities to create a just and caring society for children*, to hold political conversations about the "regulations" in which they and their institution are *willing to invest to benefit all children*, to sponsor dialogue about the *role of the public school in America and its purpose in*

> *preserving political democracy*, and to debate the importance of beginning teachers being able to *transform and restructure schools* [italics added], we will continue to conduct teacher education in settings absent mission and genuine purpose. (p. 224)

Program faculty are being asked to deliberate upon their institutional role as it relates to the creation of a just, democratic society that is beneficial to all children and how, therefore, the teachers they educate can transform schools toward these goals. Without this level of moral and political engagement at the institutional level, teacher education programs may simply reproduce tepid forms of multicultural education. Through a deliberative process inclusive of multicultural issues, a conceptual framework can offer program coherence instead of replicating worn consistencies. Buchmann and Floden (1992) explain, "While *consistency* implies logical relations and the absence of contradictions, *coherence* allows for many kinds of connectedness" (p. 4). The conceptual framework is where a faculty can articulate a coherent vision about program goals for educating future teachers multiculturally.

New NCATE (2001b) diversity expectations within a conceptual framework now give legitimacy to program faculty to make meaningful headway toward articulating a vision of multicultural education that can be transformational. Signifying a shift from previous policy, NCATE now asks for a conceptual framework that "provides a conceptual understanding of how knowledge, dispositions, and skills related to diversity are integrated across the curriculum, instruction, field experiences, clinical practice, assessments, and evaluations" (p. 13). The task rests, however, with an institution to define *diversity* either as a status quo multicultural additive approach or as transformative multicultural reform. Chapter 4 examines and offers alternatives to indeterminate diversity discourse in NCATE standards.

As a means to deepen multicultural education, teacher educators can examine the entire range of program multicultural content integration by engaging with their colleagues in self-studies and internal program evaluations to assess the coherence among social foundations and psychology courses, methodology sequences, and field experiences. Institutional self-assessment can determine specific approaches a program's curriculum and preservice teachers actually use for multicultural curriculum development and instruction. Discrete identification of approaches offers clarity over reliance upon generic claims of multicultural content integration. As Chapter 2 explains, program multicultural content integration goals can then be compared to program practices.

When teacher educators take on program analyses of multicultural education, doors can open for broadening the dialogue within the curriculum regarding the expectations and range of possibilities for multicultural content integration in the school curriculum. To arrive at this place, program faculty need to collaborate to "reconceptualize the compensatory notion of multicultural education as it now predominantly exists to a notion of multiple cultures and perspectives as *integral to all aspects* [italics added] of teacher education" (Striedieck, 1997, p. 39). The reconceptualization process can only be undertaken when a faculty have collectively expanded a program's conceptual framework by including a transformative commitment to multicultural education across the curriculum.

The making of philosophical and purposeful curricular bridges from an additive to a transformative perspective is an appropriate focal point for a teacher education faculty that seeks to strengthen multicultural education in the professional education curriculum. As Banks (1993a) acknowledges, multicultural approaches "are often mixed and blended in actual teaching situations . . . [and] the move from the first to the higher level of multicultural content integration is likely to be gradual and cumulative" (p. 207).

The developmental notion of multicultural content integration is useful to consider because, for example, involvement at the social action level may initially be an unrealistic expectation for teacher candidates who possess limited understandings of academic transformative knowledge. Both conceptual and pragmatic objectives are embedded in the design and implementation of a multicultural teacher education curriculum. This multicultural curricular condition is similar to what Bruner (1971) grappled with when he admitted that he was "puzzled . . . about the relationship between knowledge as detached (competence?) and knowledge as a guide to purposeful action (performance?)" (p. 65). The school curriculum is generally understood to be "knowledge as detached." Multicultural education knowledge, on the other hand, implies not only competence in academic knowledge but an outcome of some "purposeful action." By deliberating upon Bruner's academic quandary between knowledge and action and applying it to multicultural teacher education, faculty can design a meaningful program conceptual framework. The aim for a teacher education program then becomes the extent to which its conceptual framework for purposeful and systematic multiculturalism encourages the incorporation of transformative academic knowledge and performance applications.

Envisioning the Multicultural Teacher

A program conceptual framework permits a teacher education faculty to describe the kind of future teacher who they anticipate will graduate from their program. On the basis of a review of conceptions of multicultural education, Hidalgo, Chávez-Chávez, and Ramage (1996) developed a theoretical framework that can be used to envision the kind of multicultural teacher a college or university aspires to graduate, that is to say, future teachers who are personally committed to and see their roles as:

(1) valuing demographic diversity as an enriching social context;
(2) promoting a multicultural curriculum as a whole-school knowledge base;
(3) promoting instructional strategies that structure heterogeneous, learner-centered, and critical processes;
(4) promoting collaborative and unifying relationships among all participants . . . in the educational enterprise. (p. 765)

Building onto this framework is a vision of culturally responsive teachers who, in addition to understanding diversity as an asset to a school and affirming the cultural backgrounds of students, set high achievement goals for all students regardless of their race, ethnicity, or class (García, 1996, 1999; Gay, 2000; Ladson-Billings, 1995b).

Powell's (1997) five-year case study is encouraging in the description given for a culturally responsive teacher. Using Ladson-Billings's (1995b) theory of culturally relevant teaching, Powell (1997) provides considerable detail to help us understand the attitudinal and applied characteristics of a culturally responsive teacher. Powell's teacher, who is White, held (a) a positive image of herself and her students, (b) democratic and inclusive culturally sensitive social relations with her students and their communities, and (c) a conception of knowledge as socially constructed and capable of transformation. This teacher manifested these characteristics as

> she continuously explored students' cultural backgrounds and families, linked students' backgrounds to school culture, and assumed various leadership roles at the school that were related to racial minority students. Although [she] viewed her classroom as an extension of students' cultural and family backgrounds when she began teaching, this kind of sensitivity became a preoccupation for her, and ultimately became a prevailing theme in her decision making about her classroom curriculum and instruction. (Powell, 1997, p. 473)

This culturally responsive teacher acted to transform the classroom curriculum in her traditional school setting so that she could more completely provide students access to knowledge base connections relevant to their own lives (Powell, 1997).

Permeating the notion of a culturally responsive teacher is the multicultural value "opposing inequity, not just celebrating diversity" (Ladson-Billings, 1995a, p. 749). Irvine and York (1995) explain that becoming a culturally responsive teacher is not just a matter of studying abstract instructional techniques. Rather, culturally responsive pedagogy requires "committed, caring, dedicated teachers who are not afraid, resentful, or hostile, and who genuinely

want to teach at schools with culturally diverse populations" (p. 494). By starting with a multicultural vision of the future teacher who is culturally responsive,
programs can create curricular opportunities that support teacher candidates with
fundamental teaching skills in the context of a multicultural knowledge base.

REFLECTIVE MULTICULTURAL TEACHER
EDUCATION AND IDEOLOGY

By the beginning of this century reflective practice had become a prevalent
conceptual framework theme for programs granted NCATE accreditation. In a
study of NCATE higher education self-study reports, Wisniewski (1999) notes,
however, that the theme of reflection "may have the negative effect of communi-
cating a level of pretension not in keeping with the maze of program components described in the institutional reports" (p. 22). This "pretension" may be
accounted for by ideological obstacles that counteract authentic reflection
throughout the historical development of teacher education programs.

The status quo nature of teaching and teacher education with its historically
antitheoretical, nonreflective emphasis (Bowers, 1977; Giroux, 1988; Wildman & Nile, 1987), combined with models focused on individualistic psychological analyses, has guarded programs from reflecting upon *comprehensive*
social system critiques as part of the valued knowledge base for teaching. By
broadening reflective models to include the place of multicultural education
within the education of a teacher, program faculty and preservice teachers can
consciously incorporate in their reflective model the ideological factors that influence the infusion of multicultural reform. Teacher education programs that
attempt to structure a professional education curriculum on models of teacher
reflection have an opportunity to expand reflective practice by engaging in program transformation based on a critical orientation toward multicultural education concepts (Johnson & Ochoa, 1993; Valli, 1992; Yost, Sentner, & Forlenza-
Bailey, 2000).

Reflection That Is Multicultural

The promising practice of professional reflection may yield teacher candidates
who move beyond the technical requirements of instruction to deeper considerations and actions on complex, multidimensional topics that compose the field of
multicultural education. Unfortunately, the faculty of future teachers as a group
do not have a history of reflecting on these topics (Gilliom, 1993). Some teacher
educators appear to have limited expectations for developing culturally responsive beginning teachers by holding "strong beliefs that pre-service teachers are
incapable of reaching higher levels of thought" required for critical reflection

(Yost, Sentner, & Forlenza-Bailey, 2000, p. 46). Additionally, case studies of programs that purport to encourage reflection reveal a tendency in these programs to elude issues related to social and political curriculum transformation (Beyer & Zeichner, 1987; Valli, 1992; Zeichner, 1992).

When designing experiences to enhance reflection on multicultural theory and practice, a program can make central to reflective curricular activities concepts often presented as uncontested dominant traditional values and norms. Popkewitz (1994) offers a suggestion for those engaged in reflective models of teaching by highlighting the "need to ask what systems of ideas organize how we construct the objects that we are calling schooling, children, teaching, learning, and so on" (p. 13). To analyze this objectifying process requires teachers at all stages of their careers to deconstruct that which is considered common sense and, through critical reflection, make problematic concepts that can hinder the realization of multicultural education reform. Waiting until the student teaching phase to instill a posture of critical reflection is ineffective, especially on curricular issues surrounding multicultural education, because student teaching is too late into the teacher education program for this longitudinal teacher development process (Goodwin, 1997; Luft, 1997; Vavrus, 1994; Zeichner & Liston, 1987). The need remains to deepen critical multicultural reflection throughout the curriculum.

Too often future teachers enact value-laden multicultural education primarily as politically neutral topics. Different cultures are simply described or global phenomena are presented as having a distant relationship to students' immediate contexts (Brown & Kysilka, 1994; Vavrus, 1994; Vavrus & Ozcan, 1996). Reflective models of teacher education at their current stage of development and design (see Yost, 2000) will not overcome dominant ahistorical ideologies for the vast majority of their candidates. Nevertheless, teacher educators can make a conscious effort to expand the curricular knowledge bases from which they draw for reflective teaching in order to include an analysis of the nature and role of ideologies within a framework of cultural transmission through the pervasiveness of mass communications and popular culture (see Cortéz, 2000; McLaren, 1995; Shohat & Stam, 1994; Thompson, 1990). Reflective teacher education programs seriously concerned about multicultural education may need to create long-term networks for exchanging curricular information, efforts, and techniques that seek to overcome dominant ideologies resistant to realizing social and political justice as played out in the school curriculum.

Multicultural teacher education programs can present critical perspectives on schooling and have their teacher candidates reflect on these implications for K–12 students. Programs can also engage preservice teachers in an interrogation of the actual enactment of a curriculum and how the belief systems of teachers mediate the organization and content of their teaching. Through critical reflection, teachers' social definitions about the parameters of their professional work can be reexamined in the context of multicultural education reform goals. With critical inquiry, educators at all levels can "explore their cultural identity by examining their racial identity development" in order to unpack what it means to teach and learn in a multicultural society (E. Taylor, 1999b, p. 236). The politically charged nature of the challenge to a Eurocentric orientation, however, cannot be minimized for teacher educators operating within a reflective model. An option is to have preservice teachers, who have been considering these issues during their preparation program, write critical reflections during their field experiences and student teaching internships on their own cultural perspectives and how their orientations may influence how they approach the curriculum. Table 3.1, "Assessing Reflection for Cultural Encapsulation," presents an assessment approach with performance indicators.

For teacher candidates at the student teaching internship stage of their career, a reasonable assessment expectation is the developing level in Table 3.1. The developing teacher candidate has reached a reflective place where personal cultural values are acknowledged as influencing understandings of K–12 student performance. The skilled teacher assessment level is what we might expect of the experienced, culturally responsive teacher. The emerging level suggests a limited awareness by the student teacher intern about how cultural encapsulation affects the teaching and learning process. The unsatisfactory level indicates a deficit in the teacher candidate's multicultural knowledge base or a resistance to professional reflection on multicultural concepts.

Reflection on cultural encapsulation throughout a teacher education program can result in multicultural advocacy during the student teaching internship. Developing professional dispositions that support underserved students is a part of the role of a reflective culturally responsive teacher. Table 3.2, "Assessing Multicultural and Antibias Advocacy," sets an expectation for teacher candidates to speak out against negative characterizations of all students, especially those historically marginalized. This assessment also anticipates that teacher candidates will work with school personnel to ensure that all students experience equity.

Reflection on the alternative of transformative approaches to traditional conceptions of teaching and learning is a necessary teacher education curricular component for enlarging multicultural competencies within future teachers. Education program faculties, acting within reflective teacher education curriculum models, can make their work more authentic when they acknowledge the complexity of their task by legitimizing multicultural reflection and action. Multicultural reflection across the curriculum is a vital element for the development of culturally responsive teachers.

Making Ideological Shifts in Reflective Models

Concluding that teacher resistance to multicultural education is based simply on how teachers perceive curriculum innovations and mandates (cf. Tye & Tye,

Table 3.1. Assessing Reflection for Cultural Encapsulation

Assessment Level	*Indicator*
Skilled teacher	Teacher uses insights of cultural encapsulation to make culturally appropriate contributions to student learning and school improvement.
Developing teacher candidate	Teacher candidate is able to acknowledge and critically reflect upon his/her own received cultural perspective and come to know how that perspective influences his/her understanding of and actions toward individuals from groups different from his/her received culture.
Emerging teacher candidate	Teacher candidate is limited in being able to acknowledge and critically reflect upon his/her own received cultural perspective and come to know how that perspective influences his/her understanding of and actions toward individuals from groups different from his/her received culture.
Unsatisfactory teacher candidate	Teacher candidate makes no effort to reflect upon his/her own received cultural perspective or to come to know how that perspective influences his/her understanding of and actions toward individuals from groups different from his/her received culture.

Note: From *Student Teaching Handbook* (p. 45), by The Evergreen State College, 2000, Olympia, WA: Author. Copyright 2000 by The Evergreen State College. Adapted with permission.

1993) is only part of the story. Such a position becomes reductionist when it lacks recognition of the hegemonic force of political ideologies within our schools. Most visible ideologically are schooling practices that benefit privileged social groupings of students over those traditionally subordinated. Teacher education since its inception has been implicated in forwarding a dominant ideology. Historically schools of education have not seen their missions tied to providing preservice teachers with the intellectual and technical skills necessary for taking public positions on troublesome social and moral issues (Spring, 2001). This social transmission role of teacher education has resulted in producing teachers who find that by "identifying themselves as spokespersons for—or representatives of—the [sociopolitical] system in its local manifestation, they avoid interrogation and critique" (Greene, 1978, p. 56). Freire (1998) in his final days was even more blunt: "A bigot's *progressive* discourse, which contrasts with his or her practice, is a false discourse" (p. 42)—and, in this case, a false reflective practice.

Table 3.2. Assessing Multicultural and Antibias Advocacy

Assessment Level	Descriptor
Skilled teacher	Teacher makes a particular effort to challenge negative attitudes and helps ensure that all students, particularly those traditionally underserved, are honored in the school.
Developing teacher candidate	Teacher candidate works within the context of a particular team or department to ensure that all students receive a fair opportunity to succeed.
Emerging teacher candidate	Teacher candidate does not knowingly contribute to some students being ill served by the school.
Unsatisfactory teacher candidate	Teacher candidate contributes to school practices that result in some students being ill served by the school.

Note: From *Student Teaching Handbook* (p. 45), by The Evergreen State College, 2000, Olympia, WA: Author. Copyright 2000 by The Evergreen State College; and from *Enhancing Professional Practice: A Framework for Teaching* (p. 119), by C. Danielson, 1996, Alexandria, VA: Association for Supervision and Curriculum Development. Adapted with permission.

Beyond the current wave of experiments with reflective paradigms, the task of moving preservice teachers to critical orientations involves no small challenge to deeply embedded conservative cultural norms manifested in teacher education programs. The goal of multicultural reform in teacher education remains a crucial albeit formidable reform task in the continuing contribution to the development of an equitable society in a culturally diverse society. What happens when teacher educators do less than engage their colleagues and classroom teachers in this ideological endeavor as demanded for a culturally responsive teaching force? Programs can simply persist in preparing teachers to become one-dimensional multicultural technicians at best rather than developing into critically reflective multicultural curriculum developers.

An important step in moving to critical reflection is to make problematic Eurocentric metanarratives of human experience that fail to construct an entire historical picture in all of its complexities and competing voices. Shohat and Stam (1994) explain:

> Eurocentrism sanitizes Western history while patronizing and even demonizing the non-West; it thinks of itself in terms of noblest achievements—science, progress,

humanism—but of the non-West in terms of its deficiencies, real or imagined. (p. 298)

To counter politically dominant metanarratives, Cherry McGee Banks (1996) advocates "perspective-taking" as a technique by "creating an authentic unity" in order "to help students understand the partial nature of knowledge and to recognize that the meanings drawn from the texts are not universal" (p. 51). Engaging in multidimensional understandings of knowledge construction can serve as a foundation to aid teacher education students in critical multicultural reflection. Ultimately the responsibility rests with program faculty to create necessary conditions to make an ideological shift for developing within preservice and experienced teachers the dispositions and knowledge necessary for critical multicultural reflection.

SYSTEMATIC MULTICULTURAL EDUCATION

As teacher education faculty rethink multicultural education within a program's curriculum, a systematic approach is appropriate. Consideration should be given to incorporating multicultural concepts throughout the teacher education curriculum, reconfiguring traditional methodology and educational psychology courses, and analyzing the multicultural impact of program-arranged field experiences.

Multicultural Education Across the Curriculum

Experienced teachers who have been required to take a single multicultural human relations course are reluctant to move toward multicultural curriculum infusion (Vavrus, 1994; Vavrus & Ozcan, 1998). A foundations course based on transformative multicultural objectives can provide education students a beginning critical social orientation toward pedagogical knowledge bases for eventually incorporating multicultural perspectives into lesson plans. A single course devoted to multiculturalism in a professional education sequence—even when supplemented by a social foundations course with a critical perspective—remains insufficient, however. One solution is to infuse multicultural education across the teacher education curriculum. To do so, a teacher preparation program needs to solidify the link from its foundation courses through the student teaching internship by strengthening the multicultural content in psychology and methodology courses.

Teacher education programs can profit by using the levels of content integration proposed by Banks (1993a) (see Chapter 2) as systematic benchmarks to apply multicultural education reform across the curriculum. Applying such a taxonomy to the professional education curriculum only at the student teaching phase appears to be too late in the delivery of the program curriculum to prepare preservice teachers required to infuse multicultural concepts into their teaching experiences. Through the impetus of a multicultural conceptual framework, faculty teaching traditional pedagogical courses can move toward applications of multicultural orientations within discrete methodology areas to develop what Lynch (1986) refers to as "systematic multiculturalism" rather than applying an additive approach (p. 162). The kind of expectation for transformative multicultural knowledge development and application reaches to a more complex level of learning for teachers because it is "a synthesis-evaluation task" (Gay, 1997, p. 158). A cooperating teacher sympathetic to the multicultural goal of social action cautioned that "this would take some years building" (Vavrus & Ozcan, 1998, p. 106). It certainly will take "years" unless teachers are introduced to multicultural transformative concepts throughout their preservice and continuing education curriculum.

Reconfiguring Educational Psychology and Instructional Methodology

Many traditional teacher education courses in educational psychology perpetuate an idea that children and youth are not public members of a culturally diverse society. These curricular offerings focus primarily on the individual learner and stress execution of technique in instructional methods. Under this model young people are abstracted and objectified into controlled specimens for sterile examination. Indeed, such curricular requirements for preservice teachers tend to reduce young people to the status of individual "learners" on questionable scales of measurement and distribution. Jung (1997) pointedly described the results of this practice upon her secondary school teacher candidates:

> My students were able to display appropriate attitudinal rhetoric in reciting their altruistic beliefs about education, public school students, and teaching. Nonetheless, most of the class understood student failure as solely a student's (and by extension, parent's) problem. School-as-social-institution was typically not seen as leading to individual student failure. Neither was the teacher seen as possibly contributing to individual student failure. (p. 199)

To overcome the tendency to exclude social factors that affect student learning in the process of systematically incorporating social system variables within the curriculum, traditional educational psychology courses can be reconceptualized, for example, as the "Social Psychology of Learning, Teaching, and Schooling." Ways in which social identities develop are supported by a knowledge base ripe for reconfiguring required psychology courses for education students. Writes Gay (1999):

> Research and theory in social psychology and multicultural counseling are generating a rich pool of ethnic and racial identity development models, paradigms, and

> diagnostic techniques. Now it is possible to demonstrate how multicultural education can systematically facilitate ethnic identity development. (p. 209)

This assignment for teacher education programs extends to subject-matter teaching methodology courses. *Learning styles* is a rather uncertain term for grasping social-psychological dynamics of subject-specific learning. Approached from a multicultural perspective, learning-styles research indicates that teachers should know how to (a) incorporate the cultural context of teaching and learning into the curriculum by using the prior learning of students and including students' own personal cultural perceptions, (b) utilize affect in building interpersonal relationships with students, and (c) adjust teaching approaches that conflict with student learning styles (Irvine & York, 1995). Nevertheless, Irvine and York (1995) note that

> research on learning styles using culturally diverse students fails to support the premise that members of a given group exhibit a distinctive style. . . . Clearly, learning-styles research is a useful beginning in designing appropriate instruction for culturally diverse students, and not an end in itself. (p. 494)

Yet, when learning styles are conceived in the context of instruction being congruent with cultural backgrounds, learning gains may accrue to marginalized students of color (Gay, 2000).

Learning styles used simplistically hold the potential for stereotyping children of color and further stigmatization of an exotic Other from a White norm. Murrell (1999) explains that developmental learning needs of students from outside the dominant culture cannot be comprehended by teachers "without an analysis and synthesis of the students' experiences with the curriculum and knowledge of how they position themselves in the culture of the classroom" (p. 82). For teachers to engage in a culturally responsive analysis of student learning styles as related to discrete subject areas requires a shift away from standard ideologies of individualism and meritocracy. Such ideological orientations often create a cultural vacuum for understanding student learning.

Learning-styles approaches that either negate or simplify cultural orientations and differences can be counterproductive to the achievement of children and youth living in subordinated cultures. A multicultural teacher education program needs to incorporate in its curriculum culturally responsive content on learning styles and instructional design and implementation. Moribund forms of educational psychology and abstract instructional methodology models should be abandoned under transformative models of systematic multicultural education. In a multicultural teacher education program, curriculum and instruction methodology courses should help preserve candidates to design lessons that place a prime value on multicultural content integration. One classroom teacher, mindful of potential demands when moving up Banks's (1993a) typology, pointed out that "transformational and social action require a great deal of planning that is not introduced in an effective manner in [the student teachers'] education (methods) courses" (Vavrus & Ozcan, 1998, p. 105). Realizing that Banks's (1993a) approaches imply a sequence of developmental stages through which teachers may pass as they design lessons with multicultural content, another cooperating teacher advised, "Student teachers need to work from the basics [e.g., additive level] so they can develop confidence through success. Too much experimentation [e.g., transformation] can lead to confusion and chaos" (p. 106). Unfortunately, the responsibility for connecting teacher program elements for multicultural knowledge goals when applied to subject-matter teaching methodology is often left to the preservice teacher to figure out (Floden, 1997). To help future teachers, teacher education programs need to adopt a systematic approach to incorporate multicultural knowledge, skills, and dispositions into instructional methodology courses (e.g., see Irvine et al., 2001).

Providing preservice teachers with diverse community experiences outside campus and K–12 school boundaries continues to offer the possibility of expanding multicultural understandings (Sleeter, 2001; Zeichner & Hoeft, 1996). Besides increased exposure to diverse populations through community-based field experiences (Wiest, 1998), future teachers can be led to grapple with issues of privilege (Horton, Garcia, Scott, & Chavez, 1999). Zeichner and Hoeft (1996) caution that without across-the-curriculum multicultural education, preservice teachers in culturally diverse settings are unlikely to become the kind of culturally responsive teachers we may envision. Furthermore, when college-based supervision is limited and/or conducted without well-informed culturally responsive teacher educators, field experiences can result in the reinforcement of negative cultural stereotypes.

Multicultural incorporation throughout a teacher education curriculum can have as its culminating experience the "successful completion of student teaching contingent upon acceptable performance on multicultural criteria embedded in regular performance appraisal criteria and procedures" (Gay, 1997, p. 169). Table 3.3, "Assessing Knowledge of Multicultural, Antibias Curriculum Planning," is designed to evaluate a teacher candidate during student teaching. The antibias aims of multicultural education are advanced by a skilled culturally responsive teacher who is able to transform a conventional curriculum. A teacher education program can reasonably expect a student teacher to attempt to transform the conventional curriculum or at least add multicultural content that works toward antibias goals. The teacher candidate who excludes multicultural perspectives and antibias goals from curriculum planning should be judged unsatisfactory.

Increased multicultural content coherence throughout programs tied to student teaching performance criteria increases both the potential for the clarity of expectations and the realm of possibilities for multicultural content infusion by future teachers in their field placements. Traditional classroom management

Table 3.3. Assessing Knowledge of Multicultural, Antibias Curriculum
Planning

Assessment Level	Descriptor
Skilled teacher	Curriculum unit plans transform the conventional curriculum with multicultural perspectives and materials that advance antibias goals.
Developing teacher candidate	Curriculum unit plans attempt to transform the conventional curriculum with multicultural perspectives and materials that advance antibias goals.
Emerging teacher candidate	Curriculum unit plans add to the conventional curriculum multicultural perspectives and materials that advance antibias goals.
Unsatisfactory teacher candidate	Curriculum unit plans do not incorporate multicultural perspectives and materials that advance antibias goals.

Note: From *Student Teaching Handbook* (p. 28), by The Evergreen State College, 2000, Olympia, WA: Author. Copyright 2000 by The Evergreen State College. Adapted with permission.

expectations can be redesigned from a democratic, multicultural perspective. Table 3.4, "Assessing Democratic Classroom Management," provides a performance measure to evaluate teacher candidate performance on the basis of the provision of a management system that overtly values cultural diversity and actively encourages the democratic participation of all students.

CONCLUSION

Incorporating multicultural reform into a teacher education curriculum is a multilayered process that requires time for faculty deliberations and curriculum reorganization. When a program permits an additive approach to multicultural education to serve as a proxy for multicultural reform, the culturally responsive potential of future teachers working in a culturally diverse democracy has been compromised. It is imperative upon teacher education programs that are striving to be multicultural to initiate focused multicultural conversations within their programs and with their K–12 partner schools. Dialogue on multicultural reform and the role of teacher education and public schools needs to be articulated into goals that serve the growth of culturally responsive, multicultural teachers.

Reflection in teacher education programs remains a somewhat self-asserted, indeterminate concept in how programs may actually assess what is intended by

Table 3.4. Assessing Democratic Classroom Management

Assessment Level	Descriptor
Skilled teacher	Teacher creates classroom as a learning community by valuing cultural diversity and seeking the active participation of all student-citizens in the social and learning environment.
Developing teacher candidate	Teacher candidate's classroom management system is designed to create a learning community that consistently values cultural diversity and regularly seeks the active participation of all student-citizens.
Emerging teacher candidate	Teacher candidate's classroom management system occasionally values cultural diversity and often seeks the active participation of all student-citizens.
Unsatisfactory teacher candidate	Teacher candidate's classroom management system does not value cultural diversity or seek the active participation of all students.

Note: From *Student Teaching Handbook* (p. 33), by The Evergreen State College, 2000, Olympia, WA: Author. Copyright 2000 by The Evergreen State College. Adapted with permission.

reflection. For reflection to emerge into transformative multicultural education, teacher education programs should be vigilant in moving curriculum conceptualizations beyond additive approaches. To ensure productive multicultural reflection, an institution needs to help teacher candidates make an ideological move away from a meritocracy that blames children of color and those from lower socioeconomic classes for not succeeding academically. Multicultural reflection instead should hold a culturally responsive orientation toward questioning traditional personal and professional assumptions about teaching and learning. The manifestation of multicultural reflection can be thoughtful and caring culturally responsive teacher candidates who are not hesitant to reevaluate curricular approaches when they do not benefit all students.

The goal of graduating teachers with transformative multicultural attitudes and skills will likely necessitate the redesign of key aspects of the teacher preparation curriculum in the process of implementing systematic multicultural education. A shift is required away from decontextualized courses to a curriculum continually emphasizing culture, race, and class. Future teachers need multicultural content and skills that attend to the complexities of learning styles in interaction with cultural styles as manifested in the best practices of culturally responsive teaching (see Gay, 2000). Without a knowledge base and skills in designing meaningful instructional units from a multicultural reform perspective, future teachers can flounder in field experiences intended to demonstrate competency in multicultural content integration. Teacher candidates need opportunities to learn the importance of creating a democratic environment of respect and rapport for cultural diversity. From the first contact of preservice teachers with a program and continuing through their student teaching internship, a program should constantly reflect and reinforce multicultural knowledge, dispositions, and skills. A teacher education program can then collaborate with K–12 partners schools with a clearer vision of what is intended for the development of culturally responsive teacher candidates.

A reader of multicultural education literature over the past two decades could conclude that teacher education is stuck (cf. Haberman, 1996). A review of the 1980 ground-breaking surveys and studies sponsored and published by the American Association of Colleges for Teacher Education (see, e.g., Baptiste, Baptiste, & Gollnick, 1980; Gollnick, Osayande, & Levy, 1980) shows the highway multicultural teacher education has traveled and will need to continue to travel. I am reminded of Highlander Center founder Miles Horton's (1990) "long haul" in promoting social activism with a multicultural face. When Horton was 85, he explained, "Any educational philosophy comes out of what you do and how you deal with people. When you believe in people and in the importance of trying to create democracy, you must turn these beliefs into practice" (p. 175). Now is the time to transform multicultural reform aspirations into teacher education practices.

CHAPTER 4

Multicultural Teacher Education Standards

Governmental organizations, professional associations, and higher education processes collectively affect teacher education programs. State legislative actions and professional education standards directly influence state agencies responsible for teacher education accreditation. The National Council for the Accreditation of Teacher Education (NCATE, 2001b) standards and the Council of Chief State School Officers' Interstate New Teacher Assessment and Support Consortium (INTASC, 1992) principles and standards guide state teacher licensing agencies. These groups influence the governance responsibility of a teacher education program's curriculum, pedagogy, and evaluation through articulation of educational goals into standards (Gideonse, 1993; Murray, 2001; Tom, 1996; Wise & Leibbrand, 2001). NCATE (2001b) ultimately expects a teacher education program to "perform the key leadership role in governance and management of curriculum, instruction, and resources for the preparation of professional educators . . . [and be] responsible for the quality of all school personnel prepared at an institution" (p. 40). Although external requirements direct an institution, colleges and universities retain responsibility to document how their teacher education programs respond to established criteria.

Within the influential NCATE and INTASC standards are multicultural concepts. Through the lens of critical race theory and pragmatic antiracism (see Chapter 1), this chapter analyzes those teacher education standards devoted to multicultural discourses. The chapter asks: What are the strengths and weaknesses of national standards in furthering multicultural education reform? To what extent do NCATE and INTASC multicultural standards address racist exclusionary concepts and practices in the education of teachers? How might a teacher education program approach national standards from a transformative multicultural perspective?

This chapter examines NCATE's (2001b) *Professional Standards for the Accreditation of Schools, Colleges and Departments of Education* for what is implicitly left to an institution to determine as an appropriate emphasis and focus of multicultural incorporation. Proposed are additional performance-based assessment rubrics for transformative multicultural education in a teacher education program. They include program assessments for (a) multicultural historical foundations, (b) contemporary multicultural knowledge and skills, (c) multicultural dispositions, (d) multicultural curriculum, (e) multicultural practices, (f) institutional multicultural leadership, and (g) multicultural resources.

Proposed program assessments are offered as a way for teachers to infuse multicultural education into their classrooms and schools—not only those rich in diversity with students of color but also schools without this kind of diversity. Suggested performance assessment rubrics are forwarded in the context of how a predominantly White teaching force conservatively interprets multicultural constructs and the challenge this places before the teacher education community (see Chapter 2; Causey, Thomas, & Armento, 2000; Duesterberg, 1999; Kailin, 1999; Lawrence & Tatum, 1997a; McIntyre, 1997; Rosenberg, 1998; Sleeter, 1991, 1995a; Spring, 2001). These assessment rubrics can help move national standards and institutional deliberations beyond the use of indeterminate and additive multicultural language and toward the application of transformative multicultural concepts. To assist in this process, certain issues need to be examined that pertain to the training of NCATE Board of Examiner accreditation teams in the interpretation and application of multicultural standards.

MANAGED MULTICULTURAL EDUCATION

National teacher education standards woven into state requirements are publicly presented as a consensual paradigm. NCATE (2001a, 2001d) claims the support of 33 specialty professional associations and 46 state partnerships. NCATE (2001b) states that its standards are influenced by and aligned with INTASC (1992) principles. On the basis of a survey of state agencies and professional organizations INTASC (1995) concludes, "Clearly the standards represent what a great many members of the profession and the public believe that all teachers should know and be able to do" (n.p.). In 1998, under the auspices of the Council of Chief State School Officers (1999), INTASC initiated teacher training workshops. By the summer of 2002 the American Association of Colleges for Teacher Education, INTASC, and Alverno College were regularly cosponsoring workshops for preservice teacher educators in order to use "the [INTASC] standards to examine the design of teacher education programs," relate "INTASC core principles to classroom observations" during teacher candidate internships, and assess "dispositions in teacher education programs" (Council of Chief State School Officers, 2002, Academies/Draft Agenda for Academy I). The multicultural inquiry of this chapter seeks to understand how hegemonic national standards for institutions with teacher education programs attempt to transmit, normalize, and manage a particular interpretation of multiculturalism.

NCATE standards and accreditation processes act as a form of managed multiculturalism for state regulatory agencies and subsequently for colleges and universities. Managed multiculturalism refers to institutional restrictions on antiracist expressions. Managed multiculturalism in higher education contrasts with the application of oppositional and transformative multicultural knowledge and actions (Banks, 1993b, 1998; Goldberg, 1994). When an institution forwards an assimilationist discourse on diversity and multicultural education, managed multiculturalism can result in blithe calls for celebration of diversity and tolerance in the face of localized racist exclusions in a teacher education program's curriculum, pedagogy, and evaluation. The theoretical *intent* of standards needs to be considered alongside their *consequences* for educational practices.

During the 1990s NCATE played an important role in drawing institutional attention to issues of diversity and multicultural education reform (Gollnick, 1995; Tom, 1996). At the same time, however, much that appeared as critique under the guise of multicultural education had a minimal effect in the reform of racist and other social injustice practices (Grant, 1993; Melnick & Zeichner, 1997; Wieczorek & Grant, 2000; Wisniewski, 1999). The dependency of new NCATE (2001b) standards upon INTASC becomes suspect for actually transforming a teacher education program's multicultural practices. This is because INTASC standards, as will be illustrated, take a limited human relations approach to diversity.

NCATE (2001b) reduces multicultural conceptual space primarily to the word *diversity*. INTASC (1992) employs abstracted references to "cultural sensitivity," "cultural norms," "cultural differences," and "human diversity" (pp. 14–15, 21–22). To provide a culturally responsive teaching framework on the basis of INTASC standards requires reinterpreting and extending those standards (see Irvine, 2001, pp. 11–13). Research on state teacher education accreditation standards finds that such phrases were undefined yet were often cited as satisfying multicultural education regulations for successful accreditation (Evans, Torrey, & Newton, 1997). This contrasts with scholarship that reveals the pedagogical complexity associated with understanding and acting upon conceptualizations of cultural diversity and differences (Collins, 1993; Erickson, 1997; Gay, 2000; Hoffman, 1996; May, 1999; McCarthy, 1998a, 1998b; Montecinos, 1995; Ngũgĩ, 1993; Ogbu, 1995). Institutional accreditation standards, nevertheless, resemble the restrictive discourse of human relations on diversity. A human relations approach to multicultural education tends to avoid addressing the normalcy of localized manifestations of institutional racism (see Chapters 1 & 5; Kincheloe & Steinberg, 1998; McCarthy & Willis, 1995; McLaren, 1994; Sleeter & Grant, 1999). As is illustrated within this chapter, INTASC, NCATE, and state multicultural standards are to a large extent ahistorical, divorced from contemporary racialized social and political conditions, and difficult to assess.

Together INTASC and NCATE advance a false sense of multicultural neutrality upon state accrediting requirements. A sociopolitical linkage to managed multicultural concepts, however, is important to consider. By making explicit the connection between political influences and managed institutional positions, we can begin to more readily discern the intent of standards and their subsequent consequences for practice. Given NCATE's decision to leave unclear the meaning and implications for the concept of diversity, an evaluation of unspecified multicultural language is needed.

EXCLUSIONS AND STANDARDS

Contemporary multicultural education emerged from the civil rights era of the 1960s and 1970s when the effects of racism were a central political reason for social action. Ending racism was a primary impetus from which the civil rights movement and, subsequently, multicultural education reform originated (Watkins, 1994). In the *Initial Report of the United States of America to the United Nations Committee on the Elimination of Racial Discrimination*, the U.S. Department of State (2000) reports on the continuation of overt and subtle forms of racist exclusions as a part of the national fabric of contemporary life:

> Issues relating to race, ethnicity, and national origins continue to play a negative role in American society. Racial discrimination persists against various groups. . . . The path towards true racial equality has been uneven, and substantial barriers must still be overcome [because] *de facto* segregation and persistent discrimination continue to exist. (pp. 2, 5)

This chapter draws from a historical foundation of exclusions and focuses on contemporary racial discourse. The purpose is not to discount the negative impact of exclusionary effects on certain nonracialized groups. However, unlike other types of discrimination, racism cuts across and amplifies exclusionary practices on the basis of gender, class, handicapping conditions, and sexual orientation.

How might forms of racism in state agencies, professional accrediting organizations, and higher education institutions themselves obliquely undermine transformative multicultural education? In *Racist Culture: Philosophy and the Politics of Meaning* David Theo Goldberg (1993) provides a chronicle of racialized discourse that serves as a definitional source. He explains that an institution may be judged racist despite its professed intention:

> If it is reasonably clear that some institutional practices give rise to racially patterned exclusionary or discriminatory outcomes, no matter the institutional aims, and the institution does little or nothing to avoid, diminish, or alleviate these outcomes, the reasonable presumption must be that the institution is racist or effectively promotes racism of a sort. (p. 99)

The criterion for defining a racist institutional practice rests not necessarily upon intentions but upon the consequences of an action to promote or discourage racial discrimination.

Efforts to overcome racism include bringing to the center of professional education discourse the incorporation and influence of voices and perspectives marginalized or excluded by higher education practices. Conversely, superficial inclusion of multicultural topics across a teacher education program or a separate multicultural education course can effectively reinforce and cloak a monocultural core to a teacher education program. Exclusions and inclusions, though, are not dichotomous but are situated on a contextualized continuum (Popkewitz, 1998). Hence the development, interpretation, and application of multicultural teacher education standards can be read as a shifting racial text (Castenell & Pinar, 1993; Cochran-Smith, 2000). Depending upon the extent to which standards expect transformative movement, standards can either help to rectify or exasperate exclusionary conditions of institutional racism.

A PRAGMATIC ANTIRACIST RESPONSE
TO MANAGED MULTICULTURALISM

How NCATE and INTASC standards represent a discourse that classifies and privileges certain knowledge, skills, and dispositions over others warrants investigation. Possible exclusions within standards merit close scrutiny because teacher education standards can eventually affect the material outcome of the life opportunities for children of color. The pragmatic antiracism of multiculturalism critiques those discourses that promote overt and privatized racist exclusions (Goldberg, 1993, chap. 9; also see Crenshaw, Gotanda, Peller, & Thomas, 1995a; Delgado, 1995a). Pragmatic antiracism not only focuses on racist exclusions but incorporates orientations that have been distorted or ignored. Goldberg (1993) writes, "Incorporative undertakings are transgressive, engaged by definition in infringing and exceeding the norms of the racialized status quo" (pp. 220–221). By resisting dominant cultural control over multicultural education concepts, antiracist incorporation into teacher education standards is an oppositional and transformative alternative to managed multiculturalism. NCATE and INTASC standards, as will be demonstrated, represent an effort where some institutional racist conditions may be potentially discouraged yet fail exhaustively to demand a system committed to antiracism.

Because colleges and universities during the 1990s experienced difficulty meeting previous NCATE multicultural standards (Gollnick, 1995; Melnick & Zeichner, 1997; Tom, 1996), an institution may use whatever technical means it takes to meet NCATE interpretations of diversity to avoid the appearance of racial discrimination. Rather than encouraging a teacher education program to interrogate possible conditions of racist exclusions in curriculum, pedagogy, and evaluation, NCATE and state monitoring agencies can enable institutions to give the appearance of meeting multicultural expectations. In actuality the status quo may have been only slightly nudged. NCATE and INTASC's confusing use of the terms *diversity* and *multicultural* appears as a situation where external influences upon teacher education governance and management can result in administrative systems restraining multicultural transformation while appearing to embrace diversity (Goldberg, 1993). Undefined diversity discourse veils assimilationist practices limited to a human relations orientation to cultural understanding. Diversity approaches of this kind are intended to leave the status quo core orientations of institutions undisturbed. Consequently, transformative changes in practices are particularly constrained when human relations' additive approaches to equity and multicultural education are encouraged and managed (Banks, 1993a, 2001b; Lynch, 1986).

Expressed authoritatively, teacher education program standards assume canonized status for states and higher education institutions. One focus of multicultural education reform is to challenge canons of knowledge and practices that have the material effect of marginalizing people of color (Banks, 1993b). When organizations such as NCATE and INTASC acquire "a privileged moral position" and their authority becomes subsumed by state accrediting and licensing agencies, "racialized discourse and modes of exclusion become embedded in state institutions and normalized in the common business of everyday institutional life" (Goldberg, 1993, p. 53). Rather than a voice of multicultural authenticity, NCATE and INTASC multicultural indeterminacy is most likely a compromise among those nationally involved with managing professional teacher education. This condition reflects various political interpretations and positions on the actual existence, importance, and appropriateness in contesting potential racist exclusionary practices (Kousser, 1999; Tom, 1996).

Color Blindness and White Privilege

The nonracialized, color-blind discourse of a human relations model assumes that discrimination on the basis of racially perceived characteristics is simply one of aberrant events or a problem of the past. This perception can create an invisibility of race. A climate is set where multicultural education reform becomes a superficial expression disconnected from historical origins and contemporary social practices. When a teacher education program's governance discriminates against people of color in curriculum, pedagogy, and evaluation, color blindness may be unquestioned and accepted as normal (Schofield, 1995; Troyna & Rizvi, 1997). Standards conceived under a dominant ideology of color blindness encourage teachers and teacher educators to act as though race is nonrecognizable when it is nearly impossible in the United States to do so

(Crenshaw, 1997, 1998; Kousser, 1999; McLaren & Torres, 1999; Nieto, 1995; Powell, 1996; Winant, 1998).

Race and ethnicity are never pronounced in INTASC principles and standards underlying NCATE standards. NCATE (2001b) does not directly explain why an occasional reference to race, ethnicity, and diversity is asserted. More common is the vague usage of *diversity* terminology by NCATE and INTASC. This effectively increases opportunities for a maintenance of status quo interpretations. Nothing presumes INTASC and NCATE standards from serving assimilationist goals toward historically White norms and forms of exclusionary practices. In contrast, the pragmatic antiracist aspect of multicultural education strives to make explicit what a term such as diversity can mean. By offering alternatives to color-blind standards, transformative multicultural commitments represent a response to the hegemony of monoculturalism (see Goldberg, 1994; Vavrus, 2001a).

Diffuse use of cultural terms fits well with a mainstream human relations orientation. One explanation for this approach stems from a political system that is historically based on White privilege and property rights (C. Harris, 1993). White privilege tacitly and overtly assumes exclusionary rights on the basis of physical characteristics constituting whiteness. White privilege manifests multiple forms of racism in contemporary opportunities for schooling, housing, health care, and employment. The U.S. (2000) government officially reports, "While Whites do not believe there is much discrimination today in American society, most minorities see the opposite in their life experiences" (p. 5). The concept of White privilege highlights this experiential discrepancy.

U.S. legal history and social customs, not individualistic notions of psychological deviance, contribute to institutional racism (Daniels, 1997; Goldberg, 1993; C. Harris, 1993; Kousser, 1999; Lubiano, 1998). White privilege as used here is drawn primarily from Cynthia Harris's (1993) *Harvard Law Review* article that traces U.S. legal, historical, and economic roots of racist exclusions. Harris observes how the socially constructed concepts of whiteness and property have colluded in forging "the right to exclude" by both force and U.S. legal ratification that has historically "recognized a property interest in whiteness" (pp. 1713–1714). A central element characterizes whiteness as a property right: "The legal legitimation of expectations of power and control that enshrine the status quo as a neutral baseline, while masking the maintenance of white privilege and domination" (p. 1715). This legitimization also incorporates property as "the cultural practices of whites" (p. 1721). Chapter 5 extends Harris's analysis of White privilege and applies her approach to distributive justice as a way for an institution to reexamine its teacher education curriculum, pedagogy, and assessments from a multicultural perspective.

Although Harris (1993) and McLaren and Torres (1999), among others, use the term *whiteness* in their analyses of exclusions, they directly link it to the concept of privilege. The concept of White privilege can sharpen analyses of diversity discourse. The impact of White privilege suggests an institutional approach to understanding contemporary forms of racism as manifested through the education of teachers.

No teacher candidate, according to G. Pritchy Smith (2000), should graduate without foundational knowledge in racism and how "White norms" skew meanings of "achievement" (also see Kincheloe, Steinberg, Rodriguez, & Chennault, 1998; Popkewitz, 1998; Sleeter, 1994). Yet, through the dominant discourse of White privilege, color blindness can go unchallenged. Columbia University law professor Kimberlé Crenshaw (1997) explains, "Color-blind discourse almost singularly achieves its mighty mission by simply suspending traditional signs of race and racism" (p. 103). An impenetrable mask of color blindness makes unnecessary, therefore, the redistribution of "racial capital" (p. 103). Racial capital reflects the extent of socioeconomic advantages an individual holds based on skin color and other phenotype characteristics. For example, recognizing the negative effects of color blindness and acting to dismantle institutionally embedded forms of White privilege can make possible the equitable redistribution of racial capital.

Color blindness and White privilege can influence both NCATE and INTASC standards because little direction is given for assessing the knowledge, dispositions, and performances that are necessary for transformative multicultural education across a teacher education program (see Banks, 1993b, 1995; McCarthy & Willis, 1995; Nieto, 1997). At a subset level of generic national standards, Rodriguez (1999) also found color blindness a problem in the National Science Education Standards. Regardless as to how race is constituted, race in these national standards has been placed into a zone of assumed neutrality rather than into antiracist, culturally responsive expectations.

NCATE and INTASC standards can have the effect of forwarding a color-blind perspective for higher education where "equality would not require a fundamental dismantling of any formally white spaces, or the redistribution of white social capital" (Crenshaw, 1997, p. 106). Similarly, Cochran-Smith (2000) thoughtfully reveals her professional teacher education program experience of being implicated in a "blind vision" curriculum purportedly infused with diversity yet centered primarily around monoculturalist interpretations. Notable for their general absence in teacher education program discourse are concepts pertaining to the underlying need for multicultural education reform, such as White privilege and problems associated with color blindness. Through an avoidance of these perspectives, NCATE (2001b) standards signify that reform in teacher education may continue to support a narrow interpretation of technical proficiency and an exclusion of democratic values and moral stewardship that incorporate transformative multicultural processes.

Color-blind textbooks often give operational meaning to the knowledge base of a teacher education program (Cochran-Smith, 2000; G.P. Smith, 1998a). Thus Smith (1998a) advocates revising accreditation standards so that diversity knowledge bases are made explicit. In his writing, Smith makes operational a broad range of understandings about diversity in contrast to NCATE, which allows the term to dangle unexamined.

A TRANSFORMATIVE MULTICULTURAL
RECONCEPTUALIZATION OF NCATE STANDARDS

Smith (2000) describes a continuum of teacher education program multicultural practices. Only a few institutions articulate desired multicultural outcomes and have tried to measure them (see, e.g., Ambrosio, 2000). In the middle of the continuum are a small number of institutions that have some multicultural outcomes but have no idea how to evaluate them. The largest group, Smith contends, are institutions with teacher education faculty unaware of multicultural knowledge bases. Needed are explicit assessment standards to guide institutions toward the incorporation of multicultural knowledge, dispositions, and skills.

The following sections analyze specific NCATE standards for their potential to support transformative multicultural education. In an effort to overcome racist exclusions, various NCATE rubric assessment items are either revised or supplanted with new, transformative language. The transformative understandings that emanate from the terminology of White privilege, color blindness, and racist exclusions are consciously applied to NCATE assessments. These interdependent concepts can help to capture an intent of transformative interpretations of racism.

Although antiracism is theorized in multicultural education, antiracism is often obfuscated in practice (Nieto, 1995). Toni Morrison (1998) metaphorically expresses well this multicultural problem before the teacher education community: "How to convert a racist house into a race-specific yet nonracist home? How to enunciate race while depriving it of its lethal cling?" (p. 5). In response to Morrison's challenge, pragmatic antiracist practice is consciously placed in the foreground of assessment revisions. Transformative approaches are intended to incorporate antiracist multicultural commitments that seek to unravel and remedy the discourse of managed status quo multiculturalism.

Seven rubric assessment items are proposed as a means to advance the dialogue in helping a teacher education program move systemically toward practices inclusive of transformative multicultural education. The descriptors of the assessment rubric column headings and the grammatical structure of performance categories in the following sections are parallel to NCATE's usage.

Reconceptualizing "Candidate Knowledge, Skills, and Dispositions"

The expectation expressed by NCATE Standard 1, "Candidate Knowledge, Skills, and Dispositions," appears admirable, with its goal of teacher candidates who hold content and pedagogical knowledge and professional dispositions that lead to "positive effects on student learning" (NCATE, 2001b, p. 19). A deeper investigation suggests that much is left unsaid. The sociopolitical context of teaching and learning is left unexamined. This is accomplished primarily by the term *diversity* being unconnected to transformative multicultural practice expectations. NCATE's reticence in this area encourages institutions to access INTASC (1992) standards for clarification. However, INTASC's discourse provides little direction.

At one point INTASC (1992) refers to "human diversity" (p. 18). This nonracialized discourse shrouds the equity and antiracist needs of children and youth of color. INTASC and NCATE discourses can tacitly lend themselves to an assimilation model in which

> the goal of education becomes how to "fit" students constructed as "other" by virtue of their race/ethnicity and language, or social class into a hierarchical structure that is defined as a *meritocracy*. However, it is unclear how these conceptions do more than reproduce the current inequalities. (Ladson-Billings, 1995b, p. 467)

Although INTASC standards may be viewed as an attempt to overcome paradigms of deficits and disadvantages, they fail to pose a culturally responsive pedagogy. Culturally responsive pedagogy can help students affirm and understand their cultural identity as a positive support in their learning process. Culturally responsive orientations can also assist students in the development of a critical consciousness for becoming informed and active citizens in a pluralistic democracy (Banks, 1997, 1998; Gay, 2000; Ladson-Billings, 1995b). For students to develop a critical perspective, teachers will need to learn how to do the same. Yet INTASC and NCATE do not place such a goal in the forefront of their standards.

With a somewhat circular expectation, NCATE (2001b) expects teacher candidates to "model dispositions that are expected of educators" (p. 19), the same educators who have historically been expected to maintain the social status quo (Ginsburg, 1988; Popkewitz, 1998; Spring, 2001). To determine appropriate dispositions, NCATE suggests accessing the National Education Association's (NEA) principles of professional behavior. Written in 1975, NEA's (1975/2001) code of ethics, however, does not attend actively or transformatively to cultural diversity. NEA's (1975/2001) code is a series of reactive statements apparently intended to meet the criteria of doing the least harm to public school students and adherence to basic professional norms. The code does expect teachers not to discriminate by excluding students from programs or giving inequitable advantage to any student. If this 1975 code were revised to reflect contemporary scholarship on multicultural education, the interpretations of *exclusion* and *advantage* could be grounded in a transformative discourse.

The additive and assimilationist language of INTASC and NCATE standards can in effect silence multicultural calls to develop an attitudinal knowledge base in a critical consciousness. A transformative dispositional expectation involves acknowledging racism and other forms of discrimination in the schooling process and challenging social inequities through pragmatic antiracist actions (Banks, 1993b, 1995, 2000; Freire, 1970, 1998; Goldberg, 1993; Grant, 1993; Kincheloe & Steinberg, 1998; McCarthy, 1998a, 1998b; McLaren, 1994; Nieto, 1997).

NCATE's (2001b) expectation under Standard 3, "Field Experiences and Clinical Practice," heightens the importance for having multicultural assessment rubrics under Standard 1. A targeted goal of Standard 3 requires that teacher candidates should be competent in their work with students "from diverse ethnic, racial, gender, and socioeconomic groups" (p. 27). Yet under Standard 1, which focuses on a teacher candidate's knowledge base, no overt references are made to the actual development of multicultural knowledge, dispositions, and performances to support Standard 3. NCATE is silent on knowledge bases for diversity. In response, additions and revisions to NCATE's institutional assessment rubrics are provided in an endeavor to make explicit transformative multicultural knowledge and skills. The focus is on recognizing White privilege as part of a process to identify and eliminate racist exclusions in teacher education curriculum, pedagogy, and evaluation.

Tables 4.1–4.3 contain three additional rubric assessments that can multiculturally expand and transform Standard 1 (NCATE, 2001b, pp. 14–20).

Multicultural Historical Foundations. A transformative assessment represented in Table 4.1, "Multicultural Historical Foundations," aims to have a teacher education program help teacher candidates incorporate an informed multicultural perspective into their curriculum plans. Specifically, this additional assessment calls for a curriculum designed to redress the negative impact of a historical foundation of White privilege and property rights and its manifestation in contemporary political, economic, and educational systems through various forms of biases and racism, including color blindness. The studies of teacher candidates should include the historic opposition and resistance by people of color to acts of oppression, especially as pertains to the schooling process. Through a multicultural historical foundation, teacher education programs can help teachers understand a major rationale that underlies transformative multicultural education.

Table 4.1. Multicultural Historical Foundations

Elements of Standard	Unacceptable	Acceptable	Target
Multicultural historical foundation knowledge for teacher candidates	Candidates are not familiar with a U.S. historical foundation of White privilege and property rights and its manifestation in contemporary political, economic, and educational systems through various forms of biases and racism. Candidates do not know how this foundation influences both the curriculum plans they design and the educational and life opportunities for students of color and other diverse populations. They are unaware of a U.S. history of oppression of and subsequent opposition and resistance by people of color to racism, especially as pertains to the schooling process.	Candidates articulate how a U.S. historical foundation of White privilege and property rights manifests itself in contemporary political, economic, and educational systems through various forms of biases and racism, including color blindness. Candidates understand how this foundation can negatively influence both the curriculum plans they design and the educational and life opportunities for students of color and other diverse populations. They are aware of a U.S. history of oppression of and subsequent opposition and resistance by people of color to racism, especially as pertains to the schooling process.	Candidates demonstrate in their curriculum plans learner goals, activities, and assessments designed to redress the negative impact of a U.S. historical foundation of White privilege and property rights and its manifestation in contemporary political, economic, and educational systems through various forms of biases and racism, including color blindness. Candidates understand how transformative multicultural education can serve to benefit all students, especially children of color, in a pluralistic democracy. They are aware of a contemporary transformative multicultural challenge inherent in the U.S. history of oppression of and subsequent opposition and resistance by people of color to racism, especially as pertains to the schooling process.

Note: This is a transformative addition to existing NCATE standards. The descriptors of the assessment column headings are the same as those used by NCATE (2001b). The descriptors of "elements of standard" column and the grammatical discourse in the columns of performance are parallel to NCATE's usage.

Contemporary Multicultural Knowledge. Table 4.2, "Contemporary Multicultural Knowledge and Skills," looks for teachers who can enter teaching prepared to create interactive group curricular experiences from an antiracist orientation. Teacher candidates are expected to openly acknowledge and offer alternatives and resistance strategies to racist conditions in daily life, both inside and outside the school. This includes recognizing contemporary applications of color blindness. This additional assessment anticipates a curriculum steeped in a transformative multicultural knowledge base. A goal is to have a teacher education program play a significant role in graduating teachers who can contribute to classroom and school efforts to advance an inclusive curriculum, prejudice reduction, an equity pedagogy, and empowering school cultures for all students, especially for children of color.

Multicultural Dispositions. A transformative assessment captured in Table 4.3, "Multicultural Dispositions," calls upon a teacher education institution to enable teacher candidates to use personal and public insights of cultural encapsulation (see Chapter 3) to make culturally responsive contributions to student learning and school improvement activities. Programs are encouraged to assess the extent to which a transformative disposition toward educational inequities affects teacher candidate pedagogical enactment of curriculum. This additional assessment aims for teacher candidates who can articulate how their own antibias/antiracist multicultural philosophy of education can contribute to their efforts to create inclusive classrooms contributing to a positive impact on the academic achievement of all students.

Reconceptualizing "Diversity"

NCATE (2001b) Standard 4, "Diversity," contains performance assessments on curriculum. Transformative multicultural education opportunities exist within the targeted assessment expectation for teacher candidates "to draw upon representations from the students' own experience and knowledge" (p. 29) and to "confront issues of diversity that affect teaching and student learning and develop strategies for improving student learning" (p. 31). Institutions are also expected to solicit and value the experiences of diverse teacher candidate populations. By representing the experiences of K–12 students and teacher candidates while examining the challenges of teaching in a diverse society, each of these expectations can help direct a teacher education program to expand its multicultural curricular knowledge base.

The curriculum element under Standard 4 is focused on diverse and "exceptional" populations. NCATE (2001b) expects institutions to have curricular experiences "based on well-developed knowledge bases for the conceptualization of diversity and inclusion so that candidates can apply them effectively in

Table 4.2. Contemporary Multicultural Knowledge and Skills

Elements of Standard	Unacceptable	Acceptable	Target
Contemporary multicultural knowledge and skills for teacher candidates	Candidates are unable to recognize instances of biases and racism in daily life both inside and outside the school, including contemporary applications of color blindness. They are unaware of transformative multicultural knowledge base sources for conceiving and implementing curriculum. They have inadequate knowledge about the importance of an inclusive curriculum, prejudice reduction, an equity pedagogy, and empowering school cultures for all students.	Candidates are able to recognize racist conditions in daily life both inside and outside the school, including contemporary applications of color blindness, and have knowledge of appropriate antibias/antiracist instructional strategies. They are aware of transformative multicultural knowledge base sources for conceiving and implementing curriculum. Candidates are able to design multicultural curricular experiences based on this knowledge. They hold knowledge about the importance of an inclusive curriculum, prejudice reduction, an equity pedagogy, and empowering school cultures for all students, especially for children of color.	Candidates can create interactive group curricular experiences through antibias/antiracist strategies that openly acknowledge and offer alternatives and resistance strategies to racist conditions in daily life both inside and outside the school, including contemporary applications of color blindness. They use transformative multicultural knowledge base sources for conceiving and implementing curriculum. They contribute to classroom and school efforts by implementing pedagogical strategies to advance an inclusive curriculum, prejudice reduction, an equity pedagogy, and empowering school culture for all students, especially for children of color.

Note: This is a transformative addition to existing NCATE standards. The descriptors of the assessment column headings are the same as those used by NCATE (2001b). The descriptors of "elements of standard" column and the grammatical discourse in the columns of performance are parallel to NCATE's usage.

Table 4.3. Multicultural Dispositions

Elements of Standard	Unacceptable	Acceptable	Target
Multicultural dispositions for teacher candidates	Candidates make no effort to reflect upon their own received cultural perspective or to come to know how that perspective influences their understanding of and actions toward individuals from groups different from their received culture. They lack a transformative perspective toward educational inequities. Antibias/antiracist concepts are absent from their philosophies of education.	Candidates are able to acknowledge and critically reflect upon their own received cultural perspective and come to know how that perspective influences their understanding of and actions toward individuals from groups different from their received culture. They are developing a transformative perspective toward educational inequities. They are able to articulate an antibias/antiracist multicultural philosophy of education that informs their thinking about how teachers can create inclusive classrooms that contribute to a positive impact on the academic achievement of all students, especially children of color.	Candidates use insights of cultural encapsulation to make culturally responsive contributions to student learning and school improvement activities. They hold a transformative perspective toward educational inequities when conceiving and implementing curriculum. They are able to articulate an antibias/antiracist multicultural philosophy of education that informs their work as teacher candidates in K–12 schools. Candidates can demonstrate how their multicultural dispositions contribute to their efforts to create an inclusive classroom that contributes to a positive impact on the academic achievement of all students, especially children of color.

Note: This is a transformative addition to existing NCATE standards. The descriptors of the assessment column headings are the same as those used by NCATE (2001b). The descriptors of "elements of standard" column and the grammatical discourse in the columns of performance are parallel to NCATE's usage. The stem of each assessment is from *Student Teaching Handbook* (p. 45), by The Evergreen State College, 2000, Olympia, WA: Author. Copyright 2000 by The Evergreen State College. Adapted with permission.

schools" (p. 29). Although students of color who are placed in special education programs can be doubly harmed by exclusionary effects, the discrete discriminatory issues for students of color and those identified as exceptional can be quite different (Banks, 2000). Too often teacher education programs permit teacher candidates to select topics related to exceptional populations for a diversity curriculum project while averting racialized issues of diversity (cf. Ambrosio, 2000). This NCATE element can be strengthened by uncoupling exceptional from diverse populations and creating separate rubric assessment elements.

Regarding diverse populations, NCATE standards do not make clear which knowledge bases they refer to. NCATE cites professional organizations and publications for topics other than diversity. Nevertheless, diversity assessment expectations can be grounded by a recommendation to incorporate prominent multicultural scholarship. Useful sources include the *Handbook of Research on Multicultural Education* (Banks & Banks, 1995), *Common Sense About Uncommon Knowledge: The Knowledge Bases for Diversity* (G.P. Smith, 1998a), *Teaching Diverse Populations: Formulating a Knowledge Base* (Hollins, King, & Hayman, 1994), and *Developing Multicultural Teacher Education Curricula* (Larkin & Sleeter, 1995). To require the minimal use of these timely and valuable sources can transform a nonracialized human relations approach toward diversity.

Multicultural Curriculum. Table 4.4 modifies an existing NCATE diversity assessment standard. This modified assessment attaches the word *Multicultural* to the beginning of Standard 4 element "Design, Implementation, and Evaluation of Curriculum and Experiences" to focus this diversity assessment (NCATE, 2001b, pp. 16–17). Table 4.4 also adds transformative multicultural expectations to NCATE's (2001b) existing diversity assessment rubric. The revised assessment emphasizes the need to openly address multicultural challenges of white privilege and color blindness as historical and contemporary factors fostering exclusions in curriculum, field experiences, and program evaluations.

Racist biases cut across gender, socioeconomic class, sexual orientation, and handicapping conditions in exclusionary ways uncommon to other categorical groupings of diversity. For this reason particular attention to students of color is purposely inserted into the assessment rubric. The revisions presented in italics in Table 4.4 recognize that, as teacher candidates are required to construct a transformative multicultural curriculum, they must be mindful of the varying degrees of cultural encapsulations their K–12 students bring into a classroom (Epstein, 2000; MacLeod, 1995; Vavrus, 1994).

Reconceptualizing "Faculty Qualifications, Performance and Development"

NCATE (2001b) Standard 5, "Faculty Qualifications, Performance and Development," contains an assessment element "Modeling Best Professional Practices

Table 4.4. Multicultural Design, Implementation, and Evaluation of Curriculum and Experiences

Elements of Standard	Unacceptable	Acceptable	Target
Multicultural design, implementation, and evaluation of curriculum and experiences	The curriculum and field experiences for the preparation of educators is not designed to prepare candidates to work effectively with diverse populations, including persons with exceptionalities *and those of color. The curriculum and field experiences do not attend to the exclusionary effects of White privilege and color blindness on multicultural understandings in a diverse society.* Candidates do not have an understanding of the importance of diversity *and the harmful impact of historical and contemporary exclusions in teaching and learning.* They are not developing skills for incorporating *diversity and transformative multicultural knowledge* into their teaching and are not able to establish a classroom and school climate that values diversity *by opposing color blindness in an effort to overcome exclusions.* Assessments of candidate proficiencies do not provide data on candidates' ability to help all students learn *in a transformative multicultural curriculum . . .*	Curriculum and accompanying field experiences are designed to help candidates understand the importance of diversity *and multicultural challenges of White privilege and color blindness in teaching and student learning in a diverse society.* Candidates learn to develop and teach lessons that incorporate diversity *and transformative multicultural knowledge* and develop a classroom and school climate that values diversity *by opposing color blindness in an effort to overcome exclusions.* Candidates become aware of different learning styles shaped by cultural influences, *including those influenced by multicultural challenges of White privilege and color blindness,* and are able to adapt instruction and services appropriately for all student, including students with exceptionalities *and those of color.* They demonstrate dispositions that value fairness and learning by all students *through inclusiveness while consciously avoiding perspectives influenced by White privilege and color blindness.* Assessments of candidate proficiencies provide data on the ability to help all students learn *in a transformative multicultural curriculum . . .*	Curriculum, field experiences, and clinical practice help candidates demonstrate knowledge, skills, and dispositions related to diversity *and multicultural challenges of White privilege and color blindness.* They are based on well-developed knowledge bases for and conceptualizations of diversity . . . *that prioritizes transformative multicultural knowledge* so that candidates can apply them effectively in schools. Candidates learn to contextualize teaching and to draw upon representations from the students' own experiences and knowledge, *including those historically excluded due to White privilege and color blindness.* They learn how to challenge students toward cognitive complexity and engage all students including students with exceptionalities *and those of color, through instructional conversation mindful of historical and contemporary exclusions and student degrees of cultural encapsulation.* Candidates and faculty review assessment data that provide information about candidates' ability (a) to work with all students, *including children of color, and (b) to provide a transformative multicultural curriculum . . .*

Note: Italics represents transformative revisions to an existing NCATE (2001b) assessment expectations (see p. 29). The descriptors of the assessment column headings are the same as those used by NCATE (2001b). The descriptors of "elements of standard" column and the grammatical discourse in the columns of performance are parallel to NCATE's usage.

in Teaching." A purpose for this element is to have an institution's faculty integrate "diversity and technology throughout coursework, field experiences, and clinical practices" (p. 34). The knowledge base for diversity integration in teaching is again left undefined by NCATE.

Standard 5 problematically couples diversity expectations with technology. NCATE privileges information technology but is silent on multicultural competence. Although NCATE cites a criterion for unacceptable technology performance, no mention is made of diversity. In the acceptable assessment categories, diversity and technology are connected within the same assessment sentence. Diversity and technology, however, are two distinct knowledge domains. The confounding linkage of the two can give an impression that diversity is simply a technical concept to be engineered into a curriculum as a delivery format. Multicultural concepts are not dependent on a proficiency of passive systems such as those associated with information technology. Indeed, the best multicultural professional practices for teacher educators depend upon an active equity pedagogy consciously informed by a knowledge base that "challenges mainstream academic knowledge and . . . expands the historical literary canon" (Banks, 1993b, p. 10). Multicultural education is not about providing mainstream knowledge in a different technological manner. More accurately, multicultural education involves transforming the actual perspectives and knowledge base of a conventional curriculum.

Multicultural Practices. Table 4.5, "Modeling Best Multicultural Professional Practices in Teaching," incorporates transformative multicultural language into NCATE Standard 5. Table 4.5 corrects NCATE's (2001b) oversight in their "unacceptable" assessment by adding and defining diversity expectations. Table 4.5 adds expectations to each assessment level pertaining to faculty ability to model in their own teaching the use of transformative knowledge bases informed by multicultural challenges of White privilege, contemporary racism, color blindness, and cultural encapsulation.

Multicultural Faculty Development. NCATE's Standard 5 also contains an element devoted to teacher education faculty development and includes mention of diversity. NCATE's (2001b) supporting rationale envisions teacher education faculty who serve "as advocates for . . . public understanding of educational issues, and excellence and diversity in the education professions" (p. 36). From a transformative multicultural perspective, Standard 5 is mired in vagaries as to the extent NCATE expects professional development to support advocacy for diversity. NCATE's notion of acceptable professional development in diversity is suspect for enabling the formation and expansion of transformative multicultural competencies among teacher educators. Faculty development in diversity is dependent "upon needs identified in faculty evaluations" (p. 36). If

Table 4.5. Modeling Best Multicultural Professional Practices in Teaching

Elements of Standard	Unacceptable	Acceptable	Target
Modeling best professional practices in teaching	Faculty seldom model the use of information technology in their own teaching. *Faculty seldom model in their own teaching the use of a transformative knowledge base informed by multicultural challenges of White privilege, contemporary racism, color blindness, and cultural encapsulation . . .*	Faculty integrate diversity and technology throughout their teaching. *They incorporate transformative knowledge informed by multicultural challenges of White privilege, contemporary racism, color blindness, and cultural encapsulation . . .*	Teaching by the professional education faculty . . . integrates diversity and technology throughout the coursework, field experiences, and clinical experiences. They understand assessment technology *and can assess diversity expectations that incorporate transformative knowledge informed by multicultural challenges of White privilege, contemporary racism, color blindness, and cultural encapsulation . . .*

Note: Italics represents transformative revisions to an existing NCATE (2001b) assessment expectations (see p. 34). The descriptors of the assessment column headings are the same as those used by NCATE (2001b). The descriptors of "elements of standard" column and the grammatical discourse in the columns of performance are parallel to NCATE's usage.

professional growth in a transformative knowledge base related to diversity is not self-identified as a faculty need or highlighted in the institution's conceptual framework, a teacher education unit could successfully avoid attending to critical dimensions of multicultural education reform. Thus an accredited NCATE institution may in practice have done little internally to rectify racist exclusionary teacher education practices.

Reconceptualizing "Unit Governance and Resources"

With a prominent emphasis on technology application, NCATE's (2001b) Standard 6, "Unit Governance and Resources," conceptualizes leadership as "professional development on effective teaching for faculty in other units of the institution" (p. 38). Multicultural education is perceived as neither a factor of leadership nor a resource to be shared.

INTASC standards for leadership and resources offer an institution minimal guidance. When INTASC (1992) expects that "the teacher acts as an advocate for students" (p. 30), this requirement could be broadened to include modeling a multicultural, antiracist advocacy as a function of a teacher's leadership in moral stewardship. If, as observed above for NCATE Standard 1, leadership and resources are being envisioned in restricted technical and ahistorical terms, status quo avoidance of multicultural topics would be extended well into the 21st century.

Multicultural Leadership. NCATE (2001b) provides a narrative explanation regarding leadership: "Faculty provide leadership in developing, implementing, and evaluating preparation programs that embrace diversity and that are rigorous, relevant, and grounded in theory, research, and best practice" (p. 36). This discourse on leadership, however, does not find its way into an actual assessment rubric. To clarify this leadership possibility, a transformative assessment is represented in Table 4.6. This assessment, teacher education "Unit Multicultural Leadership," provides an additional element to Standard 6. The additional assessment presented in Table 4.6 extends leadership to other parts of the institution and community by advocating for curricular opportunities designed to redress the effects of racism. Leadership is reconceptualized as an advocacy for a curriculum infused with a transformative multicultural knowledge base that can benefit all students, faculty, and community members living in a diverse society.

Multicultural Resources. NCATE (2001b) Standard 6 also contains an element intended to identify "unit resources including technology" (p. 40) to determine the degree to which a teacher education program has the capacity to meet its governance and management responsibilities. Once again, technology

Table 4.6. Unit Multicultural Leadership

Elements of Standard	Unacceptable	Acceptable	Target
Unit multicultural leadership	The unit lacks leadership for addressing a historical foundation based on White privilege and its manifestation in contemporary sociopolitical systems, including schools. The unit is unaware of transformative multicultural knowledge base sources. The unit leadership is unaware as to how color blindness influences both the curriculum faculty design and the eventual educational and life opportunities for children of color.	The unit has the leadership to articulate how a historical foundation based on White privilege is manifested in contemporary sociopolitical systems, including schools. The unit supports the use of transformative multicultural knowledge base sources. The unit leadership demonstrates awareness as to how color blindness can negatively influence both the curriculum faculty design and the eventual educational and life opportunities for children of color.	The unit leadership extends to other parts of the institution and community by advocating for curricular opportunities designed to redress the negative impact of a historical foundation based on White privilege and its color-blind manifestation in contemporary sociopolitical systems, including schools. The unit leadership advocates for a curriculum infused with a transformative multicultural knowledge base that can benefit all students, faculty, and community members living in a diverse society.

Note: This is a transformative addition to existing NCATE standards. The descriptors of the assessment column headings are the same as those used by NCATE (2001b). The descriptors of "elements of standard" column and the grammatical discourse in the columns of performance are parallel to NCATE's usage.

application is privileged over all other forms of resource support. Table 4.7 revises this particular element to stress the importance of resources to support transformative multicultural education. If diversity does indeed hold the importance NCATE implies throughout its standards, it is reasonable to expect that an institution would need to provide resources to support diversity goals.

CONCLUSION

Located in a lone footnote by NCATE (2001b) is a reference to standards from the Council of Learned Societies in Education (CLSE). CLSE (1996) standards can be used to support teacher candidate knowledge development in the social, historical, and philosophical foundations of education. CLSE standards are the one connected place in NCATE standards where a critical pedagogical stance is embedded in teacher expectations. In practice, critical perspectives in public discourse surrounding state and national accreditation standards are rarely evoked. CLSE is an exception. The CLSE standards ask, for example, that

> the educator uses critical judgment to question educational assumptions and arrangements and to identify contradictions and inconsistencies among social and educational values, polices, and practices [and] . . . specify how issues such as justice, social inequality, concentrations of power, class differences, race and ethnic relations, or family and community organization affect teaching and learning. (pp. 20–21)

Inclusion of transformative multicultural education knowledge bases can give a clearer diversity focus to both the CLSE standards and to the entire set of NCATE standards.

Unless NCATE and state accrediting agencies adopt a critical perspective in the training of accreditation review teams, it is doubtful that a teacher education program can be expected to provide documented accreditation evidence that their faculty and students are engaged in transformative multicultural knowledge bases, depositions, and performances. The "Commitment to Diversity" conceptual framework indicator for institutions does hold the possibility for NCATE Board of Examiner evaluation teams to assess multicultural commitments across the curriculum, pedagogy, and evaluations of a teacher education program (NCATE, 2001b, p. 13). Given the human relations orientation of INTASC and NCATE, it remains questionable if these diversity commitments are capable of critical assessment. Through training with a pragmatic antiracist orientation, however, NCATE Board of Examiner teams can begin to approach diversity critically and transformatively when evaluating a teacher education program.

The goal to eliminate racist exclusionary practices in a teacher education

Table 4.7. Multicultural Resources

Elements of Standard	Unacceptable	Acceptable	Target
Unit resources including technology *and multicultural education*	Information technology *and transformative multicultural education* resources are so limited that candidates are unable to experience the use of information technology *and the application of multicultural concepts* . . .	The unit has adequate information technology *and transformative multicultural education* resources to support faculty and candidates . . .	The unit serves as an information technology *and transformative multicultural education* resource in education beyond the education programs—to the institution, community, and other institutions . . .

Note: Italics represents transformative revisions to an existing NCATE (2001b) assessment expectations (see p. 40). The descriptors of the assessment column headings are the same as those used by NCATE (2001b). The descriptors of "elements of standard" column and the grammatical discourse in the columns of performance are parallel to NCATE's usage.

program continues to be severely limited as long as accreditation teams conduct evaluations with indeterminate operational language located within state and national assessments. Regardless, a teacher education program can strive systemically to remove localized exclusions from its governance of curriculum, pedagogy, and evaluation. Just as the California state standards to prepare specialized teachers to teach limited-English proficient students show promising impact, culturally responsive standards adopted by a teacher education program faculty can be successfully imparted to *all* teacher candidates (Rios, Stowell, Christopher, & McDaniel, 1997; Walton & Carlson, 1997). In doing so, a teacher education program can actively involve itself in the employment of transformative multicultural knowledge bases with the aim of contributing to the learning and equity needs of children in a diverse society. We now turn in Chapter 5 to the actual transformative challenge of responding to racism through a teacher education program's curriculum, pedagogy, and evaluation.

CHAPTER 5

Responding to Racism Through Teacher Education

Eliminating racism in K–12 schools is an important dimension of multicultural education (Banks, 1993d; 2001b; King & Castenell, 2001a, 2001b). A teacher education program is an important location for teacher candidates and in-service teachers to become more knowledgeable about theories and practices supporting reductions in racism. Nevertheless, how a teacher education program should approach racism in its curriculum, pedagogy, and internal assessments remains a major challenge for multicultural education reform.

The topics of race and racism are often avoided in the preservice and continuing education of teachers. When offering antiracist workshops for educators, Lawrence and Tatum (1997a) and Lee (1998a) find that in-service administrators often take measured steps to restrict making school-based antiracism the organizing content of a course by excluding the words *race* and *racism* in a program's title. Such distancing can perpetuate a color blindness that denies racism as manifested in a school's policies and procedures. This avoidance is generally explained by an aversion to any terminology that may lead to conflict or other emotional responses from participants. A silence around racism reduces opportunities to create a dialogue about why these topics can cause discomfort among educators. This form of tacit censorship confounds the difficulties for addressing racist legacies and their contemporary educational manifestations that impact the life experiences of young people in a culturally diverse society.

This chapter builds on multicultural standards recommended for teacher education institutions in Chapter 4. Those recommendations include overt attention to White privilege, color blindness, and racist exclusions. This chapter continues to investigate teacher education practices that can perpetuate racism. It critiques the ineffectiveness of a human relations paradigm for examining racism. Key concepts and definitions important for understanding racism are presented. A distributive justice framework is introduced as an accountability approach to examine a teacher education program's policies and procedures. Issues surrounding teacher racial identity formation are considered as a means to help teachers be culturally responsive. Transformative antiracist teacher education practices are contrasted to restraining influences of managed multiculturalism and calls for tolerance. The chapter provides an overview of curricular efforts by college faculty who address racism in their teaching. The chapter concludes by revisiting the discussion from Chapter 4 of pragmatic antiracism within a teacher education program.

HUMAN RELATIONS PARADIGM LIMITATIONS ON ANTIRACIST EXPRESSIONS

Antiracist scholars (e.g., Goldberg, 1993; Grant & Sleeter, 1993; Memmi, 2000; Peller, 1995) explain that a human relations paradigm for multiculturalism problematically emphasizes a commonality of humankind by teaching a color-blind respect for all cultures. A human relations orientation sees issues of cultural diversity as problems to be solved through assimilation into unquestioned norms presented as universal interpretations of truth and progress. Under this model, racism is constructed as an irrational, psychological deficit. Racism is imagined as isolated acts perpetuated by individuals who deviate from universal norms of fairness.

A human relations paradigm presents affirmative action policies mainly as a correction of past injustices while denying the existence of systemic contemporary racism. This orientation is too often the case when identifying and addressing potential racist exclusions in a teacher education program's curriculum, pedagogy, and evaluation. For example, existing exclusionary teacher education practices can be forwarded as legitimate through an allegedly unbiased human relations discourse about objective, fair, and merit-based equal treatment. Legal expert Gary Peller (1995) explains a shortcoming of this perspective by noting that "once we consider the possibility that existing social practices might reflect the domination of particular racial groups, those practices can no longer provide a neutral ground from which to defend existing definitions" of merit, fairness, and objectivity (p. 143). A human relations approach to multicultural education, however, does not undertake studies of the dynamics of racialized domination and subordination or of power and conflict. Deeply imbedded is a strong belief in a color-blind individualism where all people are assumed to have an equal opportunity to succeed simply through the merit of individual actions.

Human relations solutions for racism are ahistorical and narrowly psychological. Absent are considerations of an individual's sociopolitical location within analyses of racism. Human relations universalism, explain Goldberg (1993) and Peller (1995), perceives racism as arbitrary and disconnected from a discriminatory legacy of racial identification that is politically placed on people of color. Framing racism as an irrational, individualistic, and cognitive problem permits in a human relations paradigm "a widespread cultural flight from white self-identity" (Peller, 1995, p. 149). As an approach to investigating effects of institutional racism during the preparation of culturally responsive teachers, a human relations model is severely limited by an assumption of autonomous individuals unaffected by racialized identities and political histories.

The concept of multiculturalism within a human relations paradigm is primarily confined to a superficial celebration of diversity within institutionally constructed zones of White cultural control. Outside the scope of this approach is an examination of rationalized public policies that support exclusionary practices. Dominant educational discourses about professionalism, standardization, tracking, testing, and educational excellence are conceived as politically neutral universal goals unaffected by a racial consciousness. Thus the mainstream knowledge of human relations discourse and practices inhibits possibilities for transformative multicultural analyses and actions in a teacher education program (Banks, 1993b; McCain-Reid, 1995). Because injustices are conceived as deviations from a presumption of a socially equitable status quo, transformation of educational institutions toward multicultural social justice goals is considered unnecessary within human relations studies. Unfortunately, observe Santos Rego and Nieto (2000), a human relations paradigm continues to exert influence on the pedagogy and curriculum of many teacher education programs.

RACISM AS A FIELD OF STUDY

Based on his study of multicultural knowledge bases and teacher education practices, G. Pritchy Smith (1998a) contends, "No teacher should graduate from a teacher preparation program without having thoroughly studied the *foundations of racism*" (p. 68) (also see King & Castenell, 2001a, 2001b). Smith offers alternatives to a human relations model with a succinct summary of multicultural resources about racism (chaps. 9–10). Although not explicated by Smith, any basic study of racism requires direct attention to White privilege, a critical concept for understanding existing forms of racism.

A Historical Context of White Privilege

Chapter 4 explains the need to include White privilege and the associated concept of color blindness in standards for teacher education program evaluation and accreditation. Here that discussion is expanded to emphasize the historical basis of White privilege as a primary cause of racism.

Goldberg (1993), Kincheloe and Steinberg (1998), Marx (1996), and Takaki (1993) provide excellent analyses of how notions of race as we understand them today were introduced in the early colonial expansion era of Europe. Racial hierarchies and categories were created by White Europeans to help justify the conquest and subordination of non-European populations. The American

Anthropological Association (1998) states that race "subsumed a growing ideology of inequality devised to rationalize European attitudes and treatment of the conquered and enslaved people" (para. 5). A particular population's degree of purported rationality or irrationality was said to be causally related to scales of skin color with White Western Europeans representing the most enlightened and rational ideal of humanity.

White privilege and "race-making" (Marx, 1996) are rooted deeply in the national origins of the United States. The U.S. Constitution, for example, originally considered African-Americans as White property and not fully human (National Archives and Records Administration, 2001). Just as African Americans were considered to belong to whites, the imposition of "race" on indigenous Native Americans "rendered their first possession rights invisible and justified conquest" by a White-dominated government (Harris, 1993, p. 1721). African Americans represent a unique case of property becoming citizen (Ladson-Billings, 1999a). UCLA law professor Cheryl Harris (1993) explains that throughout U.S. history "white identity and whiteness were sources of privilege and protection; their absence meant being the object of property" (p. 1721). As Chapter 1 explains, historically based racist exclusions against people of color continue to hold foundational support in a legal system designed and rationalized to support White privilege.

Defining White Privilege

Harris (1993) notes that U.S. Supreme Court decisions and public policy during the last half of the 20th century helped to transform White property and entitlement rights but did not eliminate them (see Chapter 4 for an introduction to Harris's analysis). Harris provides a definition of White privilege[1] that can inform contemporary multicultural understandings of White ideological domination of schooling processes:

> A political, economic, and cultural system in which whites overwhelmingly control power and material resources, conscious and unconscious ideas of white superiority and entitlement are widespread, and relations of white dominance and non-white subordination are daily reenacted across a broad array of institutions and social settings. (p. 1714, fn. 10)

This definition of White privilege is not necessarily predicated only upon conscious intentions. An educational institution does not need to be purposely racist to display the characteristics of White privilege and racism.

Harris's definition of White privilege can provide a baseline for analyzing teaching, learning, and schooling processes and the education of teachers. Ford (1999) foregrounds the importance in attending to White privilege because color-blind White teacher candidates "have not been marginalized, denied access, or made invisible by school curricula. They have no reason to question the texts they have grown up with and view as being right" (p. 203). Whites who complain that they do not see privilege are generally oblivious to "public, private, and psychological benefits" of their whiteness (Harris, 1993, p. 1760). Nevertheless, a teacher education program can examine its curriculum, pedagogy, and assessments to determine the magnitude to which White control of material resources, concepts, and procedures perpetuates ideas of White superiority (e.g., Cochran-Smith, 2000). A related line of inquiry is to determine how White privilege is extended to local activities of a teacher education program and its K–12 partner schools (see Chapter 8; Murrell, 1998).

White Privilege and Distributive Justice

What would teaching, learning, and schooling look like if they had been conceived in the absence of a system of White privilege in a nonracist society? The concept of distributive justice helps to address this question and is applicable to analyses of a teacher education program's discourses and practices. Distributive justice goals seek to correct conditions that have been skewed by White privilege.

Harris (1993) explains, "A distributive justice framework does not focus primarily upon guilt or innocence, but rather on entitlement and fairness" (p. 1783). Distributive justice can help move teacher education discourse away from assigning guilt and toward correcting White privileged exclusionary practices, both conscious and unconscious. Furthermore, within a distributive justice approach ahistorical color-blind discourse and claims of White victimization through "reverse racism" serve as racist detractors (Crenshaw, 1997, 1998; Goldberg, 1993, 1994; Harris, 1993; Kincheloe & Steinberg, 1998; Kousser, 1999; McLaren, 1994).

Distributive justice for a teacher education program additionally asks, What aspects of a program's discourses and practices continue to deny entitlement and fairness to transformative multicultural perspectives and outcomes? Emphasis is on providing educational benefits as they would have been "secured in the absence of racism" (Harris, 1993, p. 1783) through an incorporation of multicultural positions, representations, histories, and practices. Distributive justice strives to establish an "equality of conditions" that can lead to a "freedom from oppressive relations" (Gewirtz, 2001, p. 53). The issue of racism in a teacher program becomes one of how to reallocate pedagogical emphases and institutional resources to correct practices that White privilege has skewed and distorted. To meet distributive justice objectives requires that a teacher education program offer antiracist alternatives to conditions created and maintained through White privilege.

Clarifying the Terminology of Prejudice, Racism, and Racist

The application of racialized terminology in teacher education suffers from high variability and indeterminacy (King & Castenell, 2001a) and reflects a problematic norm found in other fields of study such as the medical health sciences (Bhopal & Rankin, 1999). Because racism as a field of study often elicits strong emotional reactions and resistance from preservice and in-service teachers, an operational definition of terminology related to racism is important to include in the multicultural education of teachers. This is especially so with White teacher populations that tend to hairsplit on definitions as a means to distance themselves from the dynamics of racism (see Duesterberg, 1999; Edler & Irons, 1998; Kailin, 1999). Therefore, it is imperative for a teacher education program to provide definitions of racialized terms.

The following sections of definitions build upon Goldberg's (1993) critique of a racist institution described in Chapter 4. These concepts are necessary to help teachers better grasp the normalcy of racism within schools and communities. The assumption underlying these terms is a perspective that views race as a political category. Although historically shifting applications of race continue to be loosely correlated with skin pigmentation, phenotypes, geographical origins of birth, and behavior, the definitions used in this chapter recognize that *race* holds no biological legitimacy (American Association of Physical Anthropology, 1996; Angier, 2000; Bhopal & Rankin, 1999; Goldberg, 1993; Gould, 1996; Seldon, 1999; Sorenson, 2001). A teacher education program can assist White teachers in their struggle to acknowledge that race is socially constructed and that *White*, too, is a politically defined racial category.

Prejudice and Racism.   The terms *prejudice* and *racism* are sometimes confoundedly used interchangeably. Prejudice is "a negative attitude toward a social group" (Stephan, 1999, p. 24). Definitions of prejudice may also include acts of physical and social harm to outgroup members. When a definition of prejudice includes injurious actions, irrational human behavior is often the assumed cause (*Oxford English Dictionary*, 1989a; Stephan, 1999). In this instance the individual—not an institution—is generally presumed as the singular cause and site for eliminating racism.

Problematic is the assumption that racial prejudice is simply an irrational impulse. The irrational conception of racism is embedded in a human relations paradigm that postulates rationality as ahistorical and neutral (Goldberg, 1993). Yet, as Chapter 6 explains about historical Eurocentrism, White European colonial nations and the United States developed the human relations roots for standards of "Reason" and rationality during an era of domination and conquest of other human beings. This colonial legacy created conditions to rationalize the maintenance of racism through public policy and legal stature (Goldberg, 1993, chap. 6; Harris, 1993; Marx, 1996; Peller, 1995; Takaki, 1993). Today many institutional bureaucracies continue to demonstrate a capacity to rationalize racist expressions. To accurately define and explain racism, an alternative to the irrationality paradigm of racial prejudice is necessary because some cases of racist acts can be defended by standards of rationality.

Goldberg (1993) recognizes multiple forms of racism and offers a definition of its common characteristics:

> *Racisms* involve promoting exclusions, or the actual exclusions of people in virtue of their being deemed members of different racial groups, however racial groups are taken to be constituted. . . . The mark of racism . . . will be whether the discriminatory racial exclusion reflects a persistent pattern or could reasonably have been avoided. (p. 98)

Inherent within racism is a belief in racial superiority (Grant & Ladson-Billings, 1997). Banks and Banks (1997) help to further make operational the meaning of racism. They add that racism is "practiced when a group has the power to enforce laws, institutions, and norms . . . that oppress and dehumanize another group" (p. 436). In schooling processes racism resembles a form of academic gatekeeping where multicultural perspectives and students of color have restrictive inclusion in White-dominated knowledge bases, policies, and procedures. Racism is evident when children of color are provided limited access to stimulating academic programs where competence is honored over deficits. Thus racism in a teacher education program or a K–12 school can exist when racially defined groups and multicultural dimensions are persistently excluded intentionally or unintentionally from White-controlled approaches in curriculum, pedagogy, and evaluation.

A definition of racism focusing on exclusions, regardless of intent, overcomes a criticism that has been leveled at the important multicultural work by Louise Derman-Sparks and Carol Burnson Phillips (1997) in *Teaching/Learning Anti-Racism*. With an intent similar to Goldberg (1993), Derman-Sparks and Phillips (1997) initially focus on racialized dominance and power but at a later point provide what they call a "shorthand definition" of racism as equaling "racial prejudice plus institutional power" (p. 10). Blum (1999) observes that the merging of prejudice with racism can be a definitional problem because "racial advantage/power does not actually depend on personal prejudice. School personnel of racial goodwill may still carry out policies that disfavor racial minority groups" (p. 867). Beverly Tatum (1999b), in her insightful book *"Why Are All the Black Kids Sitting Together in the Cafeteria?"*, recognizes this problem and sees racism as a system of advantages that "cannot be fully explained as an expression of prejudice alone" (p. 7).

Often the perceived irrational individual acting upon racial prejudice is reduced, Goldberg (1993) points out, to a problem of ignorance correctable by a study of race relations. Positive attitudinal changes under this model often wane over time and provide little explanation as to the sociopolitical origins of racist actions. Banks (2001b) concludes that "incidental teaching of race relations is usually not effective" (p. 301). Alternatively, Banks envisions a comprehensive approach to racial prejudice reduction that includes extensive interdisciplinary teacher education and institutional interventions. Banks's approach strikes a conceptually constructive balance between decreasing individual racial prejudices and stopping racist educational practices (also see Yamato, 1995). This notion of individual racial prejudice as a part of a larger social phenomenon places the concept of prejudice more clearly within a definition of racism. Therefore, individual prejudice reduction should include attention to social processes to eliminate public practices that allow racialized exclusions of groups historically targeted by racial hierarchies.

Racists. In a teacher education program that attends to racism, attention is often upon the individual teacher. Derman-Sparks and Phillips (1997) explain, "While ultimately targeting the institutionalized system of racism, anti-racism requires an immediate focus on the individual" (p. 23). Given the volatility of the "racist" label in antiracist education, a teacher education program needs to define clearly the term in a meaningful way to improve teacher understandings of the sociopolitical context of teaching, learning, and schooling. Goldberg's (1993) definition engages the complexity underlying the term:

> *Racists* are those persons who explicitly or implicitly ascribe racial characteristics of others that purportedly differ from their own and others like them. These ascriptions . . . must also assign racial preferences, or "explain" racial differences as natural, inevitable and therefore unchangeable, or express desired, intended, or actual inclusions or exclusions, entitlements or restrictions. (p. 98)

Racists consider race as constituting fixed, hierarchical categories that determine human characteristics and abilities rather than as a fluid social construction (*Oxford English Dictionary*, 1989b). Thus

> persons may also be racist where their expressions fit a historical legacy or where the effects exhibit a pattern of racialized exclusion, and these are effects the person should reasonably be clear about or it is a historical legacy to which they should reasonably be sensitive. (Goldberg, 1993, p. 98)

This definitional explanation narrows the conceptual distance between what constitutes a racist and a condition of racism. Teachers and administrators, for example, can be considered racist if they refrain from action to correct racism in an institution's policies or procedures. Even when a practice is claimed to have an unintentional racist effect, the action still remains classified as racism. Therefore, transformative multicultural education emphasizes accountability in order to eliminate and offer alternatives to curriculum, pedagogy, and assessments that sustain white privilege and racism, whether intentional or not.

Racism and Teacher Education Accountability

A teacher education program can hold both individual faculty and itself institutionally accountable in order to address racism. A program's curriculum, pedagogy, and evaluations can be analyzed for differential and exclusionary treatment on the basis of racial ascriptions under a standard of distributive justice as described earlier. Curriculum can be examined for the degree to which knowledge bases are White privileged and positioned as preferable to multicultural scholarship. Pedagogy can be critiqued for the extent to which culturally responsive teaching is practiced and supported. Geneva Gay's (2000) criteria for culturally responsive teaching can serve as a distributive justice measure to assess teaching practices. Assessments can determine the degree to which teachers are able to use "cultural knowledge, prior experiences, frames of reference and performance styles of ethnically diverse students to make learning encounters more relevant and effective" for K–12 students (p. 29). Measures can assess if teachers focus on student strengths, rather than deficits, that are "culturally *validating* and *affirming*" (p. 29). Assessments of teacher candidates can include outcome documentation of teaching internships along an inclusion/exclusion continuum incorporative of curricular antiracist strategies. Culturally responsive teaching approaches can be assessed for the magnitude to which teacher candidates openly acknowledge and offer alternatives and resistance approaches to racist conditions in daily life both inside and outside the school (see Chapter 4). As these examples suggest, opportunities exist for a teacher education program to assess and assume responsibility for the presence of racist policies and practices as part of a program's overall accountability system.

To embrace the importance of a multicultural study of racism requires naming and responding to racist social and educational practices. Efforts to censor racism are likely to be unproductive. Goldberg (1993) explains, "Racist arguments or arguments to racist conclusions by students, staff, or faculty should not be suppressed, but vigorously challenged by individuals and the institutional community at large" (p. 227). For a teacher education program to establish and maintain such an antiracist stance is rare, but possible. Moving from a knowledge base for understanding racism to the place of antiracism in transformative multicultural education is the focus of the next section.

ANTIRACISM IN TEACHER EDUCATION

As a response to racism, a teacher education program can incorporate an antiracist perspective into its conceptual framework, curriculum, pedagogy, and evaluations. Antiracism is an inherent component of transformative multicultural education. Pinar, Reynolds, Slattery, and Taubman (1995) state, *"Anti-racist education resides at the heart of education* [italics added], as it requires commitments to justice, freedom and diversity to be enacted in the context of daily institutional life, rather than murmured as a litany for a world yet to come" (p. 357). Consequently, antiracist education (see Grant & Ladson-Billings, 1997) should be a major feature of theory and practice in a program's approach to diversity and multiculturalism (King & Castenell, 2001b; Ladson-Billings, 2000; McIntyre, 1997).

Like racism and other multicultural education topics, antiracism is a legitimate area of scholarly inquiry for understanding international, national, and localized responses to exclusionary practices (Bonnett, 2000; Gillborn, 1995; Goldberg, 1993; Memmi, 1984/2000). Antiracism is part of a larger process of socioeconomic change designed to benefit children and youth in a culturally diverse society. As an aspect of transformative multicultural education, antiracist concepts and practices can help preserve and in-service teachers conceptually grasp and act upon exclusions and oppressions based on race. The development of a critical consciousness (Freire, 1970) to recognize racist exclusions can provide teachers with conceptual tools to understand other forms of oppressive exclusions as experienced through gender, class, handicapping conditions, and sexual orientation. Bonnett (2000), Derman-Sparks and Phillips (1997), and Memmi (2000) emphasize the power of antiracist concepts and practices as a transferable knowledge base for engaging in analyses of other types of social discrimination.

Defining Antiracism

Labeling who is racist or antiracist in a teacher education program or a K–12 school system is counterproductive (Derman-Sparks & Phillips, 1997; Howard, 1999; Thandeka, 1999). Focusing on an individual in the absence of social analyses marginalizes and trivializes philosophical and pragmatic understandings of race, racism, and antiracism within multicultural education. A need exists, therefore, to have a working definition of antiracism from which a teacher education program can draw.

Bonnett (2000) states that minimally antiracism "refers to those forms of thought and/or practice that seek to confront, eradicate and/or ameliorate racism. Antiracism implies the ability to identify a phenomenon—racism—and to do something about it" (p. 4). Memmi (2000) explains that antiracism, unlike a human relations paradigm, "agrees to put into question all situations of acquisition, dominance, and privilege" (p. 162). The identification of racism and subsequent antiracist actions, according to Banks and Banks (1997), means that "curriculum materials, grouping practices, hiring policies, teacher attitudes and expectations, and school policy and practices are examined and steps are taken to eliminate racism from these school variables" (p. 433). Because antiracism can potentially reveal negative practices, institutions may, however, attempt to tolerate racist expressions by limiting or discrediting antiracist inquiry and actions (see Bonnett, 2000; Troyna & Carrington, 1990).

Tolerance, Managed Multiculturalism, and Antiracism

Chapter 4 describes how organizations can manage and control expressions of multiculturalism and diversity that limit transformative effects of multicultural education. Consequently, institutionally managed multiculturalism can restrict the application of antiracism (Bonnett, 2000; Gillborn, Youdell, & Kirton, 1999; Goldberg, 1993; Troyna & Carrington, 1990). If a teacher education program is uncomfortable incorporating issues of racism, managed multiculturalism is likely to curtail antiracist orientations. Moreover, any teacher education program can profess opposition to racism but in practice still limit expressions of antiracism.

Institutions that embrace a human relations paradigm can substitute tolerance for antiracism. Conceptually, tolerance is problematic in responding to racism in both theory and practice. Tolerance suggests a sympathetic, albeit simplistic, acceptance of diversity that can deny the existence of racialized socioeconomic conditions. Tolerance implies that if people would merely accept one another's differences, racism would fade away. More significantly, tolerance can be a method to allow racism to remain undisturbed if it is rationalized as somehow having a negligible effect. Yet throughout U.S. history racialized subjects excluded by White privilege have often suffered oppression under policies of malevolent tolerance. When racism is reduced to individualized prejudice correctable through tolerance, attention is deflected away from institutional racism and antiracist alternatives.

Managed multiculturalism that promotes tolerance as a color-blind norm can lead to monoculturalist attacks on multicultural education. For example, Stotsky (1999) concludes that a "watchdog group" needs to monitor multiculturalists because acknowledgements of racist exclusions may result in "a blanket indictment of whites or the larger society" with "the net effect . . . [being] the disappearing of an American culture as a whole" (pp. 90, 133, 209). Such monoculturalist critics construe antiracism as "an anticivic moral harangue" (p. 259). López (2001) identifies a strand of monoculturalism among some higher education faculty who believe that concentrating on racism and antiracism lowers the quality of educational research. Roman (1997) observes that this kind of managed multicultural inquiry seeks to silence discourse about the contemporary effects of colonialism and racism. When racialized histories and the continuing existence of racist exclusions as reasonable arenas of scholarship and antiracist practice are denied, managed multiculturalism can curb perceived excesses of multicultural education. Implicitly, managed multiculturalism serves the maintenance of White privilege.

As an alternative to managed multiculturalism and calls for tolerance, Nieto (1998) insists that multicultural education should be grounded in the cultural difference concepts of affirmation, solidarity, and critique. Derman-Sparks (1998) juxtaposes tolerance with transformation to illustrate the social justice shortcomings of a tolerance paradigm. Although acknowledging the importance of changing individual racist attitudes and behaviors, both Nieto's and Derman-Sparks's alternatives to tolerance conceive of racism as emanating from institutional and ideological roots.

ANTIRACISM AND TEACHER IDENTITY FORMATION

In her essay on negative consequences of public school "assimilationist agendas," Nieto (1995) observes that multicultural education can fall short when enacting an antiracist perspective in teaching and learning. A teacher education program that includes studies of racial oppression and White privilege may conclude with a focus on victimization rather than transformative social action. Yet what kind of antiracist knowledge, dispositions, and skills might a program reasonably expect to develop within teachers during the span of teacher education?

Although remaining acutely mindful of systemic perpetuations of racism, transformative multicultural teacher educators recognize that the individual teacher can also be a valid analytic unit of study. To help teachers understand their socially constructed identities, Derman-Sparks (1998) presents a transformative paradigm that challenges preservice and in-service teachers "to uncover, face, and change their own biases, discomforts, and misinformation and identify and alter educational practices that collude with racism" (p. 6). Teacher education pedagogy under this approach shifts to individual teacher positionality within a racialized society where schools exist.[2] Banks (1993b) explains that "important aspects of our identity . . . are markers of *relational positions* [italics added] rather than essential qualities" (p. 5). Hence, teacher identity is dependent on shifts of positionalities according to varying social contexts (Banks, 1993b; Grant & Ladson-Billings, 1997).

Racial identity theory can help to account for how White privilege bestows upon a teacher a socially positioned racialized lens to view and respond to student competence, curricular content, and school organization (Carter & Goodwin, 1994). Teacher racial identity formation issues are potent centers to help individuals interrogate their own teaching knowledge, attitudes, and actions vis-à-vis multiculturalism. Antiracism examines these pedagogical relationships by explicitly connecting social factors to individual teacher identity development.

The incorporation in antiracist education of racial identity formation is theoretically situated within critical pedagogy where "identity formation and the development of the person are seen as thoroughly *political* enterprises, in which the people concerned are responsible for the choices made" (Miedema & Wardekker, 1999, p. 81). Antiracism's critical pedagogy can help preservice and inservice teachers to embrace a socially constructed identity oppositional to racism (Lawrence, 1997).

Illusions of a Fixed and Unified Teacher Identity

Transformative multicultural education finds a human relations paradigm, with its support for an ahistorical, transcendental identity, ineffective. The human relations assumption of a fixed and authentic identity represents a profound dilemma of being human in the 21st century. Writes Archibald (1998), "Being human brings with it the tendency to presuppose a Truth; an essence; a 'metaphysics of presence'; a unified, autonomous self" (p. 60). This human relations desire represents a search for an absolute center of identity that belies the relational positions of socially constructed identities (Althusser, 1971; Archibald, 1998; Dyson, 1994; Goldberg, 1993; Mac an Ghaill, 1999; Miedema & Wardekker, 1999; Murphy & Choi, 1997). Transformative multicultural education recognizes that individual identities result from social relations in a culturally diverse society.

A teacher's identity is influenced by hegemonic ideological values of dominant social institutions (Althusser, 1971). Because research documents that a "normal" White person can develop negative racial stereotypes at as young an age as 3 or 4 and grow in these perceptions into adolescence and young adulthood, Carter and Goodwin (1994) explain that it is imperative for teachers to understand their own racial identity formations in order to better serve children of color. Carter (1997) observes, however, "Whites, while socialized in a racially constructed world, are taught not to be aware of themselves in racial terms" (p. 199). A formidable task for a teacher program is working with teachers who act on the unfounded assumption that they have selected a color-blind identity free of a White privileged social context.

Racial Identity Formation

In "Essentialism and the Complexities of Racial Identity" Michael Dyson (1994) bridges a potential dichotomy between the individual and society that recognizes the shifting social nature of identity development:

Identity is socially and culturally constructed from the raw materials of the individual and the social, the private and the public, and the domestic and the civic. Racial identity is not exhausted by genetic inheritance. *The processes by which the meaning of race are shattered and reconstituted over time and place in American culture convincingly make the case against a narrow understanding of racial identity* [italics added]. (pp. 223–224)

Dyson captures the changing notions of historically constituted race and its implications on racial identity formation. Ethnic and racial categories publicly assigned at birth or by immigration officials are insufficient to understand the complexities of identity development. Throughout one's life a multiplicity of shifting social messages and encounters constantly bombards the privatized world of an individual's subjectivity. The public/private terrain of racial identities in teacher development should be investigated within teacher education in order that teachers can acquire a more complete understanding of the dynamics of antiracism and identity formation.

Helms's Model of Racial Identity Formation. Antiracist practitioners are drawn to Janet Helms's (1990a, 1990c; 1994; Helms & Cook, 1999) evolving approach to racial identity development in assisting teachers to unpack the positionality of their own identity formations (cf. Derman-Sparks & Phillips, 1997; Howard, 1999; Lawrence, 1997; Lawrence & Tatum, 1997a, 1997b; McIntyre, 1997; Tatum, 1999a, 1999b). Racial identity development for Helms (1990b) focuses on the social-psychological implications of racial categorization. Her model is differentiated for Whites and people of color and recognizes that the social construction and instability of racial identity formation are influenced by a "socioracial groups' differential rankings or access to resources in the political and economic societal hierarchy" (Helms & Cook, 1999, p. 84). Racial identity stages "are described in the order they are hypothesized to evolve" (p. 88).

Table 5.1 is a summary of people of color racial identity ego statuses and information processing strategies. Briefly stated, the racial identity "ego statuses," or what Tatum (1999a) interprets as "habits of mind" (p. 59), for people of color ranges from "conformity," where one devalues one's own group in favor of White standards of privilege and is usually "oblivious to [one's] socioracial groups' sociopolitical histories," *to* "integrative awareness," where one has developed the "capacity to value one's own collective identities as well as empathize and collaborate with members of other oppressed groups" (Helms & Cook, 1999, p. 87). People of color with conformity behavior, "the least sophisticated status" (p. 86), try to deny their own racialized identities while idealizing White assimilationist norms. At the other end of the spectrum are individuals who display integrative awareness by holding a positive racial identity of them-

Table 5.1. Summary of People of Color Racial Identity Statuses and
Strategies

Status	Summary and Information Processing Strategies (IPS)
Conformity (pre-encounter)	External self-definition that implies devaluing of own group and allegiance to White standards of merit. Person probably is oblivious to socioracial groups' sociopolitical histories. IPS: Selective perception, distortion, minimization, and obliviousness to socioracial concerns.
Dissonance (encounter)	Ambivalence and confusion concerning own socioracial-group commitment and ambivalent socioracial self-definition. Person may be ambivalent about life decisions. IPS: Repression of anxiety-evoking racial information, ambivalence, anxiety, and disorientation.
Immersion	Idealization of one's socioracial group and denigration of that which is perceived as White. Use of own-group external standards to self-define and own-group commitment and loyalty is valued. May make life decisions for the benefit of the group. IPS: Hypervigilance and hypersensitivity toward racial stimuli and dichotomous thinking.
Emersion	A euphoric sense of well-being and solidarity that accompanies being surrounded by people of one's own socioracial group. IPS: Uncritical of one's own group, peacefulness, joyousness.
Internalization	Positive commitment to and acceptance of one's own socioracial group, internally defined racial attributes, and capacity to objectively assess and respond to members of the dominant group. Can make life decisions by assessing and integrating socioracial group requirements and self-assessment. IPS: Intellectualization and abstraction.
Integrative awareness	Capacity to value one's own collective identities as well as empathize and collaborate with members of other oppressed groups. Life decisions may be motivated by globally humanistic self-expression. IPS: Flexible and complex.

Note: From J.E. Helms and D.A. Cook, *Using Race and Culture in Counseling and Psychotherapy: Theory and Process.* Copyright © 1999 by Allyn and Bacon. Reprinted/adapted with permission.

selves while recognizing the importance of cultural differences and exhibiting flexibility to support the objectives of others who suffer from discrimination. Table 5.2 summarizes White racial identity ego statuses and information processing strategies. The racial identity statuses for White people extend from "contact," where an individual holds "satisfaction with racial status quo, obliviousness to racism and one's participation in it," *to* "autonomy," where one demonstrates a "capacity to relinquish the privileges of racism" (pp. 90–91). Although one racial identity status theme may predominate for both people of color and Whites, Helms's model theorizes that most individuals move among identity statuses depending upon each individual's social context.

The reliability and interpretation of the model have proven unstable when psychometric scales are applied. In her own meta-analysis of studies that used the model with White populations, Helms (1999) is unable to explain measurement errors on either the basis of methodology or the theoretical underpinnings of the model. Tatum (1999a) notes the model is sometimes used too rigidly and ahistorically. Howard (1999) advises that the model's statuses should be used as "merely an approximation of actual experience" (p. 94). The model also falls short in conceptualizing and acknowledging a White antiracist identity. Despite potential problems associated with the use of this model, it has proven useful with White teacher populations—the primary concern of this chapter—by offering a schematic to understand racial identity formation in broader and more complex ways than a dualistic racist/antiracist conceptualization of racial identity.

White Antiracist Identity Formation.   Transformative multicultural education necessitates the presence of teachers whose clarity of their own racial identity serves to affirm the identity of all students. To better serve their students, White teachers in particular should not be immobilized in White shame, guilt, and confessionals as they grow to recognize and reject the premises of color blindness and White privilege (Derman-Sparks & Phillips, 1997; Giroux, 1999; Howard, 1999; Katz, 1978; MacLeod, 2001; McIntyre, 1997; Tatum, 1999a, 1999b; Thandeka, 1999). Because the ideology of White privilege can act "to delegitimate antiracist activity and to make accommodation to racism seem commonsensical and sane" (Roediger, 1999, p. 242), White teachers should develop the capacity to maintain an oppositional, antiracist identity.

Tatum (1999a) sees the role of "White ally" as a viable aspect of a White antiracist identity. A White ally is an "actively antiracist White person who is intentional in ongoing efforts to interrupt the cycle of racism" (p. 61). Winant (1997) contends that Whites can ally themselves with antiracist causes supporting people of color without abandoning their whiteness as some antiracists suggest (cf. Ignatiev & Garvey, 1996). Ellsworth (1997) warns against a fixed White ally role that can position Whites paternalistically within antiracist prac-

Table 5.2. Summary of White Racial Identity Statuses and Strategies

Status	Summary and Information Processing Strategies (IPS)
Contact	Satisfaction with racial status quo, obliviousness to racism and one's participation in it. If racial factors influence life decisions, they do so in a simplistic fashion.
	IPS: Obliviousness, denial, superficiality, and avoidance.
Disintegration	Disorientation and anxiety provoked by unresolvable racial moral dilemmas that force one to choose between own-group loyalty and humanism. May be stymied by life situations that arouse racial dilemmas.
	IPS: Suppression, ambivalence, and controlling.
Reintegration	Idealization of one's socioracial group; denigration and intolerance for other groups. Racial factors may strongly influence life decisions.
	IPS: Selective perception and negative outgroup distortion.
Pseudo-Independence	Intellectualized commitment to one's own socioracial group and subtle superiority and tolerance of other socioracial groups as long as they can be helped to conform to White standards of merit.
	IPS: Selective perception, cognitive restructuring, and conditional regard.
Immersion	The searching for an understanding of the personal meaning of whiteness and racism and the ways by which one benefits from them as well as a redefinition of whiteness.
	IPS: Hypervigilance, judgmental, and cognitive-affective restructuring.
Emersion	A sense of discovery, security, sanity, and group solidarity and pride that accompanies being with other White people who are embarked on the mission of rediscovering whiteness.
	IPS: Sociable, pride, seeking positive group-attributes.
Autonomy	Informed positive socioracial-group commitment, use of internal standards for self-definition, capacity to relinquish the privileges of racism. Person tries to avoid life options that require participation in racial oppression.
	IPS: Flexible and complex.

Note: From J.E. Helms and D.A. Cook, *Using Race and Culture in Counseling and Psychotherapy: Theory and Process.* Copyright © 1999 by Allyn and Bacon. Reprinted/adapted with permission.

tice. Writes Ellsworth (1997), "Because racism never operates twice in the same way with the same meanings and effects, the specifics of when and how our help as white people is appropriate, wanted, or useful are crucial" (pp. 267–268). Duesterberg (1999) cautions against Whites who act as allies by asserting an essentialist representation of race and constructing overly simplistic and fixed dichotomies of "friend/enemy, oppressed/oppressor, knowledgeable/ignorant" (p. 762). Ellsworth (1997) and Yamato (1995) conclude that ultimately White antiracists should proceed to some form of social action by taking responsibility to obstruct racism for the benefit of those it harms.

Blewett's (2000) case study of White antiracists working outside of academia and Lawrence and Tatum's (1997b) experience with in-service teachers reveal that the notion of White allies supporting people of color is riddled with the issue of trust. In the context of a historical legacy of White privilege and racism, a White with a strong antiracist identity understands why people of color might distrust Whites who claim to be antiracist. Like the people of color with whom Whites may be seeking to ally themselves, White antiracists also distrust "many white people, particularly those in power" (Blewett, 2000, p. 181). Supporting this apprehension is Kailin's (1999) documentation of White teachers who recognized instances of school-based racism but were "too silent to behave as allies" (p. 742). Given the instability of a White antiracist identity, Cochran-Smith (1995b) refers to Whites as "uncertain allies" (see pp. 567–568).

Despite the importance of the thorny issue of trust/distrust, White antiracists attempt to move beyond this point by taking actions than can lead to beneficial changes in the political status quo. Because a White antiracist identity in the United States is nearly invisible in history textbooks and the mass media, antiracists can, however, become estranged from other Whites. Thus support from people of color is considered critical in the maintenance of an active White antiracist identity and in building multiracial coalitions. Howard (1999) passionately confirms this vital connection as an ally with people of color in his own career as a White antiracist educator. Yet, in the absence of people of color to provide direct support, any teacher—regardless of his or her racial identification—needs to find like-minded multicultural advocates to sustain social action (Lawrence & Krause, 1996; Lee, 1998b; Tatum, 1999b).

Howard (1999) describes a White antiracist identity as an individual who is a "transformationist" (see pp. 106–109). A White teacher with a transformationist identity is active in challenging Eurocentric perspectives and dismantling white privilege. A transformationist is an advocate for marginalized populations who are silenced by color blindness and White privilege. In a transformationist identity status a White teacher acts in congruence with culturally responsive teaching. Howard, too, recognizes that a White transformationist identity requires continuous maintenance because a transformationist can cycle through antiracist engagement and then withdraw to a perceived comfort zone of White privilege.

Blewett's (2000) antiracist subjects did not necessarily move developmentally along a theorized racial identity scale (also see Thompson & Tyagi, 1996). Through her case studies Blewett found four shared identity dimensions among White antiracists: (1) knowledge of structures and ideologies of racism; (2) the importance of social action; (3) self-awareness "to counteract racist socialization"; and (4) a commitment marked by a willingness to take sociopolitical risks for antiracist social change (p. 80). A multicultural challenge for a teacher education program is how to bring White teachers to an understanding of the importance to develop and value an antiracist identity. This necessitates helping teachers sustain a multicultural commitment in the face of dominant ideologies that minimize the importance of antiracist pedagogies (Causey, Thomas, & Armento, 2000; Lawrence & Tatum, 1997a; McIntyre, 2000).

ANTIRACIST TEACHER EDUCATION PEDAGOGIES

A White antiracist identity is both difficult to attain and maintain in a nation whose history and social practices are embedded in White privilege and color blindness. A teacher education program, however, can be an institutional place where an antiracist identity is positively promoted and supported (Cochran-Smith, 1995a, 1995b). Explicit transformative multicultural knowledge, dispositions, and skills from a teacher education program can move White teachers into an antiracist, transformationist identity. Mindful of dominant counterforces that discourage antiracist practices, a teacher education program can represent a secure space to develop an identity oppositional to racism. Next, we turn to both the challenges and possibilities for aiding teachers in the formation of an antiracist identity.

Racialized and Color-Blind Discourse Tensions

Given that we live in a racialized society, some expressions of race may be benign and distinguishable from racism (Goldberg, 1993). However, in teacher education practice this distinction is often blurred. Linda Valli (1995) perceptively reveals a major dilemma when addressing race and diversity with preservice teachers. She grapples with seemingly contradictory maxims in teaching: "*If you don't see the color, you don't see the child* and *Teachers should be color blind*" (p. 121). In reconciling this dichotomy, Valli found, "White student teachers had to first see the color of the child in order to design a multicultural curriculum, but then they had to move beyond color sightedness to value a multicultural curriculum for everyone" (p. 125). Valli recommends that teacher educators heighten their awareness about how teachers can attach color-blind desires to progressive instructional methods such as whole language and integrated curriculum development. In doing so, teachers can assume that these pedagogies make it unnecessary to attend to K–12 student diversity and multicultural education. Teacher candidates who cling to such beliefs unquestioningly direct student behaviors toward White privileged cultural expectations. Valli concludes that a teacher education program should consciously analyze and deconstruct this dualistic maxim to help teacher candidates be culturally responsive.

Lawrence and Tatum (1997a) state that antiracist education should examine "the ways racism influences schools and the people in them, teach students about the racial stratification that exists, and empower learners to take responsibility for and/or challenge the racial status quo" (p. 164). The following sections provide an overview of higher education transformative multicultural pedagogical efforts. These summaries represent faculty considerations when teaching college students, including preservice and in-service teachers, to critically analyze racism and move toward a transformationist, action-oriented antiracist identity. Although strategies and issues are presented separately, they are often interactive in practice.

Analyses of Racism.   Leading transformative multicultural scholars incorporate into their own teaching analyses of racism and oppression (e.g., Banks, 2001a; Cochran-Smith, 1995a, 1995b; Nieto, 1999; Shor & Freire, 1987; Sleeter, 1995a, 1995b, 2001). Besides having faculty present analytic information, preservice teachers can construct their own research questions to investigate racism (Sleeter, 1995a). Macro-analyses can be applied to local power relationships in a school or community to ground analyses of racism (Banks et al., 2001; Chan & East, 1998; Duesterberg, 1999; Oakes, 1996). When historical and contemporary structures and discourses of racism frame multicultural education, preservice and in-service teachers are exposed to transformative possibilities that can counter metanarratives based on White privilege.

Without fundamental analyses of racism, White teachers can remain colorblind to the need for culturally responsive teaching. Strategies that depend solely upon an informational approach to multicultural education tend, however, to have a limited effect in assisting White college students to appreciate and form an antiracist identity (Duesterberg, 1999; Fox, 1999).

Shifting Positionality.   Building upon analyses of racism, multicultural education effectively engages White teachers when they can realize how their relational social positions influence their racialized perspectives. Sleeter (1995b) describes the importance in having teacher candidates examine their own positionality because "the impact of systemic and persistent discrimination is a very difficult concept for most White teachers to grasp since they do not experience racial discrimination themselves" (p. 20).

Anecdotes from multicultural education colleagues indicate that using behavioral checklists of White privilege (e.g., McIntosh 1988/1995; Olsen, 1998) can lead to productive opening dialogues with White teacher candidates. Films that document evidence of racism are effective in helping shift the positionality held by Whites (Banks, 2001a; Cochran-Smith, 1995b; Gillette & Boyle-Baise, 1996; Katz, 1978; Khan, 1999; Sleeter, 1995a, 1995b). Teacher educators can access the journal *Multicultural Review* for multicultural resources, including films. Each issue of *Multicultural Perspectives*, the official journal of the National Association for Multicultural Education, also contains a variety of reviewed multicultural resources that can help teachers clarify their positionalities.

Simulations through role playing and researched narratives can help White teachers to see the positionality of people of color more realistically (Banks, 2001a; Derman-Sparks & Phillips, 1997; Ford, 1999; Greenman & Kimmel, 1995; Sleeter, 1995a, 1995b). Dialogue groups among students with differing backgrounds can contribute to awareness of various individual and group positionalities in comparison to one's own relational identity (Zúñiga & Nagda, 1993). A goal with these pedagogical approaches is to problematize the normalcy of color blindness and White privilege by exposing teachers to both the unstable terrain of racial identities and the dynamic relationship among culturally different positionalities.

Multicultural Autobiographical Research.   Autobiographical research is based on an analytical narrative of the experiences of the writer. Multicultural autobiographical research strives to deepen individual understandings of positionality. Clark and O'Donnell (1999) suggest that criteria for analyzing autobiographical research ought to acknowledge that "each and every autobiography has to be contested with critical and reflective analysis in order for learners to realize that their point of entry into the debate is not the only one, that the way they view and perceive the world is not the only way" (p. 6). Racial identity formation is generally a central focus for multicultural autobiographical research. An unfocused autobiographical assignment on "diversity," however, can result in color-blind drivel (Subrahmanyan, Hornstein, & Heine, 2000).

Focusing on White racial identity formation through theory and autobiographical research can help anchor the responsibility of White preservice and in-service teachers in a culturally diverse society (Clark & Medina, 2000; Ford, 1999; Ladson-Billings, 2000; Sleeter, 1995a, 1995b). When exposed to analyses of racism and White privilege, preservice students can engage in reconstructing their autobiographies cognizant of their whiteness (Cochran-Smith, 1995b). Banks (2001a) has teacher candidates use a "family history project" that includes "ways in which race, class, and gender have influenced their family and personal histories" (p. 12). Reid (1995) initiates the autobiographical process by asking teacher education students "to write about their first encounter with color, their own and those of others" (p. 239). Banks (2001a) observes, however, that White teacher candidates experience difficulty in articulating the place of race in their family histories. Schoem (1993) notes that college students also have trouble integrating theoretical knowledge of racial identity formation with their personal experiences.

The teacher education admissions process can be used to both screen applicants on multicultural criteria (Haberman & Post, 1998) and initiate autobiographical research. For example, the Evergreen State College (2001) requires applicants to write a short essay that responds to the following statement:

> It is virtually impossible to be raised in the culture of the U.S. without being taught racial, ethnic, gender and socio-economic class biases; yet teachers today must be prepared to work with children from many backgrounds. They must also be prepared to demonstrate a commitment to the highest ideals of U.S. society and of public education. (p. 12)

In their response applicants are asked to examine "your background, behaviors and experiences that have prepared you to face these issues. In light of your experiences consider challenges you may face in meeting the expectation to become an advocate for multicultural and anti-bias teaching" (p. 12). A multicultural application essay can serve as a springboard to formally initiate autobiographical research in a teacher education program.

When directing students to construct their autobiographical narratives through a multicultural lens, Gillette and Boyle-Baise (1996) find that initial drafts begin superficially despite students expending considerable time on conceptualizing and writing from a multicultural perspective. Gillette and Boyle-Baise emphasize to their students the "role of place, voice, and perspective" (p. 281) and have multiple drafts completed. Multiple drafts allow for perspectives to be refined in the context of curricular analyses of racism and racial identity formation (also see Causey et al., 2000; Ford, 1999).

Tatum (1999a) finds White antiracist autobiographies promising for what they offer other Whites as turning points in racial identity formation that can result in movement away from racism. She is concerned, however, when autobiographical research wallows in confessionals and "White angst" that can detract from the very real daily struggles against racism faced by people of color (p. 62). Part of the overall success of an autobiographical research pedagogy is contingent upon teacher educators themselves enacting antiracist identities that serve as models for their students (Bollin & Finkel, 1995; Carter & Goodwin, 1994; Fennimore, 2001; O'Loughlin, 2001; Subrahmanyan et al., 2000). As Chapter 4 explains, faculty should strive to model antiracist practices as a condition of teacher education accountability and accreditation.

Experiences With Populations of Color.   I have pointed to the inconsistency of research supporting the value of field experiences with populations of color. Alone and unmediated without analyses of racism, examinations of social positionality, and research into racialized autobiographies, White teacher education students may actually leave a diverse field site with reinforced racial stereotypes (Armaline, 1995; Bakari, 2001; Ford, 1999; Goodwin, 2001; O'Loughlin, 2001). This outcome correlates with Gordon Allport's (1954) conclusion that certain conditions should exist in order that constructive contact can occur between Whites and people of color. These conditions include working cooperatively for a common purpose in which participants are of equal status. Allport added that "the effect is greatly enhanced if this contact is sanctioned by institutional supports" (p. 281).

As Chapters 2 and 3 note, a combination of factors in a school setting can affect the multicultural quality of the experience, such as the degree to which a cooperating teacher values transformative multicultural education and the extent to which multicultural content is incorporated in the curriculum. The Bank Street College of Education is an example of a teacher education program that consciously attends to these issues. Bank Street faculty strive to find field sites where student teacher interns can have experiences in "democratic forms of community in which antiracist and egalitarian norms are pursued" (Darling-Hammond & Macdonald, 2000, p. 26). Bank Street preservice teachers participate with cooperating in-service teachers whose classrooms support equity in a participatory "mini-society" that connects "to children's family, community, and cultural roots" (p. 26).

A growing body of research suggests that teachers in racially diverse settings need time to reflect critically upon their experiences (Armaline, 1995; Bassey, 1996; Bollin & Finkel, 1995; Causey et al., 2000; Duesterberg, 1999; Finney & Orr, 1995; Ladson-Billings, 1995a; Sleeter, 1995a, 1995b, 2001; Wieczorek & Grant, 2000). Field reflections need to be interwoven with multicultural course work to foster the aims of culturally responsive teaching. The University of California at Berkeley, for example, offers two courses concurrently with field experiences: "Education in the Inner Cities" and "Teaching Linguistic and Cultural Minority Students." Taken together with internships, the courses serve to address the teacher's role juxtaposed to "the gnarly issues of race, class, and first- and second-language development" (Snyder, 2000, p. 118).

Oakes (1996) and Sleeter (1995a) consider promising the practice of placing teacher candidates both in a culturally diverse school setting and in a community agency serving populations of color (and ideally headed by people of color). Sleeter (1995a, 2001) finds community-based experiences that incorporate service learning more valuable than K–12 placements for problematizing unacknowledged racist attitudes of preservice teachers. By investigating school and community practices through "situated pedagogies" (Ladson-Billings, 2000, p. 210), a teacher education program can assist teachers to see localized manifestations of "how racial meanings are used and interpreted" (Duesterberg, 1999, p. 759; also see Chan & East, 1998). Derman-Sparks and Phillips (1997) and Lawrence and Tatum (1997a) discovered that an antiracist action research project with a field experience can frame localized racist exclusions within a larger context of White privilege. Lawrence and Tatum (1997a) found that when in-service teachers were expected to engage in some form of antiracist action, many made curricular changes inclusive of multicultural histories and perspectives. Teachers also took steps to interrupt racist assumptions about the competence of children of color within both individual classrooms and school policy responses to achievement.

Anticipating Emotional Reactions.   A course in multicultural education may be the first college course in which teacher candidates encounter issues of racism, White privilege, and antiracism (see, e.g., McCain-Reid, 1995; Young & Buchanan, 1996). When college faculty emphasize racism and White privilege in multicultural education, inevitably students, especially Whites, react emotionally to a disequilibrium that has been created within their formerly assumed stable and normalized White identities. Emotional reactions may include *anger* expressed as "This is a racist class for talking about White people this way" or "Why am I only hearing about this now?" or falling sullenly silent and simply disengaging from learning because "My professor is so negative and doesn't look at all the good things America has done"; *denials* such as "I haven't discriminated against anyone" or "Racism isn't a problem here" or presuming contemporary racism rests only with the likes of the Ku Klux Klan; and *despair* expressed in tears of shame or as "The situation is hopeless. What can one person do?" Fear of emotional reactions can serve as a rationale for a faculty member either to avoid issues of racism or to present racialized information antiseptically and removed from local conditions. When unanticipated by multiculturally committed faculty, preservice and in-service teacher anger, denials, and despair can impede efforts to impart transformative multicultural knowledge, dispositions, and skills.

Sleeter (1995a) sees value in recognizing and eliciting emotions from teacher candidates early in a teacher education program. She explains that course materials "should provide an emotional jolt, clearly illustrate unequal conditions, and provide a range of concrete examples of structural inequalities that can be used for analysis later" (p. 424). Schoem (1993) also assumes that strong emotional reactions ought to be recognized as a normal and accepted aspect of any course attending to transformative multiculturalism. Derman-Sparks and Phillips (1997) conclude,

> At the heart of White students' transformation is a nondefensive acknowledgment
> of their participation in a racist society. The energy that once was consumed in
> defending and hiding their racism or feelings of guilt and inadequacy can now be
> applied to learning how to be anti-racists. (p. 107)

It is critical to help White teachers understand that emotions emanating from
their own internalized racism are a function of a history of rationalized institutional racism.

Extended Pedagogical Time.   Because learning about racism is directly
connected to processes of White identity formation, sufficient time is required
for preservice and in-service teachers to construct new information that directly
affects their personal and professional self-conceptions. Although some positive
movement among White teachers toward an antiracist identity may be observed
in one course, additional time is necessary to help teachers maintain transformative perspectives and actions (Lawrence & Tatum, 1997b). When Derman-
Sparks and Phillips (1997) and Lawrence and Tatum (1997a) observe positive
development with teachers in antiracist studies, they attribute this success in
part to their students having had adequate time to investigate a series of interrelated topics and experiences. Subrahmanyan et al. (2000) note that extended
pedagogical time allows groups of preservice teachers to share in significant
investigations of personal and professional responses to racism.

For teachers to become multicultural demands extensive time to understand
themselves as changing subjects and to learn that "multiculturalism is a way of
being, perceiving, thinking, and acting in the world" (Ford, 1999, p. 14). Developing a multicultural perspective requires more than just time to acquire an
objective knowledge base. Extended time is necessary for teachers to thoroughly
integrate a transformative multicultural orientation. Chapter 8 details the rationale, advantages, and challenges when designing and implementing a multicultural teacher education learning community in which education student dialogue
can be supported and the learning of topics considered socially controversial
can be explored in extended time formats.

Reconceptualizing the Teacher Education Curriculum.   For preservice
and in-service teachers to value and affirm an antiracist identity requires more
than an assignment within a multicultural education course in a teacher education program. Both a safe and courageous learning environment should be structured in order to allow education student dialogue on such volatile topics as
racism and White privilege to unfold affectively and cognitively. Subrahmanyan
et al. (2000) find it useful to have all courses in a semester "blocked" together
to help preservice teachers construct transformative multicultural education concepts through an inquiry process that can be applied to their teaching. Their

restructuring goal is to expand the block concept to two semesters so that student teaching internships can be framed by multicultural course work at both the beginning and the end of the experience.

Alverno College, Bank Street College, the University of California at Berkeley, and Wheelock College are positive institutional examples of teacher preparation programs that infuse multicultural concepts and internships throughout the curriculum for their respective teacher candidates (Darling-Hammond & Macdonald, 2000; Miller & Silvernail, 2000; Snyder, 2000; Zeichner, 2000). The collective experience of these colleges is based on the critical need to incorporate transformative multicultural knowledge, dispositions, and skills throughout the teacher education program.

CONCLUSION

Teacher educators who work on the multicultural education of preservice and in-service teachers have observed the discomfort the vast majority of Whites have with issues of race, racism, and antiracism. Problematically, a significant number of teacher education programs demonstrate a reluctance to address these "taboo subjects" in their curriculum, pedagogy, and evaluations (Santos Rego & Nieto, 2000, p. 423). Yet, as Banks (2000) notes, teacher education programs should be reformed to enable teachers to "examine their own personal knowledge and values" in a transformative multicultural context (p. 39). This personal racial identity investigation by teachers needs to be related to racism perpetuated in school systems and local communities along with a vision of antiracist alternatives.

Multicultural teacher educators find promising curricular practices that incorporate analyses of racism, shifting positionalities, autobiographical research, and experiences with populations of color. Simultaneously, there exists a growing awareness of the need to anticipate emotional reactions from White teachers, the importance of extended pedagogical time to investigate issues of race, and the challenges of a fragmented teacher education curriculum. Hence a growing and viable experiential knowledge base exists to assist teacher education programs to incorporate a transformative multicultural education perspective through curriculum, pedagogy, and evaluations.

Pragmatic antiracism, as introduced in Chapter 4, is an approach for a teacher education program in order to incorporate previously excluded or distorted multicultural orientations. Pragmatic antiracism decenters a political status quo norm of White privilege and color blindness. Through this process race can be brought to the forefront of multicultural education. Antiracism by teachers can be an expression of a multicultural social action commitment to culturally responsive teaching.

Although a combination of curricular approaches show promise in reducing racism among teachers, considerably more research into antiracist teacher education is needed. Deliberations and actions for antiracism should examine both what is included and what is excluded in a teacher education program. Although incorporating antiracist knowledge and pedagogical approaches is very important, a program's "solution" to racism can never be complete. Racism and other forms of oppressions continue to take different and contradictory forms in diverse settings. Pragmatic antiracism for a teacher education program necessitates a commitment to flexible approaches that tackle the multiple and changing faces of racism.

CHAPTER 6

Globalization and Multicultural Education

Significant numbers of racially and ethnically subordinated people who live outside the United States and Europe awaken daily to inhumane living and working conditions. Lack of access to minimum conditions for basic health care, caloric intake, sanitation, and primary and secondary education are among a list of inequities for at least 1.3 billion people who must live on less than $1 a day (United Nations Educational, Scientific, and Cultural Organization, 2001). In effect, global inequities disproportionately reduce the life quality and expectancy of the people of Latin America, the Caribbean, Asia, and sub-Saharan Africa (see U.S. Bureau of the Census, 1998). Suffering the most within these regions are children and women and racial and ethnic minorities, individuals historically least empowered politically to change their living conditions.

Global poverty stemming from concentrations of wealth and racial and ethnic discrimination are perceived as remote and disconnected from the primary interests of most U.S. citizens.[1] This public perception influences a general belief that global social justice issues are beyond the purview of the multicultural education of teachers. A scarcity of models exists for helping teachers form an identity that can support global understanding for K–12 students (McLaren & Torres, 1999; Torres, 1998). Teacher education programs should incorporate global cultural identification (Banks, 2001b) that is built upon a transformative and antiracist teacher identity. Although containing constructive perspectives, global education texts for teachers tend to only approximate this aim for teacher identity formation (cf. Diaz, Massialias, & Xanthopoulos, 1999; Merryfield et al., 1997). Ambiguous human relations approaches to multicultural and global education that focus primarily upon cultural tolerance make obscure global economic disparities (Macedo & Bartolomé, 1999). The global dimension of multicultural education generally shies away from taking an overt transformative stance on moral implications of unequal material and political resource distributions. An understanding of these dynamics can help teachers increase student awareness and actions for considering possibilities to create a better world for all people.

The near absence of a critical global perspective in teacher education programs is unfortunate because we are situated in the most financially and politically privileged and influential nation in the world. This near invisibility of globalization concepts in multicultural education suggests a fundamental knowledge base gap. Banks (2001a) confronts this multifaceted challenge for multicultural education. He writes, "My work on global identification and issues is incomplete and episodic. . . . Global issues remain mostly an unrealized and hoped-for goal" (p. 14). The complexity as to what global identification can mean, however, does not easily lend itself to social psychological identity formation models (Best & Kellner, 1997, pp. 273–280; Cvetkovich & Kellner, 1997b). Banks's candid assessment captures a dilemma for the development of culturally responsive and relevant teachers who hold a transformative global identity.

Approaching globalization for multicultural education demands that educators, in Carlos Alberto Torres's (1995) words, "think politically about education" (pp. 255–331). The negative social cost of global capitalism in comparison to its presumed benefits is a valid and significant concept for a teacher education program to examine. Economists Samuel Bowles and Herbert Gintis's (1976) ground-breaking critique on capitalism's adverse impact on schooling led to further educational analyses in the late 1980s and early 1990s that were more closely tied to teaching and teacher education (e.g., Ginsburg, 1988; Giroux, 1988; Liston, 1988; Liston & Zeichner, 1991; McLaren, 1989; Shapiro, 1990). As globalization becomes more visible in our daily lives, researchers continue to provide relevant analyses of the political economy of education (e.g., Apple, 1996, 2001; Engel, 2000; McLaren & Farahmandpur, 2001a, 2001b; Spring, 1998; Torres, 1995, 1998). Critiques of globalization tend to counter a master metanarrative whose stories describe the purported advantages of global standardization and homogeneity. By focusing on the relationship between (a) publicly funded, governmental structures designed to assist corporate capital accumulation and (b) the unmet social needs for the vast majority of the world's population, students in a teacher education program can critically situate and articulate teaching and learning in a local-global nexus (see Cvetkovich & Kellner, 1997a). This chapter describes how discriminatory effects that hamper educational equity within the United States can be analyzed and related to global economic processes and outcomes.

This chapter examines multicultural education in the light of globalization. Globalization is analyzed for both its liberating potential through global solidarity and its oppressive qualities through corporate globalization. In explaining historical links between globalization and colonialism, emphasis is placed upon Eurocentrism and the Eurocentric concepts of progress, development, civilization, and 21st-century expressions of manifest destiny. The chapter focuses on how global economic production of inequities is manifested in the United States and in other nations. Highlighted are globalization's role in fostering antidemocratic employer intimidations, declines in public funds for education, social injustices created through debt burdens and unmet local needs, and neo-colonial practices. The global economic effects on education are described to examine how students are reconstituted as a form of human capital under a meritocracy myth perpetuated by school–business alliances. The undermining impact of global economic ideologies on multicultural education is presented with particular attention to the establishment of the Interstate New Teacher Assessment and Support Consortium (INTASC, 1992). The final sections of the chapter discuss implications of globalization for the multicultural education of teachers.

GLOBALIZATION AS A MULTICULTURAL CONCEPT

Globalization is a contested concept that incorporates cultural studies and political economy (Cvetkovich & Kellner, 1997b; Dorman, 2000; Held, McGrew, Goldblatt, & Perraton, 1999; Jameson, 1998a, 1998b; Ruigrok & van Tulder, 1995; Wallerstein, 1999). Jameson (1998b) explains that globalization is less a specialized field of study and more "a space of tension" between (a) "transnational domination and uniformity [and (b)] liberation of local culture from hidebound state and national forms" (pp. xiii–xiv). Hence one aspect of globalization incorporates capitalism's international profit quest to standardize cultural differences and subordinated populations. In popular education this approach is often referred to as *corporate globalization*. Another side of globalization, however, reveals a capacity to free politically dominated groups from parochially and internationally sanctioned acts of oppression. This perspective is generally stated as *global solidarity* for emancipation. Theoretically discomforting as it may appear, globalization carries with it this seeming paradox between oppression and liberation. For example, a global document such as the United Nations Universal Declaration of Human Rights (1948) can provide a global solidarity foundation for fundamental freedoms to oppressed populations. Yet other forms of universal standardization such as an advocacy and application of corporate globalization can have dire consequences for historically marginalized racial and ethnic groups. Globalization contains a potential for emancipation though encased in a historical legacy of suffering and violence.

Like multicultural education, globalization is interdisciplinary and falls outside canonized knowledge bases. Both multicultural education and globalization are defined within conceptual matrices that encompass status quo maintenance of privileged populations as well as transformative possibilities for the emancipation of subordinated populations from cycles of oppression. A human relations paradigm considers globalization and multicultural education as nearly completed and unified projects moving along a predestined, unswerving historical path. This fixed-system model theorizes that growth in financial capital and global markets causes aggregate improvements in human well-being and cultural understanding. Conversely, a transformative approach recognizes tensions and contradictions inherent in globalization and multicultural education for improving the human condition. In this spirit Mahalingam and McCarthy (2000) note "the need to rescue the best intuitions in multiculturalism from a full-scale corruption and incorporation by the interests of global capitalism" (p. 6). A transformative paradigm renounces a finalizing narrative that projects a global economy in its current form as inevitable and necessary. Instead, transformative multiculturalism favors such local-global concepts as difference, plurality, and solidarity against oppression. Transformationists offer critique and possibilities to truth claims in a metanarrative that trumpets the current direction of a global capitalist economy and cultural homogeneity.

Although globalization as a communicative process can bring attention to cultural diversity, the outcomes of globalization processes can limit expressions of cultural differences. In *Hybrid Cultures* Néstor García Canclini (1995) discusses this multicultural tension of globalization. García Canclini contends that such standard dichotomies of cultures as subordinate/dominant, traditional/modern, and rural/urban can be overly restrictive. Such distinctions need to recognize new global conditions to extend concepts "of culture and of hybridization of the traditions of classes, ethnic groups, and nations" (p. 206) so that emergent cultural forms can be incorporated into studies of globalization. Indeed, the spaces of global tension among the economic, political, and cultural dimensions are actually an inseparable multicultural composite. Separating culture from economics and politics and, more specifically, human rights from property rights is a counterproductive and "banal distinction" under current conditions of U.S. global hegemony (Jameson, 1998a, p. 70). Yet the meanings and implications attached to hybrid or borderland multicultural spaces within a political economy are not necessarily self-evident or easily revealed. For that reason, a historical perspective on globalization is necessary for a teacher education program to help teachers grasp the multicultural significance between economic exploitation and the lived realities of oppressed populations.

GLOBALIZATION AND COLONIALISM

Contemporary corporate globalization processes and outcomes can be traced to the initiation of European colonialism in the 15th century. Whereas prior to 1492 capital accumulation was limited to regional conflicts, Columbus's arrival in the Americas marked in many ways the beginning of globalization. No longer would the states of Europe be peripheral to non-European regional economic dominance. The beginning of a world system that placed Europe at the center initiated the global dominance of finance capital and its accumulation over other forms of socioeconomic production and exchange. Unlike previous historical epochs, capital accumulation has continually been supported and maintained by government officials through the subjugation of people throughout the world (Arrighi, 1994; Chomsky, 1999; Cvetkovich & Kellner, 1997b; Dussel, 1995, 1998; Held et al., 1999; Leys, 1974; Ngũgĩ, 1993; Takaki, 1993; Wallerstein, 1984, 1999; Zinn, 1995).

The aim of this section is not to review 500 years of history; its purpose is to note a historical thread of colonialism that is related to current practices of corporate globalization. Rather than assuming the existence of an exclusively postcolonial world, teachers can be introduced to contemporary configurations of colonialism that do not necessarily require seizing or colonizing physical territories through military occupation, as described later in this chapter. An important starting point for education students is an understanding as to how a Eurocentric paradigm perpetuates oppression.

Historical Eurocentrism

Central to transformative multicultural education are theories and practices intended to critique and offer alternatives to the dominance of Eurocentrism (Banks, 1993b, 2001c; Freire, 1970; Gay, 2000; Goldberg, 1993; McCarthy, 1998b; McLaren, 1994, 1995; Santos Rego & Nieto, 2000; Shor & Freire, 1987; Sleeter & McLaren, 1995). But how did Eurocentrism become hegemonic and remain a significant force into the 21st century? How were political and economic elites able to globally circulate specific kinds of discourses and ideologies that fall within Eurocentrism?

With the arrival of Europeans into North America, European nations initiated a world economic system through military seizures of lands and the forced labor of colonized people. The purpose of colonization was to provide raw materials to produce inexpensive goods to benefit colonizing nations. Dussel (1998) describes this as the "first *world* hegemony. This is the only world-system that has existed in planetary history, and this is the modern system, European in its center, capitalist in its economy" (p. 9).[2]

The existence of the United States as a nation is an outcome of European expansion. Arrighi (1994) explains, "U.S. capitalism and territorialism were indistinguishable from one another" (p. 59). To manage its new "vacant" territories, the U.S. government modeled itself after European colonialism by dominating and committing nearly total genocide of indigenous peoples and using various combinations of slave and forced labor (Adams, 1995; Takaki, 1993; Zinn, 1995).

As European nations competed to manage this newly formed world system, European conquerors produced and reproduced an ideology intended to justify the necessity of their brutal exploitation. Under a Eurocentric ideology only Europeans were assumed to have legal rights. Non-Europeans, that is, people of color, had no rights and were considered less than fully human. Within a civilizing mission premised on Christian superiority, a form of commerce and social relationships based on capital production and accumulation became justified. The bodies of the conquered and enslaved became *the Other*, people devoid of any human potential beyond merely a means to European economic growth and wealth. Eurocentrism placed Europe at the planet's center because only its history and social mores were assumed to be of global significance. Under Eurocentrism other groups of people were believed not to possess a history or a coherent culture worthy of recognition (Dussel, 1995, 1998; Goldberg, 1993; McLaren, 1995; Mignolo, 1998; Wallerstein, 1999). This perception persists into the 21st century and took, for example, a recent African archeological finding to cause the Smithsonian Institution to reconsider a paradigm that contends "modern human behavior" originated only in a "creative explosion" in Europe (Wilford, 2001, p. A1).

Without the existence of the labor and lands of the Other, most global economic production systems in place today could not exist. Sophisticated management systems of non-Western countries exist through financial collaboration of Europe and the United States. These arrangements are backed by the real threat of military intervention and financial controls. Eurocentrism remains a globally disseminated ideology that defends continued economic inroads into other nations at significant social costs to millions of people. In 2001 tensions were reported between non-Western nations and European and U.S. governmental leaders over an anti-Eurocentric provision in a United Nations' document developed for the World Conference Against Racism. The United Nations' planning report states, "Theories of superiority of certain races and cultures over others promoted and practiced during the colonial era continue to be propounded in one form or another even today" (Crossette, 2001, p. A8). Under this contemporary political atmosphere, much of the world continues as a subordinated periphery to the dominant centrality of a Eurocentric myth.

Progress, Development, and Civilization.   Eurocentrism contains a peculiar notion of "progress" that contends that European and U.S. thinking and actions inevitably lead to a better world. Historical evidence and contemporary global conditions suggest otherwise (Wallerstein, 1999). Nevertheless, Eurocentric progress informs the concepts of development and civilization, all of which underlie conventional conceptions of schooling.

Inherent to Eurocentric colonial logic is development. Western Europe and the United States are assumed to be politically, economically, and culturally "developed." Lands populated by the Other are perceived as "undeveloped." Economic exploitation is explained as a missionary duty to develop both people and material resources. Development continues to signify a rationale for capital accumulation at the expense of politically disenfranchised populations (Dussel, 1995).

Eurocentric development is imbedded within an ideology of "civilization." Civilization is used as a process that results in a product labeled culture (Mignolo, 1998). Eurocentric civility is hostile to cultural differences and, therefore, attempts to regulate what counts as legitimate culture. One example of this regulation is how multicultural linguistic relationships become defined. Under progress, development, and civilization, colonial languages maintain a hegemony to the detriment of indigenous languages (Macedo, 2000). These Eurocentric concepts continue to shape a multitude of local-global social relations between privileged and oppressed populations both inside and outside of schools.

Manifest Destiny Into the 21st Century. Within a capitalist economic system a Eurocentric belief of "manifest destiny" retains its necessity in subduing politically subordinated populations purportedly for their own welfare. At the end of his U.S. presidency William Clinton proclaimed the manifest destiny of Eurocentric globalization. In a historic visit to Hanoi he declared that a capitalist global economy "is the economic equivalent of a force of nature [that] is not going away" (Sanger, 2000, p. A8). Conceiving the economy as beyond public controls, President Clinton insisted that the Vietnamese must learn to manage these "natural" forces because their "next job may well depend on foreign trade and investment" (Sanger, 2000, p. A8). His imagery is similar to 19th century manifest destiny conceptualizations of a "wild" frontier as a region to be "tamed" by burgeoning capital growth, wage labor, and individualized property ownership. Clinton's comments give a disingenuous impression that Vietnam, a nation formerly occupied by the French and the United States, is on equal financial terms internationally for negotiating how trade and investment might best benefit its own people.

The manifest destiny of Eurocentrism equates culture in the 21st century with consumerism. Sklair (1998) observes,

> The cultural-ideological project of global capitalism is to persuade people to consume above their "biological need" in order to perpetuate the accumulation of capital for private profit. . . . The cultural-ideology of consumerism proclaims, literally, that the meaning of life is to be found in the things we possess. (p. 297)

People are objectified economically as a resource for consumption. The market economy aspect of Eurocentrism strives to narrow political activity under slogans of progress, development, and civilization in order to maintain consumption for capital accumulation. This benefits a small but dominant tier of the population (Kincheloe & Steinberg, 1998). As discussed later in this chapter, business interests come to expect teachers to "develop" students into marketable forms of human capital.

Gerald Vizenor (1994) in *Manifest Manners* weaves a colonial history into the current era to illustrate how the histories and cultures of indigenous people are only highlighted by dominant cultures in ways that will not shake the centrality of Eurocentrism. Cultural differences are homogenized "into an acceptable and serviceable cultural product" (Gellner, 1999, p. 190). The cultures of people of color are either packaged for consumption or called upon to fill cultural and spiritual voids of Eurocentrism (McCarthy, 1998a; Vizenor, 1994). White preservice and in-service teachers are often prone to believe that they do not have a culture when they are unable to recognize their own Eurocentric cultural premises and contradictions. Some express a romanticized longing for cultures of the Other, unaware that their own cultural encapsulation can have a deleterious effect on teaching and learning (see Chapters 3–5).

By attempting to domesticate cultural diversity under an assimilationist ideology, contemporary monoculturalist educators (cf. Stotsky, 1999) strive to manage multicultural expressions that contest the exploitative aspects of development and civilization (see Vavrus, 2001a). Although 19th-century usage of the terms *savages* and *barbarians* has generally slipped from Eurocentric representations of people of color, a manifest destiny of White privilege in the 21st century postulates the superiority of its civilizing mission in continuing the development of the Other as a White property right (Harris, 1983; Kincheloe & Steinberg, 1998; Spring, 1998).

GLOBAL ECONOMIC PRODUCTION OF INEQUITIES

Markets of exchange predate capitalist accumulation for profit. People throughout the world have historically depended on local markets for the exchange of goods and services. Although profiteers existed prior to 1492, global capital accumulation *as a central societal feature* was only instigated under European colonialism (Dussel, 1998; Wallerstein, 1999). Today, in the context of globalization, the phrase *market economy* is used nearly interchangeably with *global economy*.

The global economic emphasis on markets is premised on theoretical underpinnings of orthodox or classical economics. This model envisions markets as self-regulating by assuming that individual consumers freely determine their own choices and collectively set the price they are willing to pay for commodities. Labor is assumed to be mobile and, therefore, workers and their families will relocate to where their skills are needed and their labor rewarded. Classical economics theorizes that accrued profits are reinvested into improving and expanding production, a common argument for providing large corporations "tax breaks."

Actual global and domestic economic practices contradict the premises of classical economic theory. Consumer needs are not independent of corporate advertising intended to influence tastes and perceived needs. Industrial jobs that formerly constituted the economic backbone of the U.S. economy are being exported to cheaper labor markets with few, if any, social benefits or labor protections. *Business Week* affirms that displaced workers and their families are not necessarily able to find equivalent employment and wages even if they move elsewhere within the United States (Kite, 2001).

Unprotected "sweat shop" workers, who labor under inhumane working conditions in newly located U.S. industries in tax-free zones of countries outside the United States, have difficulty earning a living wage (e.g., Greenhouse, 2001a). The decline in taxation rates for corporations and for a population's wealthiest segments provides less funding to education and health care (Chossudovsky, 1997; Waters, 2001). Rather than fostering prosperity, the global economy in its present form produces an increase in social, economic, and political inequities that portend negatively for the goals of multicultural education.

Global Economic Effects Within the United States

The public is regularly inundated with news that imposition of measurable, "basic skill" standards at all levels of the schooling process is necessary for giving the United States a global economic advantage. Research scholarship, however, challenges undocumented claims of a causal link between (a) quantifiable standards of academic achievements and (b) U.S. economic competitiveness (Apple, 1996, 2001; Aronowitz & DeFazio, 1997; Bowles & Gintis, 1976; Brown, Halsey, Lauder, & Wells, 1997; Brown & Lauder, 1997; Pagano, 1999). Nevertheless, this global economic ideology finds governmental support among U.S. presidents, legislators, governors, and educators who act on a corollary discourse surrounding the patriotic welfare of the United States and measurable educational standards. Unacknowledged is the outcome of global expansion that the U.S. economy underwent during the last quarter of the 20th century. Most visible are the economic gains for the leadership and large stockholders of transnational corporations and financial institutions and growing inequities for large segments of the rest of the population (see Hartman, 2001). In this context, U.S. foreign policy drives its domestic policy (D. Leahy, personal correspondence, August 28, 2001).

Current U.S. global economic activities are detrimental to the vast majority of its citizens. Increases are recorded in the number of families who fall below the federal government's established poverty line—including nearly 20% of all children or more than 12 million youngsters—and are evidenced in a rise in the number of hours individuals are expected to work annually, the equivalent of four extra 40-hour weeks (Collins, Leondar-Wright, & Sklar, 1999; Sengupta, 2001; Terry, 2000). The poor, who are disproportionately people of color, must allocate 60% to 70% of their income for housing rent, double the 1975 percentage (Bernstein, 2000). Decreases are recorded in the minimum wage as measured in real dollars, in the buying power of 85% of the public, and in the bargaining power of labor unions to protect worker benefits and working conditions. Meanwhile, manufacturing jobs are being relocated to cheaper labor markets in countries outside U.S. borders. Such a practice causes a further decline in the bargaining power of labor unions and the overall earnings of an average citizen. Many formerly well-paying jobs are now substituted with unemployment, lower paying service positions, and a combination of part-time jobs without benefits (Brown & Lauder, 2001; Collins et al., 1999; Ruigrok & van Tulder, 1995).

Poor children tend to experience lower academic achievement than their wealthier peers do (deMarrais & LeCompte, 1995; Persell, 1977, 1997). When parents have to work multiple jobs and long hours to economically provide for their families, they can have difficulty, in comparison to middle-class and wealthy parents, giving their children educational assistance and resources or conferring with classroom teachers. Global economic practices can further accentuate achievement dilemmas for students from families of low socioeconomic status.

Antidemocratic Intimidation.   A market ideology contributes to political conditions that limit public criticism of business practices (Frank, 2000). Individuals employed by mobile industries—those that could locate in countries with cheaper labor—are faced with antidemocratic intimidation. This occurs when workers organize for fundamental labor rights as subscribed to by the U.S. government and articulated by the International Labour Organization (1964) of the United Nations. A Cornell University study covering the 2-year period 1998–1999 concluded that "capital mobility and the threat of capital mobility have had a profound impact on the ability of American workers to exercise their rights to freedom of association and collective bargaining" (Bronfenbrenner, 2000, p. 53).

The Cornell study revealed that over half of U.S. employers threatened to shut down or move their industries if workers successfully organized unions to protect fundamental workplace rights. Tactics included threats of firings, "electronic surveillance, illegal unilateral changes in wages and benefits, bribes, threats to refer undocumented workers to the INS [Immigration and Naturalization Service], promises of improvement, and promotion of union activists out of the [union organizing] unit" (Bronfenbrenner, 2000, p. vi). Employer-directed antidemocratic intimidation is apparently not a direct function of the financial stability of a company. Rather, a global economic specter is raised to suppress employee expressions that seek fair working conditions and a living wage.

Students from working-class families already tend to encounter a disconnection between their homes and the middle-class, professional values of schools. One outcome is "ability" tracking that tends to have a negative effect on students from lower socioeconomic families in regards to an equal access to valued school knowledge and pedagogies (deMarrais & LeCompte, 1995; Oakes et al., 1992; Persell, 1977, 1997). This home-school difference can be heightened by unstable parental employment that includes workplace intimidations, the prospect of layoffs, and forced job relocations. A teacher education program can help raise teacher awareness about how globalization can destabilize the lives of their students and further reduce working-class students' access to equitable learning. Framed in a local-global context, tracking systems can be reevaluated for reproductive effects of inequities, effects that rarely enhance life opportunities for economically poor children. In order to advocate for low-income students and their families, teachers can also learn how to make community connections with local labor unions to support the preservation of jobs offering a livable wage and social benefits.

Racist Scapegoating. In an anxious climate created by economic uncertainties, White employees in mobile industries can look for a scapegoat to account for erosions in their purchasing power. Unfortunately, race can be used to misrepresent this decline. Because Whites historically have been more economically privileged than people of color, affirmative action policies are perceived as victimizing Whites. Through a historical practice of White privileged property rights (C. Harris, 1993), economic insecurity can lead to racist conclusions.

Both Apple (1996) and Giroux (1998) pose scenarios of young people developing White solidarity in the absence of an antiracist identity to account for the economic decline of the average U.S. citizens. Racist actions by the sons of White British workers whose textile plants have been moved abroad lend credence to these speculations (Hoge, 2001; Lyall, 2001). Yet the identification of poor and middle-class Whites with the interests of White business leaders has a long history counterintuitive to notions of interracial class solidarity (Bonnett, 2000; Goldberg, 1993; C. Harris, 1993; McLaren & Farahmandpur, 2001a; McLaren & Torres, 1999; Ogbu, 1997; Woodward, 1974). Racism can augment the profits of capitalism. In 2001 the *Wall Street Journal* reports on a 20th century history of "capitalism and racism in a cruel partnership" that resists "debate over compensating victims of 20th century racial abuses involving businesses" (Blackmon, 2001, p. A1). Implicated businesses, however, deny responsibility to victims of racial abuse (Blackmon, 2001). Today, meanwhile, predominantly White corporate leaders who close plants in the United States and ship jobs to Mexico and other countries publicly declare that they are helping poor people of color (Frank, 2000).

If young people lack educational experiences grounded in transformative multicultural education, they are likely to have difficulty understanding the complexities surrounding their occupational opportunities in the context of global economic practices. When teachers without a multicultural commitment educate students, Eurocentric curricula and pedagogy can skew interpretations of White youth's socioeconomic opportunities toward racist conclusions. In noncollegiate vocational education tracks in secondary schools, for example, Whites tend to be placed in courses that generalize to skills for middle-management positions while African American and Latino youth are "more frequently enrolled in programs that train for the lowest-level occupations" (Oakes, Gamoran, & Page, 1992, p. 590). Despite this racialized curriculum differentiation, research points out that "participation in vocational education does not enhance students' chances for securing employment related to training, avoiding unemployment, or securing higher wages than those of nonvocational high school graduates" (Oakes et al, 1992, p. 593). Thus color-blind teachers and administrators, who lack a knowledge base that makes connections among White privilege, local labor markets, Eurocentrism, and global economic effects, can unintentionally promote racist expressions by their students that are institutionally reinforced by insidiously ineffective curricular patterns of differentiation.

Erosion of Public Education Funds.   A tax base that could support K–12 and higher education continues to be significantly reduced. Business advisory groups chastise state legislators to run government more efficiently with fewer tax dollars. Affected are U.S. teacher salaries, for example, which rank 22 out of 26 for industrialized nations (Wilgoren, 2001). Governors and presidents run as education candidates who support public funds for standardized testing outcomes. Yet governmental leaders are reluctant to allocate necessary resource inputs since the tax base for public services has been allowed to decline. Simultaneously, public officials seek greater public control over values, cultural expressions, and individual economic options (Apple, 1996; Gellner, 1999).

Calls by businesses to privatize public education and reduce social services and minimum health assistance are one response to stagnating tax resources. A related market recommendation is to reconceptualize schools as commercial enterprises (Anderson, 1998; Bowman, 2000). Concurrent with market solutions for decreasing public funds for schools are some states that offer tax-free zones to businesses in a desperate attempt to bring any kind of jobs to their regions. This process accrues negligible funding for public education and is mirrored in poverty-stricken countries outside the United States. Most affected are schools located in poor areas with disenfranchised racial and ethnic populations.

Global Economic Effects Outside the United States

Structural economic adjustments being imposed in the United States are a mild indicator of what much of the world experiences. The global economy serves to recolonize former European colonies through U.S. advocacy of a "one world" concept that is manifested in austere policies of the World Bank and the International Monetary Fund (IMF) (Ruigrok & van Tulder, 1995). A Ford Foundation–sponsored report explains that "huge capital flows, moving daily between the financial centers of advanced and advancing countries, bypass people caught in abject poverty" (Qureshi & von Weizsäcker, 1995). Hamelink (1993) concludes, "What is generously termed the *global economy* would rather seem the *economies of few*" (p. 376). Meanwhile, the U.S. government allows itself to carry its own substantial public debt and, in turn, economically peripheral nations are given structural adjustment shock treatments for their debts.

The debts of these nations are accrued without the democratic consent of the majority of people living within those nations. Privileged neocolonial leaders make unilateral, undemocratic decisions with little consideration for the social conditions of people living in poverty (Chossudovsky, 1997; Kahn, 2000b; Weissert, 2001). Leys (1974) defines neocolonialism as "the formation of classes, or strata, within a colony, which are closely allied to and dependent on foreign capital, and which forms the real basis of support for the regime which succeeds the colonial administration" (p. 26). Today IMF, World Bank, and World Trade Organization practices are conducted exclusively in collaboration with neocolonial leaders (Chossudovsky, 1997; Parenti, 1995).

To pay off just the debt *interest* owed to Western banks, funding for education and health is significantly reduced for millions of poor people. For many of these nations per capita foreign debt is greater than annual per capita income (e.g., Vukelich, 1999). Because such financial burdens exist, former colonies that now pursue economic growth policies under IMF and World Bank rules tend not to improve the quality of their educational systems (Nussbaum, 2000). An international analysis of world education indicators reports, "Countries that faced an economic crisis in the 1990s must meet the double challenge of building sustainable educational reform in an unstable macro-economic environment" (Organisation for Economic Co-Operation and Development & UNESCO Institute for Statistics, 2001, p. 9). Within this global financial mix transnational industries primarily produce textile and luxury goods for European and U.S. consumers that are neither affordable by nor beneficial to local populations. At the same time merchants and small farmers are denied business loans to produce affordable domestic goods and grow local crops (Burbach, Núñez, & Kagarlitsky, 1997; Chossudovsky, 1997; Kahn, 2000a; Moody, 1997; Thompson, 2001).

Like U.S. workers who watch their jobs being displaced to former colonies, non-Western workers with families consent to work under threats of replacement with any of the unemployed masses within their own nations. Safe working conditions, a minimum living wage to support a family, and health and retirement benefits are nearly nonexistent. Global economic practices can also intensify the illegal use of forced labor (Bales, 1999; Greenhouse, 2001a). Under competitive labor conditions for scarce jobs in regions where a serious decline in small businesses as well as locally-owned farms stems from the demands of corporate globalization, ethnic strife is accentuated and multicultural coalitions for global solidarity against oppression are undermined.

GLOBAL ECONOMIC IDEOLOGY AND EDUCATION

For education, state privileging of *private* corporate business interests tends to obscure schooling goals for educating a democratic citizenry informed about the civic responsibilities of *public* participation in a culturally diverse society. Missing are transformative educational processes and practices where "a sense of crisis is brought to our choices" and a dominant metanarrative is reevaluated (Cherryholmes, 1988, p. 172). Instead, an air of status quo compliance encapsulates teachers, administrators, and school boards. The global economy is passively perceived as inevitable and even necessary by "a public education establishment unwilling to take on the logic and dominance of corporate regulations" (Leahy, 1998, p. 3).

Corporations not only look to markets outside the United States for profiteering but also see K–12 schools as new sources of income (Bowman, 2000; Lehman Brothers, 1998; Wyatt, 1999). The *New York Times* recounts that "the race to invest in education marks the triumph of a market mentality that has consumed the nation in the late 20th century" (Wyatt, 1999, p. A21). A market ideology shapes educational goals toward an economics of human capital.

Students as Human Capital

Governmental and business attention to "basic skills" standards—whether for seventh graders or beginning teachers—is based on the concept of human capital. Traditional human capital theory emphasizes lifelong earnings and occupational status correlated to an individual's formal educational attainment level. Today, however, governments and transnational corporations redefine human capital by making the aim of an individual's education the eventual production of goods, services, and knowledge to benefit a market economy. As Bourdieu (1998) points out, the dominance of a Eurocentric human capital component of market ideology serves to construct education and society exclusively within global economic expectations.

Market ideology filters directly into public schools through a contemporary articulation of human capital theory, a master metanarrative that can negate a transformative multicultural conception of education. Human capital theory views students for their potential economic value to private industry. According to this model, schooling is a financial investment in young people to increase their value as an economic resource (Woodhall, 1997). Students are understood to have no life outside their ultimate economic value. Under this logic, democracy is weakened and inequalities exist because human skills prior to formal education are not economically developed and distributed. Education is blamed for domestic economic failures (cf. U.S. National Commission on Excellence in Education, 1984) that are actually connected to governmental economic policies supportive of transnational corporate capital accumulation. Consequently, teachers can become alienated from humanistic conceptions of child and adolescent potential by serving as representatives for capital accumulation (Robertson, 2000).

The economic construction of individuals for their profit-enhancing productivity potential is a dominant U.S. policy (Apple, 2001; Bowles & Gintis, 1976; Brown & Lauder, 1997; Carnoy, 1997; Spring, 1976, 2001). This is similar to neocolonial practices that extract material resources from subordinated people. In the case of a student, the individual is also objectified as a potential economic component.

Economist Lester Thurow (1999) wonders, "How does one put together a democracy based on the concept of equality while running an economy with ever-increasing degrees of economic inequality" (p. 1)? Thurow's question highlights that a model of students as human capital is not intended to produce an equitable society (see Bourdieu, 1998). Held (1995) explains that "market relations are themselves power relations that can constrain democratic process" (p. 246). Yet a market ideology contends that capital growth and democracy are codependent. This position overlooks more socially oriented economic possibilities that emphasize citizen participation in a democracy not necessarily predicated on serving capital accumulation (see Dorman, 1997; Held, 1995; McLaren, 1997; McLaren & Farahmandpur, 2001a, 2001b; Torres, 1998; Wallerstein, 1999).

Meritocracy and Inequality. Although business-governmental alliances maintain that success in schools and workplaces is predicated on merit, this assertion holds mythic qualities (Bowles & Gintis, 1976; Gould, 1996; Shea, 1989). In practice, *equal opportunity* under a meritocracy actually legitimizes "occupational and social inequalities because the doctrine of meritocracy is based on the idea of giving everyone an equal chance to be unequal" (Brown et al., 1997, p. 13). When educational levels of attainment are equal, for example, Whites remain economically privileged over people of color (Carnoy, 1997). Under globalization one group of U.S. workers is sorted along the lines of high-skilled, "knowledge"-based jobs for industrialized nations while others are left with reduced employment possibilities. Increasingly, skilled jobs are being exported to educated populations who are willing to work at significantly lower salaries than their U.S. counterparts (Moody, 1997, chap. 6; Shea, 1989).

Both conservative and liberal economic conceptions of the school curriculum are constructed within conventional theories of human capital that are embedded in a myth of meritocracy. President Clinton, for example, shaped his economic policies within this paradigm; President George W. Bush continues the same practice. The Clinton administration's strategy (1992–2000) assumed that "the federal government must help prepare workers to adapt to the economic forces at work in the rapidly changing, worldwide economy" (Pitsch, 1994, p. 1). With this premise, lifelong education becomes reconfigured from a self-fulfilling experience in the arts and sciences to one that mirrors "just-in-time" production strategies to reduce taxable warehouse inventories. The expectation is for individuals to gain just-in-time workplace competencies. Thus, regardless of how diligently people develop the merits of their human capital, mobile transnational industries and finance capital can force continuous reeducation/training patterns in an unstable job market.

    School–Business Alliances.   Schools are conceptualized as locations to lay a foundation to meet global economic human capital goals. Although even classical economists have long recognized that schools are not cost-effective institutions for providing training needs, the school reform movement of recent decades has invoked school–business alliances to make schools more responsive to the needs of capital formation and social-order expectations. These loose partnerships have rarely considered issues of inadequate public funding for schools in general and teacher preparation and staff development specifically (see Darling-Hammond, 1997b). Legislators have instead tended to collaborate with business leaders "to weaken institutional pressures on increasing state expenditures for education" (Brown et al., 1997, p. 24).

    Business chief executives who have sought to directly influence the school curriculum base their claim on a theorized shrinking and poorly prepared labor pool. Corporate leaders primarily use school–business ties and government-supported committees to forward their views. For example, most of the 73,000 school–business partnerships of the 1980s grew "out of opportunism" to use the school curriculum to help identify an educated mobile labor pool (Weisman, 1991, p. 5). This limited notion of the purpose of education undermines the goals of multicultural education.

Global Economic Interpretations of Multicultural Education

Curricula advocated by business advisory committees to develop problem-solving skills typically search for technical solutions for transnational corporations rather than building local and regional democratic economies. For example, initial drafts of the state of Iowa's 1993 Education Strategic Planning Council report had as its first reform principle the ability of high school graduates to compete in a global economy. This was later revised to a concern for engaging in an interdependent world. The original thinking behind this schooling goal was built upon a governor-initiated committee recommendation that "state government should assume an intermediary and policy setting role to direct educational resources toward employment shortage areas" (Governor's Target Alliance, 1990, p. 21). This goal was altered only when members of the council, especially classroom teachers, objected to the narrowness of that particular interpretation of the concept of "global education."[3] The state, though, inserted into its final rationale statement concern over "global economic competition" and "shortages of skilled workers" (Iowa Department of Education, 1994, p. 1).

Business and governmental interests in implementing multicultural education typically stem from corporate needs to handle diverse work forces and markets rather than from a support for democratic schools inclusive of the voices and histories of women, laboring classes, and disenfranchised racial and ethnic groups (Bonnett, 2000). An increase in the accessibility to foreign language instruction, for example, is advocated not to build a multicultural democracy but to have "trained people familiar with languages and cultures of potential trading partners" (Governor's Target Alliance, 1990, p. 21) and of regions that are perceived as threats to U.S. political and economic interests (cf. Talbot, 2001). Although appearing to expand democracy with state codes for global and multicultural education curriculum infusion, a state government can find itself actually supporting transnational corporate interests for capital growth at the expense of domestic and global multicultural democracy.

Transformative multicultural education goals contain a focus on global equity to eliminate human suffering and promote human dignity. A teacher education program can legitimately deliberate on market ideological forces that work against considerations of transformative multicultural education. One starting point for transformative multicultural inquiry on global issues asks, "What is the relationship between social inequality and the suffering that accompanies it and the schooling process" (Kincheloe & Steinberg, 1997, p. 24)? Social inequities perpetuated directly and indirectly by public school policies and procedures can be studied when a teacher education program considers transformative multicultural possibilities.

A teacher education program and its graduates can become implicated, however, in the growing chasm between the rich and poor when they support schooling processes that serve a market ideology to the detriment of multicultural goals. For example, a college noted for having an exemplary teacher education program is lauded for its partnerships with a public high school whose curriculum studies implementation of the North American Free Trade Agreement (NAFTA) as a positive social development (Koppich, 2000). Such a partnership unreflectively overlooks that Eurocentric conceptions of "free trade" are rarely conducted on equal terms (Burbach et al., 1997; Chomsky, 1998; Leys, 1974; Rohter & Rich, 2001; Ruigrok & van Tulder, 1995). When a teacher education program unquestionably supports a curricular goal tied to a public

policy like free trade that contributes to environmental degradation, social inequities, and workplace abuses (see Athanasiou, 1996; Thompson, 2001), transformative multicultural education is undermined (see Vavrus, 2001b). Research
indicates, however, that preservice teachers are able to learn from and make
connections with children from families of displaced workers who are negatively affected by NAFTA (Horton et al., 1999). To do so, a teacher education
program needs to include critical local-global analyses in curricular and pedagogical strategies.

In the opening decade of the 21st century, entrenched transnational economic goals serve to distort understandings of multicultural education (Spring,
1998). Global economic objectives can also negatively impact diversity standards that are intended for beginning teachers and their teacher education programs.

Global Economic Influences on Teacher Education Standards

The ideological conflict between a market ideology and transformative multicultural education is evident in the underpinnings of the Interstate New Teacher
Assessment and Support Consortium (INTASC, 1992) sponsored by the Council
of Chief State School Officers. The INTASC preamble holds as one of its
"truths to be self-evident" a call to K–12 teachers to help develop students who
can help ensure for the United States a "competitive position in a global economy" (p. 8). As argued in Chapter 4, diversity standards for teacher education
programs suffer from indeterminate language. From an economic perspective,
McLaren and Farahmandpur (2001a) note the importance of analyzing "capitalist social relations" (p. 13) for the way in which mainstream parameters influence what can be accepted as *diversity*. INTASC, and subsequently the National
Council for the Accreditation of Teacher Education (NCATE), omits standards
that can encourage an examination of the relationship between (a) global economics and (b) oppression of women, children, and historically marginalized
racial and ethnic groups.

In an era of a global decline in jobs with benefits suitable for maintaining
a basic standard of living, INTASC reflects an economic perspective on schooling most interested in "efficient learners" who can "adapt to continuous changes
in jobs and career paths" (Organisation for Economic Co-operation and Development, 1998, pp. 5–6). Equally unfortunate for transformative multicultural
education, INTASC chose to frame a global economic imperative as synonymous with a promotion of democracy. INTASC and NCATE standards fall prey
to a dominant ideology that creates silences around roots of racism and concentrations of wealth by failing to address White economic privilege (see Chapters
4 & 5). INTASC and NCATE inscribe on a teacher identity compliance to social
relations under global capital accumulation.

IMPLICATIONS FOR MULTICULTURAL TEACHER EDUCATION

Transformative multicultural education is positioned to incorporate studies of globalization. The totality of globalization as a subject of study is challenging for finding an appropriate place in a teacher education program's curriculum. Current topics germane to transformative multicultural education, however, can be altered to include attention to globalization. Bennett (1999, chap. 8), for example, provides classroom teachers with pertinent instructional ideas for developing multicultural lessons with a critical global perspective. Such activities need to be grounded in a knowledge base that helps teachers understand the importance of transformative concepts and actions.

A teacher education program can seek assistance from an organization like Global Source Education (2001). Global Source Education provides workshops for K–12 teachers that can include higher education faculty. Interactive programs include opportunities to consider teaching globalization across academic disciplines and from a human rights perspective. Global Source Education emphasizes trade issues and local effects while incorporating media literacy and issues of social responsibility.

The following sections are suggestions for a teacher education program to consider when incorporating globalization concepts.

Human Rights and Globalization

As noted earlier, globalization holds within its core the potential to extend basic human rights to oppressed people. A teacher education program can incorporate into its curriculum internationally recognized rights documents such as the "Aims and Purposes" of the International Labour Organization (1964) and the Declaration of Human Rights (United Nations, 1948). Imbedded within each of these documents are clear multicultural statements related to recognizing the rights of marginalized populations. Comparisons can be made between these documents and local, national, and global political and economic practices. Further multicultural connections can be made between human rights and schooling conditions that foster an inclusive curriculum, prejudice reduction, an equity pedagogy, and an empowering school culture for all students (e.g., Garcîa, 2001).

Schooling Practices Under a Global Economy

A teacher education program can make visible links between origins of European colonialism and current global economic practices. For example, tracking practices that disproportionally have a negative impact on students who are poor and of color can be compared to neocolonial educational systems that primarily serve a privileged population. How White privilege in the United States is extended to global economics is a valid multicultural issue for teachers to understand (Kincheloe & Steinberg, 1998). The interrelationship between race and economic class can be explored (Bonnett, 2000; McLaren & Torres, 1999; Winant, 1994). Through this process, teachers can learn why it is important to resist undemocratic and racist schooling practices that are replicated as models for global pedagogies (see Ladwig, 2000).

A teacher education program can extend its analysis to public school policies that ultimately define a student as a form of human capital and blur visions of a student as a democratic citizen. Teachers should learn that participation in global capitalism is not synonymous with democratic citizenship (Torres, 1998). A program can help teachers to construct a democratic rather than an economic instrumental goal for schooling in a culturally diverse society.

Democratic Economic Practices

Democratic dispositions and actions are an important aspect of transformative multiculturalism. A teacher education program can help teachers to make connections among local, national, and global democratic possibilities, as governmental decisions affect the life opportunities of the children of agricultural and industrial wage earners (e.g., Horton et al., 1999). An erosion of democratic public control over the behavior of transnational corporations negatively affects the ability of (a) local school districts to generate sufficient tax revenues for public education, (b) the federal government to make meaningful social investments to rebuild decaying school infrastructures, and (c) non-Western nations to provide decent working and living conditions for their citizens. Since the current global economy "is not an automatic or self-producing process" (Held et al., 1999, p. 437), a teacher education program can help teachers to realize that public responsibility exerted in order to redirect the economy toward the common good is a reasonable expectation in a democracy.

Private business leaders working with government officials have generally been successful in narrowing democratic alternatives for publicly controlling economic decisions. A teacher education program can provide teachers a knowledge base that recognizes how such unequal distributions of power can actually destabilize democracy. Teacher educator Julie Kailin (1999) emphasizes that "dimensions of individual and institutional racism must also be related to an examination of power relations and placed within the context of American capitalism which is, at this moment, the most powerful imperialistic force in the world" (p. 747). Viable democratic options do exist that prioritize fundamental social and educational needs over corporate interests (e.g., Chomsky, 1999; Dorman, 1997; Wallerstein, 1999). Because transnational corporations do not operate politically independent of a national home base (Ruigrok & van Tulder,

1995), multiculturally educated citizens can hold corporations and governmental officials accountable for democratic practices and the multicultural needs of schools.

A teacher education program can help teachers to navigate through the complexities of democratic practice. Anderson (1998) writes, "Habits of authentic participation that give voice to subordinate groups have a ripple effect that affects power relations in other settings such as [school] district offices, state legislatures, community organizations, and corporate offices" (p. 594). Teachers can lend a public voice to democracy while being mindful that negative responses may be elicited when economically privileged groups are challenged by democratic involvement of the public. A teacher education program can provide teachers with basic knowledge, skills, and dispositions that attend to equity issues of school financing. To increase corporate responsibility for support of public school funding, organizations of teacher education programs can build collaborative relationships with educational associations for K–12 teachers and administrators in order to pressure elected governmental officials for laws that create equitable and democratically responsible tax systems with corporate restraints. These coalitions might include the American Association of Colleges for Teacher Education, the National Education Association, the American Federation of Teachers, the National Association of Multicultural Education, and their respective regional and state chapters.

Immigrant Children and Families

The multicultural education of teachers includes attention to immigrant children in public schools. Rightfully, the importance of cultural and linguistic backgrounds of immigrant students is incorporated into multicultural education. Yet an assimilationist orientation toward immigrants can prevail in schools that create tensions between teachers and immigrant families (Katz, 1999; Simon, 1997; Trueba & Bartolomé, 2000). Too often educators look sadly upon the conditions of an immigrant's country of origin while unreflectively framing the United States as a savior for the poor. Nevertheless, in a study of children of immigrant families Suárez-Orozco and Suárez-Orozco (2001) "found classrooms where teachers are resentful and feel burdened by their new charges, convey pessimism about the immigrant students' abilities to learn, and fail to engage them" (p. 146). For immigrant children of color who live in racially segregated, poor neighborhoods, overlooked are U.S. governmental policies that may have worsened living and working conditions for an immigrant's home nation and perpetuated the existence of substantial numbers of U.S. children living in poverty.

A teacher education program can take an inquiry approach toward the relationship between immigrant countries of origins and U.S. global economics.

Take the case of a Mexican immigrant student and the questions that can be investigated. For example, what are the structures of inequality in Mexico that induce Mexican families to come to the United States? How have trade agreements with the United States affected social inequities? What are the global economic influences working for and against Mexico to invest in its own industries and school systems? What are the advantages to U.S. industries when they relocate in Mexico? What are the costs to U.S. workers? to Mexican workers? to the Mexican environment? What populations in Mexico and the United States benefit the most economically when a transnational industry is established in Mexico? Why might U.S. policies toward Mexican "illegal" immigrants be more lax during U.S. produce harvests than in other seasons? What are the living conditions and social service supports provided to "illegal" immigrants who are employed in the United States? These sample investigative questions can encourage multicultural explorations into the relationship between U.S. policies and the lives of immigrant children.

Such an inquiry approach can help preserve and in-service teachers develop an understanding of immigrant women who come to the United States as domestic workers when they could not support their families in their countries of origin. Often their home country conditions are reflective of IMF and World Bank financially imposed structural adjustments that eliminate social welfare programs and jobs benefiting local economies. In the United States many immigrant women and their children find themselves again facing limited access to social services or outright conditions of forced labor as a partial function of U.S. internal structural adjustments that cause a decline in basic services (Brinkley, 2000; Chang, 2000; Greenhouse, 2001b; Skrobanek, Boonpakdi, & Janthakeero, 1997). An inquiry approach can help teacher education students to unpack the complex conditions under which immigrant children find themselves when they are in schools (see González, 1999; Igoa, 1995; Suárez-Orozco & Suárez-Orozco, 2001; Valdés, 1996; Yon, 2000).

Teacher Global Identity Formation

Chapter 5 drew attention to the importance of an antiracist, transformationist teacher identity. Through transformative multicultural education, globalization studies can further help teachers to form an identity supportive of the emancipation of oppressed people. In an investigation of poor immigrant youth of color in Toronto schools, Yon (2000) explains that "while globalization erodes national identities, these and other identities are also being strengthened as resistance to globalization" (p. 15). Teacher global identity formation facilitated by a teacher education program should resist configurations of globalization that privilege economic competition over emancipatory expressions of social justice solidarity with victimized industrial and agricultural workers, oppressed women, and subordinated racial and ethnic groups (see McLaren & Farahmandpur, 2001b).

Globally influenced and locally formed identities merge in complex ways. This suggests a reconceptualization of assumptions based on a dichotomy between local and global identities. Cvetkovich and Kellner (1997b) explain "links between different locations [are] unpredictable and contingent rather than representative of a single transnational condition or national identity" (p. 25). For the students in Yon's (2000) study, the local cultures of their school and neighborhoods in Toronto intersected with globally circulated identities. A global identity that acknowledges "the spaces of everyday life" (p. 25) can make transformative multicultural connections among different cultures, global situations of oppression, and localized experiences. A culturally responsive teacher should have a global identity that strives to encompass local-global cultural interactions. A global identity for teachers should reject the premises of Eurocentrism and incorporate experiences and reasoning of the Other as valid concepts (Dussel, 1995; Goldberg, 1993; McLaren, 1998). As Banks's (2001a) observation in the opening section of this chapter suggests, global identity formation remains a largely untapped area of exposure for preservice and in-service teachers.

CONCLUSION:
WHAT DOES IT MEAN TO BE A TEACHER UNDER GLOBALIZATION?

Britzman (2000) explains that dominant political forces advance teacher educator "definitions of professionalism [that] preclude complications of selves and then ask for compliance and conformity" (p. 200). A teacher education program's response to globalization requires a transformative redefinition of professionalism and subsequent deliberations upon Britzman's question, "What inhibits our capacity to respond ethically to others, *to learn something from people we will never meet and to be affected by histories that we may never live* [italics added]" (p. 202)? Transformative multicultural education encourages teachers to reach out beyond their usual comfort zones to oppressed people and to incorporate those histories and contemporary experiences into a critical pedagogical knowledge base.

Wayne Au's (1999, 2000) high school teaching is an example of an embryonic K–12 and teacher education curricular shift away from Eurocentrism and toward making meaningful connections between localized, familiar curricula and globalization (also see Hoff, 2000; Hudak, 2000; Whang & Waters, 2001). Au, the 2002 recipient of the American Association of Colleges for Teacher Education Advocate for Social Justice–Early Career Award, completed a teacher education program that placed a strong emphasis on civic responsibilities associated with teaching in a culturally diverse society (see Chapter 7). He defines professionalism in a manner that attends to ethical social issues as a legitimate aspect of curriculum development. Acknowledging the questions of his students as a valid source of inquiry, Au helps culturally and economically diverse youth who have been unsuccessful in traditional high schools articulate their own answers to issues of globalization (see Students of Middle College High School, 2000).

By incorporating research-based rationales for global solidarity against oppression into multicultural knowledge bases, dispositions, and skills, a teacher education program can establish a foundation for teachers to resist compliant professionalism. Educating for multicultural democratic citizenship (Banks, 1997, 2001b; Torres, 1998) is an important aspect of global awareness and should be brought to the forefront of a teacher education program's curriculum, pedagogies, and evaluations. The absence of transformative multicultural education can limit a teacher's ability to form a democratic concept of citizenship that is inclusive of local and global responsibilities to the poor and disenfranchised. Hence a teacher education program holds promise as an important site for incorporating a critical perspective on globalization in the multicultural education of teachers.

CHAPTER 7

Weaving the Web of Multicultural Democracy

In *Teachers for Our Nation's Schools* John Goodlad (1990) calls for teacher education programs to develop profound democratic consciousness within education students. He argued that this awareness can help teachers understand and resolve the inevitable tensions that arise when unquestioned instructional routines are examined in light of "both the governance structures and processes of [a] political democracy and the requisites of humane citizenship" (p. 52). Such an examination is essential. Given increasing cultural diversity in public schools and society and gnawing inequities fueled by socio-economic class disparities, teachers should be prepared to make professional decisions about how best to meet the educational needs of all students. Goodlad (1996) explained that a disposition toward "moral stewardship," a formative teacher ability "to be honed in professional education programs" (p. 113), should characterize an educational mission in a democratic setting.

Teacher education programs tend to shy away from confronting schooling practices that work against the best learning and self-esteem interests of children and youth. Many teacher education programs socialize preservice teachers into status quo social climates of K–12 schools, an outcome of program faculty who collectively tend to "avoid interrogation and critique" about the political nature of schooling (Greene, 1978, p. 56). This avoidance most acutely manifests itself in inadequate approaches to examining public school education from a multicultural perspective (Barreto, 1997; Grant, 1993).

Teacher education programs wishing to weave democratic and multicultural perspectives throughout their programs face significant dilemmas. Arising from conflicting public and personal values and representing sizable areas of contention, these challenges can be represented by statements labeled "provocative declaratives," a concept that Marie Fielder (faculty emeritus, University of California at Berkeley) introduced to us at The Evergreen State College. These statements are deliberately formulated to elicit reactions to values and beliefs held by groups of people. Subsequent conversations bring forth contradictory

Editor's note: This chapter was originally published as: Vavrus, M., Walton, S., Kido, J., Diffendal, E., & King, P. (1999). Adapted with permission.

and moral perspectives to help participants clarify unexamined assumptions that drive their actions and the actions of others. Provocative declaratives do not stand independently from one another or necessarily represent discrete points of view; therefore, such statements on a similar topic may overlap or contradict one another.

This chapter presents examples of six provocative declaratives that our teacher preparation program has developed for its internal program discussions. Designed from the perspective of a teacher education program, the statements cover issues of democratic public schools; teacher candidate resistance to a program's conceptual framework; theory and practice conflicts with K–12 schools; racist, classist, sexist, and homophobic teacher candidates; technical teaching proficiency; and appropriateness of requiring democratic practices in internships. These pronouncements highlight issues that a teacher education program can encounter.

Absolute affirmation or denial of any of the provocative declaratives can lead us at Evergreen into conflict with either our professional values or the norms of public schools and state legislatures. Our program has evolved as we have responded to issues and values embedded in each statement. This chapter presents attempts to create and provide a teacher education program that examines what it means to teach in public schools in a democratic and culturally diverse society.

DEMOCRACY AND TEACHER EDUCATION: CONTENDING WITH PROVOCATIVE DECLARATIVE 1

1. Given current teaching practices in K–12 public education and most student teaching contexts, preparing teachers to create democratic classrooms is unrealistic and professionally irresponsible.

We deliberate upon this frequently voiced position and conclude that our graduates should understand public schooling within a multicultural democracy even if democratic practices are not used extensively in public school classrooms. We act upon the premise that schooling without equity and student voice is contrary to democratic goals and practices. Stevens and Wood (1995) ask, "How democratic can a society be that provides unequal education?" (p. 312). Efforts to replace unequal education with democratic classrooms can, however, be undermined by "conventional pedagogy [as] a particular form of cultural reproduction which endorses, models, and transmits Eurocentric cultural values and ignores or denigrates other cultural heritages" (Gay, 1995, pp. 164–165). This undemocratic tension is manifested in structural perpetuation of social class inequalities within schools and classrooms and in disjunctive relationships between schools and their communities (Persell, 1997; Zeichner, 1991).

Evergreen's combined initial certification and master's degree program provides a curriculum that infuses a democratic knowledge base. Faculty attempt to confront and alter undemocratic and biased teaching behaviors of future teachers. Processes are not without their imperfections. We perennially meet with resistance from some education students and cooperating teachers as well as from our own unexamined assumptions. Previous chapters point out how unreflective attitudes and behaviors of preservice and cooperating teacher toward transformative teaching can thwart multicultural and democratic expressions. Nevertheless, faculty accept individually and collectively the professional responsibility to advance the goal of democratic schooling opportunities for all learners.

Fundamental to this process is a commitment to democratic, collaborative, interdisciplinary faculty curriculum planning and instruction. Faculty teams of teacher educators, arts and science faculty, and full-time teacher practitioners on leave from their K–12 schools design learning experiences that lead students to question and investigate the multifaceted relationship of democracy to public schooling. Throughout this interdisciplinary curricular process, program practices mirror our expectations for preparing elementary and secondary teachers with an aptitude toward democracy along with appropriate corresponding process skill. The program catalog states,

> We believe the program's success lies as much in the learning processes used to investigate the content as it does in the content itself. Though we teach particular subject matter content, our processes are also "content." Community building, seminars, collaborative learning, group problem solving, extensive field experiences and critical and reflective thinking are not just ideas [our] students read about and are then directed to use when they teach. Rather, these are the processes used daily in the program to help graduate students learn to become skilled, competent professionals who can assume leadership roles in curriculum development, child advocacy, assessment and anti-bias work. (The Evergreen State College, 2001, p. 3)

This statement is in congruence with Cunat's (1996) challenge for the enactment of democratic education when she writes, "Form must match content" (p. 130).

Democratic education holds the expectation that a teacher education program create a process to engage future teachers to "help them develop the skills and attitudes necessary to become people who can and will contribute to the making of a vital, equitable, and humane society" (Cunat, 1996, p. 130). Responding to her own posed question, "What is democratic education?" Cunat (1996) provides the following components:

- a learning community that recognizes and validates the individuality and responsibility of each participant
- students learning cooperatively and reflectively to engage in experiences that are determined by aims and objectives determined at the local level

- a curriculum integrated with social development and social conscience: a sense that individuals can have a reflective and dynamic impact on the society around them and that individuals carry a responsibility to effect necessary social and political change. (p. 130)

Along with the discussion here, Chapter 8 continues an examination of these conceptual and structural elements in a teacher education learning community.

"Democracy and education" was the original organizing conceptual theme for the creation of a teacher education program at Evergreen in the mid-1980s and remains central to the program curriculum. Faculty understand that a deep interrogation of the political context of schooling is critical because, as Dewey (1916) explained, "The conception of education as a social process and function has no definite meaning until we define the kind of society we have in mind" (p. 112). To this end, faculty generally incorporate into the curriculum interdisciplinary primary texts rather than conventional textbooks that tend to reduce or ignore the complexity of significant educational topics (see Soder, 1996). Readings are intended to broaden standard representations of what it means to consider the place of schooling in a democracy. The following list is a sample of readings that teacher candidates are assigned to broaden their democratic knowledge base. They include

- Banks's (2001b) *Cultural Diversity and Education*;
- Bigelow's (1997) *Rethinking Columbus: Teaching About the 500th Anniversary of Columbus's Arrival in America*;
- Christensen's (1990) essay "Teaching Standard English: Whose Standard?";
- Chomsky's (1999) *Profit Over People: Neoliberalism and Global Order*;
- Cohen's (1994) *Designing Group Instruction: Strategies for the Heterogeneous Classroom*;
- Delpit's (1995) *Other People's Children: Cultural Conflict in the Classroom*;
- Dewey's (1938/1974) *Experience and Education*;
- Freire's (1970) *Pedagogy of the Oppressed*;
- Gardner's (1993) *Frames of Mind: The Theory of Multiple Intelligences*;
- Gastil's (1993) *Democracy in Small Groups: Participation, Decision-making, and Communications*;
- Gates and West's (1996) *The Future of the Race*;
- Gould's (1996) *The Mismeasure of Man*;
- Hammond's (1998) *Fighting to Learn: Popular Education and Guerrilla War in El Salvador*;

- hooks's (1994) *Teaching to Transgress: Education as the Practice of Freedom*;
- Igoa's (1995) *The Inner World of the Immigrant Child*;
- Kozol's (1991) *Savage Inequalities: Children in American Schools*;
- Loewen's (1995) *Lies My Teacher Told Me*;
- Moll's (1990) edited collection of analyses in *Vygotsky and Education*;
- Orenstein's (1994) *Schoolgirls: Young Women, Self-Esteem, and the Confidence Gap*;
- Piaget's (1968) *Six Psychological Studies*;
- Shor and Freire's (1987) *A Pedagogy for Liberation: Dialogues on Transforming Education*;
- Spring's (2001) *The American School, 1642–2000*;
- Takaki's (1993) *A Different Mirror: A History of Multicultural America*;
- Tatum's (1999b) *"Why are All the Black Kids Sitting Together in the Cafeteria?" and Other Conversations about Race*; and
- Tocqueville's (1840/1984) *Democracy in America*.

With these books, education students write analyses, engage in seminar dialogue, compare information to field experiences in communities and schools, and scaffold new information onto previous understandings and experiences.

DEMOCRATIC CONSCIOUSNESS AND MORAL STEWARDSHIP: CONTENDING WITH PROVOCATIVE DECLARATIVES 2 & 3

2. It is not legitimate for a teacher education program to require its teacher candidates to adopt a specific conceptual framework or emphasis to successfully complete program requirements.
3. It is legitimate for the values embedded within teacher preparation programs to conflict with current political parameters and curricular practices of public schools.

Centering the program on public education within a multicultural and democratic context requires us to address the requirements of moral stewardship and the likelihood that our program conflicts with current political parameters and public school practices. Despite the challenges that arise from such a position, we conclude that students should minimally be able to articulate, explain, and take actions related to the importance of a conceptual framework that is at the heart of their program. We agreed that they should be able to examine teaching and schooling practices in light of sound theory and to test theory with practice.

To accomplish these goals, the program uses an interdisciplinary approach to weave democracy through three major themes or elements that inform the program's curriculum, pedagogies, and evaluations. All of the themes embody an anticipated disposition toward moral stewardship. The first theme, *democracy and schooling*, relates directly to issues of democracy. The faculty state,

> We look at schooling from the perspective of what it means to work and learn in a democracy operating within a state-supported, advanced capitalist economy. We help students both to understand the evolution of our current democracy and to critique the practices that exclude particular groups from equitable participation in our society. Democracy is presented as a multidimensional concept. Prospective teachers are guided toward professional action and reflection on the implications for the role of a teacher when enacting (a) democratic school-based decision making that is inclusive of parents, community members, school personnel and students and (b) democratic classroom learning environments that are learner-centered and collaborative. (The Evergreen State College, 2001, p. 3)

Because socioeconomic equity is skewed adversely for significant segments of the U.S. population, the program helps teacher candidates understand how current forms of corporate capitalism can negatively affect democratic participation in and out of schools (see Chapter 6).

The second theme, a *multicultural and anti-bias perspective*, is indispensable for recognizing efforts toward establishing a democratic consciousness for moral stewardship among our preservice teachers. We construct the curriculum on Evergreen's strong commitment to diversity because faculty contend

> that both teaching and learning must draw from many perspectives and include a multiplicity of ideas. We believe in preserving and articulating differences of ethnicity, race, gender, and sexual orientation rather than erasing or marginalizing them. We seek to expose [our] students to the consequences of their cultural encapsulation in an effort to assist future teachers in the acquisition of a critical consciousness. We believe that future teachers must be ready to provide children and youth with culturally responsive and equitable schooling opportunities. (The Evergreen State College, 2001, p. 3)

Transformative multicultural topics and approaches are continually spiraled throughout program activities and connected to democratic education.

Our third theme, *developmentally appropriate teaching and learning*, is critical to the understanding and reduction of an individual's personal degree of cultural encapsulation (see Chapters 3–5) and to the development of teachers who are committed to providing an equitable and meaningful curriculum for all students. Program faculty write,

> We understand that no instructional model or limited set of methods responds to the complex cognitive processes associated with K–12 subject matter learning. Our curriculum reflects the social, emotional, physiological and cognitive growth pro-

cesses that shape how children and youth receive, construct, interpret and act on their experiences of the world. We also understand that the competence of students is performance-based. A broad-based curriculum that is interdisciplinary, developmentally appropriate, meaningful and guided by a competent and informed teacher, as well as by learner interests, results in active learning. (The Evergreen State College, 2001, p. 3)

The three themes of the Evergreen teacher education program are interrelated in theory and practice. Beginning with our first conceptual framework theme, democracy and schooling, we place U.S. democracy in the context of its economic system, advanced capitalism, and consider how that economic system shapes collective understandings and possibilities for conceiving and enacting democracy. Teacher candidates are guided in their examination of schooling practices as they might relate to larger social phenomena within U.S. society. This curricular inquiry brings to the forefront of explorations about K–12 teaching and learning economic influences on social relations that can produce systemic inequalities in the organizational structure of the classroom and school (see Giroux, 1988; Kozol, 1991; MacLeod, 1995; Oakes et al., 1992).

Drawing on Dewey's (1916, 1938/1974) insights and concerns, the curriculum strives to offer an organic whole to comprehend how young people learn. Critical for long-term student multicultural learning can be the democratic participation of elementary and secondary school students in instruction and the social system inside and outside of school. Thus we have come to see the importance of K–12 students taking part in democratic governance of classrooms. Besides serving as a constructivist motivational approach to involve students in their own learning, a democratic classroom offers children and youth an opportunity to experience democracy to better understand the responsibilities of participatory citizenship in a culturally diverse society. Critical for Evergreen teacher education faculty is the need to provide preservice teachers a grasp of both classroom social systems and broader institutional and societal contexts in which they will teach.

Faculty often use concepts of "liberatory education," "emancipatory education," "participatory democracy," and "social transformation" interchangeably (see Freire, 1970, 1998; Shor & Freire, 1987) and as compatible with professional sensibilities they anticipate graduates will acquire. The faculty ground these concepts by helping students imagine, design, and enact liberatory or democratic classrooms. By proposing a vision of teaching based on an emancipatory knowledge base (e.g., O'Loughlin, 1992), the program sets the groundwork for collaborative efforts in school settings that involve our teacher candidates and graduates. Faculty do not intend democratic work of this nature to reinforce or promote repressive schooling and social practices such as those that limit democratic and multicultural expressions of children and youth through state-sanctioned elitist political and economic ideologies.

Two examples clarify how we support students in constructing an understanding of democracy and public schooling. The first addresses a project that students have undertaken in the first weeks of the program. The second focuses on field experiences.

Students come to Evergreen with a wide range of definitions and conceptual understandings about democracy. Many assure us that they understand democracy. Yet when they attempt to explain how democracy in the United States functions for diverse groups of people and to apply democratic principles to their lives, group interactions, and public schooling, their ability is often weak. Education students' notions of how equity affects public education are often naive (also see Ross & Yeager, 1999); they have seldom grappled with questions of equity in public schooling in a democratic society prior to enrollment in our program. The first extended learning activity creates conditions requiring them to confront and explore interrelationships of democracy, equity, excellence, and equality. They are expected to apply these ideals as they pertain to poor children's experiences in public schools, laws governing school financing, alternatives to public education such as charter schools, home schooling, and religious schools, and the public's beliefs about the roles of excellence, equity, and equality in public education.

We start this extended activity by inviting students to recall conditions that have supported their own learning. Through reflective writing, individuals begin to identify what helped and hindered their learning process. We provide written descriptions of four project options focusing on the issues of democracy and public schooling in the previous paragraph. These options reflect the four learning preference quadrants Kolb (1985) describes. Students select the option that most appeals to them based, at least in part, on what they had identified as supporting their ability to learn. Once in option groups, they follow a set of discussion guidelines leading them to a more complex understanding of how people learn. In this first step, faculty model a teaching/learning relationship that respects candidates' current experiences and beliefs. A cooperatively based method helps them examine, correct, and expand their existing knowledge. Faculty also create curricular experiences on how to use an individual's experiences and interests to heighten commitment to an externally imposed instructional goal.

The most significant learning often occurs in the second step of the learning activity when groups attempt to work together for 3 weeks to complete the options that they selected. Although we provide information about expected processes and outcomes and suggestions for resources, we do not tell teacher candidates how to work together, schedule their time, or solve problems of group dynamics. As the work develops, education students learn a great deal about public schooling; they also confront and learn about democracy in action. Each group and individual struggle with problems of authority, group process, effective and ineffective problem solving, and functioning democratically in a learning community. The often-heated conversations about this experience provide the foundation for subsequent workshops that explore what it means to teach school in a democratic society.

In addition to on-campus learning experiences, we continually confront preservice teachers with questions about democracy and schooling as they engage in field observations and student teaching. They begin field observations in the first quarter of the program. For three quarters, they divide their time between public school classrooms and campus. All students spend time in an urban, rural, and suburban school and in elementary, middle, and high school. Field expectations carefully lead them through observations and experiences that focus their attention on school environments, student–student interactions, student–teacher interactions, questioning approaches, implied theories of learning, management policies, curricular choices, and equity issues. Student journals based on these focused observations provide the basis for weekly seminar discussions in which the faculty and the students explore educational practices and their implications for the diverse groups of children who attend public schools.

In the second or third quarter of the program, the students begin teaching lessons approved by their faculty and their cooperating classroom teachers. These lessons, as well as all lessons taught during two quarters of student teaching in their second year, are assessed using performance-based assessment rubrics (The Evergreen State College, 2000). The students, college faculty, and classroom teachers all participate in this assessment. The rubric domains of instructional planning and classroom environment include specific descriptions of enactment of democratic principles in public school classrooms. If students are unable to demonstrate the qualities and abilities included in assessment expectations owing to school constraints, the faculty engage them in discussions and written reflections to help them realize that alternatives are possible to what they are encountering.

THE INTERRELATIONSHIP OF DEMOCRACY AND DIVERSITY: CONTENDING WITH PROVOCATIVE DECLARATIVE 4

4. In preparing future teachers for a democratic society, teacher preparation programs should not recommend for certification or licensure students who are openly racist, classist, sexist, or homophobic—regardless of the candidates' subject area knowledge and teaching skills.

As we developed the curriculum and examined the implications of living, teaching, and working within a culturally diverse society, we concluded that teachers who are openly biased toward others on the basis of ethnicity or race, socioeconomic class origins, gender, or sexual orientation would poorly serve children and adolescents. Hence much of our curriculum incorporates texts and experiences that heighten preservice teachers' understanding of the negative effects of racism, classism, sexism, and homophobia on children's lives. We grapple with appropriate avenues to counsel candidates overtly biased in these areas out of the program. As we take each case individually when we perceive a violation of the democratic, multicultural values of the program, we struggle with our responsibilities regarding recommending to the state individuals for teacher certification. To avoid denying a certification recommendation, we ideally strive to have the interactive experience of teacher candidates with the program's curriculum, pedagogies, and formative evaluations preclude such an outcome.

For these reasons, the multicultural and antibias perspective theme does not stand separate from democratic considerations; the faculty view it as a litmus test of the vitality of U.S. democracy. The curriculum is influenced by Freire's (e.g., 1970, 1998; Shor & Freire, 1987) work and his powerful analytic insights into populations silenced by a dominant economic element that attempts to negate the lives and culture of subordinated groups. "The power of the dominant ideology is always domesticating," Freire (1998) observed, "and when we are touched and deformed by it we become ambiguous and indecisive" (p. 6). We realize all of us have been touched and deformed to varying degrees by dominant ideologies in the United States. The program wants students to interrogate their respective positions so that as beginning teachers they are not ambiguous and indecisive in the face of racism and equity (see hooks, 1994).

Banks's (1993b, 1996, 2001b; Banks & Banks, 1993) scholarship is an important source for faculty when they approach the program's curriculum, pedagogies, and assessments from a multicultural perspective. His work helps us understand that to engage in transformative multicultural education, we should realize "that all knowledge reflects the power and social relationships within society, and that an important purpose of knowledge construction is to help people improve society" (1993b, p. 9). To use knowledge to improve society from this perspective requires advocacy of some form of social action against the forces of status quo thinking and dominant behaviors that reproduce unequal relations on the basis of skin color, ethnic origins, gender, or sexual preference. Although we realize the limitations of curriculum transformation for reconstructing society, we understand the vitality of a curriculum that recognizes diverse perspectives leading to the social reconstruction of schools and society. Freire (1998) concluded, "It is true that education is not the ultimate lever for social transformation, but without it transformation cannot occur" (p. 37).

Research documents that institutional disregard of children from disenfranchised socioeconomic groups, especially for children of color, has a negative impact on their subsequent school achievement (e.g., Comer, 1980, 1996; Deloria & Lytle, 1984; Delpit, 1995; Deyle & Swisher, 1997; Kozol, 1991; Persell,

1977, 1997). We strive, therefore, to prepare future teachers who hold an anti-bias perspective so they can be voices of advocacy in their schools and communities. To do so entails recognition of the unquestioning origins of most teacher candidates and demands both an individual and institutional examination of what it means to be culturally encapsulated (Banks, 1993a; Haymes, 1995; McLaren, 1995; Sleeter, 1995a, 1995b; Sleeter & McLaren, 1995; Vavrus, 1994). We recognize that all of us are culturally encapsulated to varying degrees. We seek to help students understand how each of our received cultural perspectives influences our actions toward individuals from groups different from our own cultural origins.

INSEPARABILITY OF TEACHING AND LEARNING FROM DEMOCRACY AND DIVERSITY: CONTENDING WITH PROVOCATIVE DECLARATIVE 5

5. Issues of technical proficiency in teaching along with a sound knowledge base in learning theory should ultimately take priority over other topics within the teacher education curriculum.

The program's third theme—developmentally appropriate teaching and learning—is inseparable from the enactment of a democratic society with a diverse population. For that reason, we resist making reductionist teaching skills the penultimate goal of our program. Nevertheless, the faculty expects candidates to act on complexities inherent in the interaction of teaching and learning. Planning and delivery of this aspect of the curriculum is informed by the importance of learner-centered classrooms where student learning is accurately and authentically described and assessed (Darling-Hammond, Ancess, & Falk, 1995). Because all learners are idiosyncratic in how they construct, process, and interpret information and events, the curriculum incorporates information that highlights constructivist theory as a necessary link to comprehend the social and intellectual development of children and youth (Piaget, 1968; von Glasersfeld, 1991; Vygotsky, 1978). Within this constructivist context, education students learn about and practice skills often considered central to the preparation of beginning teachers such as curriculum design, lesson planning, technology application, assessment, materials development and selection, and the like (see Danielson, 1996).

The program does not, however, offer a linear, cookbook approach to resolve this entanglement of teaching and learning variables; neither does it minimize the uncertainties that teachers experience on a daily basis in their classrooms. Thus "being prepared for uncertainties includes understanding them" (Floden & Buchmann, 1993, p. 217). The program curriculum and pedagogies emphasize the complexity and multidimensional aspect of learning by correcting a common belief of future teachers that learning results only from the selection of activities by teachers and through the transmission of information from the teacher to the students. We help teacher candidates construct an understanding that learning stems from the interaction of learners with their entire social environment (Kliebard, 1992).

MOVING DEMOCRATIC CONCEPTS INTO STUDENT TEACHING: CONTENDING WITH PROVOCATIVE DECLARATIVE 6

6. Incorporating democratic education concepts into full-time student teaching distracts from the sharpening of technical teaching skills beginning teachers require.

Faculty oppose creating a dichotomy between democratic education and teaching proficiency. Leading up to full-time student teaching, faculty engage students in individual and group projects such as the one about democracy and public schooling described earlier. By shaping projects and a learning community environment, faculty stimulate openness toward personal and professional investigation among education students. Teacher candidates are guided initially in their understanding of these curricular topics and activities through an exploration of their sense of themselves, equity, and authority. This often results in creating a state of disequilibrium in individual education students as faculty challenge preservice teachers' previously held knowledge and perceptions through selected curricular experiences.

For example, teacher education students who come into the program devoutly believing that the United States is a just and economically equitable society are stunned to discover through a self-selected project that there are children attending decrepit schools in crowded classrooms with out-of-date textbooks and limited instructional and library resources. They are further shaken when they realize that the children who attend these schools are predominantly poor and of color. They learn through interviews with community members that many people regret the situation but are unwilling to allocate funds equitably in order to improve education for all children. Students confront genuine problems, not hypothetical possibilities. Our curricular goal is that graduates leave the program with a teaching and learning knowledge base purposefully constructed within the social realities of the United States.

The curriculum moves education students away from a misconception that discrete disciplines or subjects should constitute the whole of the curriculum (Kliebard, 1992). In this process, we endeavor to translate impersonal and bureaucratic language of educational goals and standards by rearticulating state discourse within our conceptual framework's emphasis on democracy and multicultural education. For learning to flourish under calls for educational reform, a teacher education curriculum should emphasize how K–12 students ought to be involved democratically in learning and classroom environments that let learner thoughts and voices be heard and engaged (Beyer, 1996; Cohen, 1994; Dewey, 1938/1974; Gastil, 1993; Jones, 1996).

CONNECTING DEMOCRACY TO PROFESSIONAL PRACTICE

All six provocative declaratives remind us of the complexities and challenges for maintaining fidelity to multicultural, democratic commitments. This recognition has lead faculty to continually build mutually beneficial relationships with practicing teachers. Refining a student teaching performance-based assessment rubric provided a powerful avenue for collaborating with local K–12 teachers. Together we infused the curricular themes devoted to democracy, multiculturalism, and developmentally appropriate teaching and learning into student teaching assessment expectations. Working with practitioners brought us closer to expanding a dialogue about the contested space for democratic practice encountered by our graduates. The program's handbook for student teaching has become an opportunity to further share with K–12 teachers and administrators our understanding of democratic education as related to the preparation of teachers and to hear their views and concerns. The following sections briefly highlight four examples of connections that are made between democracy and classroom practice.

Democratic Classroom Management

Through a modification of Danielson's (1996) work, classroom management expectations include an assessment that calls for teacher candidates to "build a democratic classroom management system . . . designed to create a learning community that consistently values cultural diversity and regularly seeks the active participation of all student-citizens" (The Evergreen State College, 2000, p. 34). This requirement provides a student teacher college-supported legitimacy to learn in a public school setting what a "performance-based" democratic environment can be. Teacher candidate ideals of democracy are tested against school-based realities to create a learning "environment of respect and rapport" (p. 34).

School-based Democratic Decision-making

Professional decision-making requires that each teacher candidate "maintains an open mind and participates in team or departmental decision making in a democratic manner" to promote a disposition toward collaborative deliberations with colleagues (The Evergreen State College, 2000, p. 46). Throughout the program teacher education students learn that lasting collaboration should be nonhierarchical and recognize skills and professional goals of teaching colleagues (see Conoley, 1989). The aim is to graduate teachers who "ensure that decisions are democratic and based on the highest professional standards" (p. 46).

Democracy and Cultural Encapsulation

The program places a high value on education students becoming practitioners who reflect upon their cultural encapsulation. The student teaching assessment rubric requires that

> each teacher candidate acknowledge and critically reflect upon his/her own received cultural perspective and come to know how that perspective influences his/her understanding of and actions toward individuals from groups different than his/her received culture . . . [so that as a future teacher each graduate will] use insights of cultural encapsulation to make culturally appropriate contributions to student learning and school improvement activities. (The Evergreen State College, 2000, p. 45)

By highlighting the concept of cultural encapsulation throughout the program, we seek to discredit authoritarian misrepresentations of teacher and school system neutrality when students of color in particular are suffering from unequal and inappropriate treatment in many public school classrooms. Consequently, we emphasize advocacy for K–12 students by asking that teacher candidates work "within the context of a particular team or department to ensure that all students receive a fair opportunity to succeed" (p. 46). A program aim is to recommend those teachers for certification who "make a particular effort to challenge negative attitudes and help ensure that all students, particularly those traditionally underserved, are honored in the school" (p. 46). In this process teacher candidates receive our professional support so that they can have confidence in interrupting racism and other forms of discrimination.

Multicultural Curriculum Development

The program requires that all teacher candidates during their student teaching internship demonstrate how their curriculum plans and teaching "attempt to transform the conventional curriculum with multicultural perspectives and materials which advance anti-bias goals" (The Evergreen State College, 2000, p. 28). Transformation is differentiated from an additive approach as the program strives to break a schooling cycle that marginalizes multicultural education (see Chapters 1–3).

EVALUATIVE FEEDBACK

At the conclusion of the fall 1997 student teaching experience, we surveyed all participants—faculty, teacher candidates, cooperating teacher mentors—to gain information on perceptions about the program's student teaching component. One part of the survey asked for opinions on the democracy theme of the program.

Regarding barriers to creating democratic classrooms, one faculty member noted, "Without the mentor teacher's support, it was very difficult to sustain the effort." Another stated that teacher candidates "often were limited by the structures and culture of the classroom they were in." In some cases when teacher candidates did not find democratic classrooms in practice, they simply sought to fit in the best they could. One student teacher intern stated, "Much of the rubric does not apply to student teaching if the cooperating teachers don't subscribe to that philosophy. . . . I found myself thinking a great deal about what it would be like to be able to implement [the program's] philosophy in my own classroom." Another preservice teacher noted,

> I implemented some strategies I considered as democratic, but felt the pressure from my teacher mentor for lack of time to implement learner-centered and collaborative learning. I did not have an opportunity to practice democracy in classroom management due to constant monitoring and comments by my teacher mentor to be in constant control of the students. . . . I brought up concerns I had with students concerning a cultural/language problem between several students and a gender bias problem—it was ignored.

These observations underscore the challenges to implementing multicultural classroom democracy in mainstream schools.

When teacher candidates were given the opportunity to develop and participate in democratic processes in their student teaching sites, they felt empowered. One described the importance of being "rooted strongly in both theory and practice. In my particular experience, I feel the environment I was in fostered [democratic theory and practice] strongly as well." Another student teacher reflected, "I feel that this was an excellent forum for me to learn about curriculum building. We explored democracy from many perspectives, all of which enriched my understanding of our social and educational systems." A cooperating teacher noted that it was "good to see [the student teacher] already sensitized to this [diversity/democracy] issue and very ready and able to practice a multicultural perspective." Another cooperating teacher noted that "democracy really comes through in candidate's philosophy of teaching and strategies for problem solving (i.e., classroom management)."

Many teacher candidates are hesitant to assert themselves in their field placements. As one observed, "What you may wind up with is a clash of values and no way to resolve them in such a brief span of time." Accordingly, we continue to place priority on the identification and development of a cadre of K–12 teachers who will allow our students to practice democratic teaching and become colearners with all of us in this process. However, even cooperating teachers who agree with our philosophical orientation and goals sometimes are frustrated with their own settings. A cooperating teacher noted, "I believe the HUGE, difficult concept [i.e., democracy and schooling] is given only as much attention as each school community/teacher offers. In a culture and time of incredible rules and state requirements it is VERY tough to honor Mr. John Dewey!" The task remains foremost, nonetheless, for a teacher education program such as ours that commits to the multicultural education of teachers and advocates for democratic schooling.

CONCLUSION: BENEFIT OF COLLECTIVE SHARING AND ACTION

Program faculty at Evergreen remain mindful of sociopolitical constraints when promoting democratic education. They are committed to finding means to deliver a graduate preservice teacher education curriculum that attends to K–12 school reform and improvement efforts while retaining a social reconstructionist spirit that is embedded in the program's conceptual framework. Program development experiences with K–12 practitioners has enriched our collective ability to work within the complexities of conflicting expectations for teachers and schools. To include critical colleagues, the program has also invited a panel of cooperating teachers and an external advisory board of K–12 teachers and administrators to participate in this dialogue. This was part of an effort to infuse democratic practices into teacher preparation and articulate a democratic, multicultural knowledge base for a state board of education accrediting body (see The Evergreen State College, 1998, pp. 15–17, 24–33). Our goal here has been to act publicly upon the state's educational reform efforts in ways that mirror our core beliefs and program experiences for future teachers.

Weaving the web of multicultural democracy for a teacher education program is not a static, compartmentalized concept that can be reduced to a simple technique. Program faculty interact in status quo political environments that drive many assumptions underlying public schooling. Thus a basic requirement for us is regular and collective sharing among ourselves. Faculty also endeavor to broaden conversations to include new cooperating K–12 teachers in the discourse surrounding democracy and multicultural education. The program finds inspiration from other programs struggling with these issues, such as those located at Bank Street College (Darling-Hammond & Macdonald, 2000) and the University of Nevada at Las Vegas (Gallavan, Troutman, & Jones, 2001).

Freire (1998) stated that when "trying to escape conflict, we preserve the

status quo" (p. 45). Confronting conflict will and should continue to be norma-
tive behavior for us. We find hope from Freire (1998) when he advised, "We
must redefine our understanding of the world; though it is historically produced
in the world, this understanding is also produced by conscious bodies in their
interactions with the world" (pp. 52–53). Freire comprehended the potential for
human agency that is addressed in Chapter 1. This understanding of teacher
capacity for social action impels us to continue to define our actions as necessary and vital if we actually are to understand that schools are historically produced. Through faculty interactions and practices, a teacher education program
can make a contribution to the realization of democratic schools that exist to
enhance the lives of all children.

CHAPTER 8

Learning Communities for Multicultural Teacher Education

Making transformative multicultural education central to the education of pre-service and practicing teachers has many challenges. Taken as a whole, the scope of multicultural education can be daunting. Multicultural education as a reform effort not only addresses curricular content integration and what is valued through the process of knowledge construction but also includes racial prejudice reduction, an equity pedagogy, and the creation of empowering school cultures (Banks, 1993d, 2001b). To implement various dimensions of multicultural education requires an environment in which sustained deliberations can arise for educators in teacher education programs and public schools. Issues of equity, racism, and power are unavoidable in addressing transformative dimensions of multicultural education yet, as earlier chapters point out, are potentially volatile for classroom and professional development discussions. Conversations can become strained and difficult in steering reflective consideration toward multicultural reform goals. In some cases racialized topics in particular are glossed over or simply avoided. Educators involved in developing substantial learning experiences that focus on social justice and antiracist/antibias education note that academic structures often truncate interactions and the grasp of multicultural concepts (Adams, Bell, & Griffin, 1997; Derman-Sparks & Phillips, 1997; Zeichner, 1996). Given the dilemma of stifled reflection and decision-making around multicultural education, what institutional steps might a teacher education program initiate to overcome a reluctance by faculty and preservice and in-service teachers to engage in multicultural education reform?

Learning communities offer a potential solution to the quandary of abbreviated academic study that can avert multicultural goals. The expression *learning community* fundamentally implies that a group of individuals are learning together in a supportive atmosphere toward a common purpose. The work of this community is guided by knowledge acquisition. Ample opportunities exist for both affective and cognitive responses. This learning in turn not only benefits the individual members of the community but contributes to shared understandings and new points of view for all participants. Community in this sense combines both a task orientation toward a goal as well as the development of a bond among community participants imbedded in a democratic ethos (see Calderwood, 2000; Merz & Furman, 1997). The realization of a learning community focused upon multicultural education is an undertaking that, while providing the groundwork for rewarding outcomes, takes thoughtful planning and continuous assessment.

This chapter explores how teacher education can create a setting that allows the investigation of thorny yet crucial multicultural education issues. Described is the relationship among learning, community, and democracy. Given the generally fragmented nature of the teacher education curriculum and many staff development programs, a learning community provides a holistic option to learn about and act upon multicultural education dimensions. Darling-Hammond and McLaughlin (1999) explain that "the possibilities for individual teacher learning are increased greatly as professional communities move from individualistic or 'balkanized' cultures to 'collaborative' cultures, and towards what can be described as 'learning communities'" (p. 381). Because multiple usage of the term *learning community* can obfuscate an understanding of the concept for multicultural teacher education, the chapter sifts through various applications of it. Paralleled with the question of who might constitute the membership of a learning community are pragmatic and ethical considerations of where and with whom a teacher education program should initiate one. The chapter also outlines structural and pedagogical features for conceptualizing a learning community that places multicultural education at its core.

LEARNING, COMMUNITY, AND DEMOCRACY

The organization of teaching and learning throughout the history of U.S. schooling was rarely intended to create a community of learners. Instead, the intent was upon having *stratified classes* of students rather than creating *democratic social groups* (Dewey, 1916, 1938/1974; Spring, 2001). The varieties of social-psychological learning needs brought to public schools by individual students have historically been dismissed in favor of standardized understandings of learning and intelligence and the reified groupings of students deemed marginal (Banks, 2000; Gould, 1996; Spring, 2001). Concurrently, the conventional structure of formal education has been and continues to be based upon the arrangement of students into classes for bureaucratic efficiency and the reinforcement of dominant power relationships in U.S. society.

Against the grain of this history, Dewey (1916, 1938/1974) chastised traditional schooling arrangements that dismiss the importance of an individual's relationship to the conditions of teaching and learning. To create a learning experience, Dewey (1938/1974) contended that educators should account for how learning environments positively "interact with personal needs, desires, purposes, and capacities" (p. 44). Because "education is essentially a social process," he understood that educational quality should be judged by "the degree in which *individuals form a community group* [italics added]" (p. 58). For Dewey, the subjectivities of students should be acknowledged within a community-of-learners context in order for the social-psychological aspect of teaching and learning to be accurately understood by faculty.

Dewey (1916) located the purpose of schooling in the larger context of a democratic society. More than a government based on electoral politics, democracy "is primarily a mode of associated living, of conjoint communicated experience" (p. 101). Schooling under a democratic ethos requires conditions of community for learning and teaching. In a democratic learning community activities become inseparable from products. To focus only on outcomes of learning renders the education process as simply "materialistic" (p. 143). A democratic learning community for Dewey involved participation that honors a freedom of interaction built upon a development of social relations and shared interests.

Dewey (1916) conceived of a democratic community founded upon "good will," which he equated with "intelligent sympathy" (p. 141). Good will or intelligent sympathy in social groupings results when individuals can empathetically see across their self-interests and biases—be they socioeconomic or racial—to work toward common learnings and understandings. In this context Dewey warned against one group acting under the guise of benevolence by dictating to others what was in their best interest. In contemporary terms we can characterize the application of intelligent sympathy as Noddings's (1992) notion of caring communities in schools and classrooms. Critical for Noddings is open-ended dialogue as a process in "a common search for understanding, empathy, or appreciation" (p. 23) where affect interacts with cognitive knowledge acquisition. In a democratic learning community, means are not disassociated from ends.

Pondering the purposes of higher education, Gutmann (1999) asks, "Is there an ideal academic *community* by democratic standards" (p. 185)? For some, according to Gutmann, this would mean a focus on the acquisition of knowledge for its own sake while rejecting standards of accountability established by the state or professional learned societies. This particular ideal would result in the denial of students to an academic community seeking education for a professional purpose, such as a career in public school teaching. Gutmann warns, however,

> In excluding scholars and students who are interested in socially useful knowledge, a community of learning therefore misses a democratic opportunity: to cultivate a sense of social responsibility among future professionals and to criticize society on the basis of shared . . . standards. (p. 188)

Such an academic community can present professional technical skills as secondary to the social histories of the broader society in which the profession is located. A democratic academic community that studies the work of a teacher would place an emphasis upon social and political relationships inherent in learning, teaching, and schooling.

How, then, can a democratic academic learning community for multicultural teacher education be conceptualized? Fundamentally, structures and pedagogies are required to enhance the development of a social grouping of students into a sense of community rather than into isolated classes. Because learning involves social processes, democratic standards provide the basis to find shared interests through a freedom of interaction on multicultural perspectives. Grounded by the active participation of diverse voices, a learning community should emulate democratic processes that permit individuals to learn across parochial interests. Extending Gutmann's (1999) observations of a democratic academic community, professional education for teachers should involve situating the work of teaching and learning within the multiple social and political forces that influence schools. Grant (1997) explicitly notes that the development of culturally responsive teaching skills requires an interdisciplinary academic foundation "shaped by multicultural perspectives and experiences that have been acquired working with race, class, and gender issues and culturally diverse groups of people" (p. 17). Hence, a narrow focus on the execution of technical skills associated with teaching rids a learning community of its academic grounding and fails to account for basic democratic learning community criteria. In summary, placing a learning community in a democratic context allows for a multifaceted investigation of multicultural education reform goals in a teacher education program.

RANGE OF UNDERSTANDINGS OF LEARNING COMMUNITIES

The concept of learning communities is used in a variety of ways. Jean MacGregor (2000), codirector for the National Learning Communities Project, has outlined contemporary trends in the use of learning communities. The most common applications of the term include (a) a "community of learners" broadly encompassing any group of individuals intentionally coming together to learn, (b) thematic higher education interdisciplinary programs connecting formerly discrete courses, (c) individual K–12 classrooms where cooperative learning and/or thematic teaching predominates, (d) on-line or virtual activities connecting participants via the Internet for a particular purpose, (e) faculty and staff development where the approach resembles study groups upon specific topics, (f) "learning organizations" in which an institution learns from its own activities, and (g) community-based projects such as a local community development effort with the capacity for individuals to learn and take action together. All of the ways in which learning communities are employed can have applicability to multicultural teacher education. Yet the scope of functions can render learning communities as another educational buzzword devoid of actual intention and application. In line with the focus of this book, the emphasis here is upon institutionalized, sustainable academic learning communities rather than informal educational networks that strive to create communities of learners (see, e.g., Lieberman, 1996; D.R. Taylor, 2000). Into this environment come multicultural researchers who find the concept useful in furthering multicultural education reform.

K-12 Multicultural Learning Communities

Most discussions of multicultural learning communities focus on K-12 schools and consider the interactions among students and between students and teachers. Concentrating on improving student achievement in culturally diverse settings, Nieto (1999), for example, recommends that learning communities be inclusive of students and teachers. She recognizes that student learning cannot be improved simply on the basis of technical teaching skills. Furthermore, substantial learning growth does not necessarily occur when multicultural education takes a token or additive approach to instruction. Instead, Nieto explains, students need a transformative curriculum in a caring classroom environment reflective of a "meaningful" learning community (p. 162). The reason to have a supportive schooling atmosphere is that *"the way students are thought about and treated by society and consequently by the schools they attend and the educators who teach them is fundamental in creating academic success or failure"* (p. 167, emphasis in original). Nieto's learning community insight on the role of teachers and administrators for student academic success is critical in advancing an equity pedagogy in an empowering school culture.

Cochran-Smith (1997) advocates the implementation of learning communities in K-12 settings. She sees learning communities as places for "significant work" that can improve academic achievement (p. 49). "Communities of learners" offer a place for a curriculum that is learner-centered. Central to the enterprise of a learning community that serves diverse students is a collaborative curriculum design and cooperative learning opportunities to develop critical thinking and a substantial grasp of subject matter. Instruction moves away from a transmission of information and toward teachers and students working together with a transformed curriculum characterized by multiple perspectives and interpretations. Teachers hold high expectations for all students who understand that learning is a shared responsibility with their classmates and teachers. Cochran-Smith's processes and goals for a learning community can contribute positively to the aims of transformative multicultural education reform.

When a learning community involves a targeted group of students of color, student academic success can be improved (Battistich, Solomon, Kim, Watson, & Schaps, 1995). Scribner and Reyes (1999) found that a learning community's impetus that started at the institutional level of the school resulted in a significant increase in the number of high-performing Latino students. To develop a common learning vision, teachers and administrators involved in a school-based learning community "examine their own beliefs about what they do, how it gets done, their students, their students' parents, each other, and the larger community within which they work" (Scribner & Reyes, 1999, p. 190). The goal for the learning community becomes the development of localized multicultural applications and inclusive pedagogies.

A caring learning community focuses on student achievement in a collaborative classroom climate. Nieto and Rolón (1997) point out that in bilingual settings the need is heightened for "centering pedagogies" that provide a safe environment for students by relating directly to experiences of students and families (pp. 104–109). A nonauthoritarian relationship between students and teachers is a critical component at the classroom level. Learning communities require an institutional commitment at the school level with enactment that takes place in the daily routines of the classroom (Nieto & Rolón, 1997; Reyes, Scribner, & Scribner, 1999).

The Holmes Professional Development School Model

The Holmes Partnership is the largest consortium of colleges where institutional representatives have articulated the need to increase attention to both multicultural education dimensions and the creation of learning communities. A primary goal of the consortium is devoted to "Equity, Diversity, Cultural Competence":

> Actively work on equity, diversity and cultural competence in the programs of K–12 schools, higher education, and the education profession by recruiting, preparing, and sustaining faculty and students who reflect and deeply understand the implications of the rich diversity of cultural perspectives in this country and our global community. (Holmes Partnership, 2000)

For preservice teachers the specialized knowledge of teaching for which Holmes advocates would be transmitted through professional development schools that are passionate about the issues of equity and diversity (Holmes Group, 1990, 1995).

The Holmes Group (1990) in its design for professional development schools placed the creation of learning communities in public schools as a high priority: "The ambitious kind of teaching and learning we hope for will take place in a sustained way for large numbers of children only if classrooms are thoughtfully organized as communities of learning" (p. 7). Echoing Dewey's (1938/1974) position on the positive relationship between community and learning, Holmes (1990) writes, "Lasting and powerful learning involves the mastery of discourse and active participation in community . . . [because] without community, academic work lacks meaning" (pp. 12, 24).

The Holmes Group (1990) proposal understood the liberal arts aim of learning community discourse as generalizable to not only all levels of K–12 education but also higher education. Specifically, the Holmes learning community model goes beyond the individual classroom to incorporate continuous staff development of teachers at all career stages. Professional development schools would be expected to become places where teachers, teacher educators, and school administrators are learner-participants in learning communities. Central to a school-based teacher education curriculum is "thoughtful, long-term inquiry into teaching and learning" in collaboration with college professors and K–12 practitioners (p. 7). Pedagogical inquiry would be framed by "a major commitment . . . [to] overcoming the educational and social barriers raised by an unequal society" (p. 7). Learning communities in such a collaborative environment "will act as a bridge in the long process of creating a democratic culture" (p. 22). By having mutual understandings around the importance for advancing social justice goals in a schooling context (see pp. 29–43), learning communities as proposed by Holmes offer a theoretical possibility in the preparation of teachers for multicultural education reform.

Learner-centered, Knowledge-based Accountability

The National Commission on Teaching and America's Future (NCTAF, 1996) recommended as part of its "action agenda for change" that "schools be restructured to become genuine learning organizations for both students and teachers—organizations that respect learning, honor teaching, and teach for understanding" (p. 101). Specifically, NCTAF's concern sprang from disjointed learning structures within schools: "Lack of coordinated time and shared responsibility among teachers reduces accountability for the overall learning experience" (p. 102). Confounding the fragmentation of deliberations and responsibilities for student achievement, Darling-Hammond (1997a) also notes on behalf of NCTAF that students attending schools in low-income areas too often lack access to qualified teachers.

Chapter 2 emphasizes that qualified teachers holding a teaching license in the subject area in which they teach is just but one piece of the multicultural puzzle. Darling-Hammond (1992) has made the case for professional accountability to support "practices that are *learner-centered* and *knowledge-based* rather than procedure-oriented and rule-based" (p. 13). Therefore, "where knowledge about appropriate practices exists, it will be used in making decisions" (p. 14). Darling-Hammond (2000a, 2000b, 2000c) has connected the learning communities concept of learner-centered academic success to successful teacher education programs. Collaborative cultures of common visions are the foundational hallmarks of the teacher preparation programs in her case studies. The most convincing case studies are marked by institutions that have infused transformative multicultural perspectives throughout the curriculum and where faculty see themselves as colearners and fellow participants with their preservice teachers (Vavrus, 2001b).

Darling-Hammond's (1992, 1997a, 2000a, 2000b, 2000c) and Darling-Hammond and McLaughlin's (1999) scholarship suggests further ways to think about learning communities. For the creation of a *classroom* learning community within either a public school or a teacher education program, a precondition is a commitment by an *institution* to provide the assistance and climate necessary to become a learning organization. The academic climate should promote collegial learning and deliberations around multicultural education reform. Teacher educators and public school teachers and administrators are more likely to be successful in an organizational setting that values principles of a learner-centered, culturally responsive curriculum when they attempt to implement a learning community model to enhance multicultural education reform dimensions. Ultimately, educators should be held accountable to assist their students—be they K–12 students, preservice teachers, or in-service teachers—to meeting multicultural learning goals.

THE PARTICIPANTS AND LOCATION OF A LEARNING COMMUNITY

Who are the ultimate participants in a reform-minded learning community? The previous section suggests no educational level is left untouched. With an eye toward improving the learning of all students in a society challenged to meet the democratic aims of equity and social justice, children and youth in our public schools need to receive an education in a secure learning community environment. To create a learning community, teachers themselves need to have experienced a democratic learning community as a continuous aspect of school-based staff development inclusive of multicultural education dimensions. Preservice teachers need experiences in learning communities facilitated by teacher educators who are willing to restructure a teacher education curriculum. "Developing a multicultural perspective," Nieto (1999) explains, "means working with colleagues in collaborative and mutually supportive ways" (p. xviii). Consequently, from the students, teachers, and administrators in a public school to preservice teachers and their college faculty in a teacher education program, all are potential participants and colearners in a learning community.

Where, then, should teacher educators focus their energies to create learning communities that allow a rich investigation into topics surrounding multicultural education purposes? Multiple possibilities exist. Nieto's (1999) work was situated on her college campus and in her individual classroom with groups of preservice and practicing teachers. Like Cochran-Smith's (1997), Nieto's (1999) goal is the development of culturally responsive teachers who are capable of creating a learning community in their public school classrooms. For Reyes et al. (1999) and Nieto and Rolón (1997), another place to start a learning community is with an entire public school staff. The description of a democratic learning community in Chapter 7 highlights the location on a college campus of a learning community approach serving as the curricular model of a teacher education program. The Holmes (1990, 1995, 2000) proposals call for a learning community located in a pubic school where there is a fertile blending of deliberations among preservice teachers, classroom teachers, school administrators, and teacher educators.

Darling-Hammond (1992, 1997a, 2000a, 2000b, 2000c) grasps well the complexity of locating learning communities across preservice, in-service, and K–12 classrooms. A lasting classroom learning community can be sustained in an institution committed to transformative multicultural education. She clearly sees the need for learning communities that serve multicultural education reform to happen simultaneously in public school classrooms, staff development activities, and teacher education programs. One without the others could render ineffective the concept of democratic, multicultural learning communities. Yet teacher educators are somewhat limited by the parameters of their job definitions to transform an entire system of education from preservice teacher education through public school classroom instruction.

Limitations of the Professional Development School Approach

The first step for teacher educators should be an examination of their own campus-based teacher education program structures and curriculum. As research described in Chapter 2 indicates, teacher candidates tend to take an additive rather than a transformational approach toward multicultural education knowledge integration. Thus the foundational and methodological curriculum is a site to begin restructuring of a teacher education program.

The college campus is where the preponderance of the education of future teachers takes place. Kennedy's (1999) research reveals that "university-based pre-service programs had more influence on teacher learning than school-based programs did" (p. 83). Therefore, working within the college and university academic setting is preferable to initiating an off-campus, field-based, learning community as *the* learning community for a teacher education program.

To start a learning community approach to teacher preparation through a professional development school, as the Holmes (1990, 1995, 2000) organization advocates, does not, however, guarantee a transformational approach toward multicultural education. In fact, a specific action plan was not forthcoming to reform collegiate teacher education academic processes because the Holmes

(1995) consortium did not consider its partnership "the proper forum for thrashing out the details of the many policies that will affect field-based faculty" (p. 71). When the Holmes proposal was actually implemented in various forms during the 1990s, Murrell (1998) discovered that the design and organizational framework in professional development schools

1. inhibits the questioning of the underlying political questions and sociocultural dynamics that produce inequalities in schooling; . . .
2. inhibits the development of conceptually rich, culturally aware, and politically astute definitions of equity, diversity, and quality schooling; . . .
3. maintains the political status quo by failing to address real needs, interests, and agendas of urban communities supposedly served by [professional development schools]. (p. 27)

Thus central lines of multicultural education inquiry are actually diluted or, more seriously, silenced.

Newly designed standards for professional development schools by NCATE (2001c) begin to attend to this concern. NCATE requires a college that seeks accreditation for a professional development school to "systematically analyze data to address the gaps in achievement among racial groups" (p. 16) and to compare curricular and pedagogical practices with learning outcomes. Furthermore, teacher candidates and school partners are expected to "be able to teach from multicultural and global perspectives that draw on the histories, experiences, and diverse cultural backgrounds of all people" (p. 16). Questions remain, however, over the extent to which these new standards can make a transformative shift to act on multicultural issues of democracy, White privilege, racism, and globalization that are raised in previous chapters.

Where To Begin Pragmatically and Ethically

Murrell's (1998) findings raise both pragmatic and ethical issues regarding the location of learning communities for multicultural teacher education. Pragmatically, the professional development school model, despite its proposed merits and intended social justice ideals, contains elements that appear to constrain transformative multicultural discourse. The limitations of teacher preparation placed in a K–12 professional development school setting may function from a lack of necessary conditions to build a community of trust through shared expectations. Classroom teachers, school administrators, teacher educators, and preservice teachers need extensive time and dialogue outside the normal public school workday to develop learning communities. Given the time constraints placed upon public school educators, a professional development school may not be a practical location for preservice teachers to have their first and only experience in a learning community model. Indeed, future teachers may be so soured by such an experience or come away with such an arrested understanding of multicultural education that they end up reproducing in their teaching tepid notions of curriculum and instructional arrangements in the name of multicultural reform.

A learning community requires a secure environment in which education students have sufficient time with their faculty. Preservice teachers organized into learning community cohorts can come to know one another as active learners and shapers of multicultural knowledge rather than passive depositories of information, technologies, and techniques (see Freire, 1970). A university-based learning community potentially extends time for students to learn cooperatively in heterogeneous groupings with their peers. Teacher candidates can come to see their faculty members as colearners with them in the quest to understand and actualize multicultural education reform. The importance of acknowledging the temporal aspect of a learning community finds emphasis with Calderwood's (2000) caution that "the accommodation of difference and its balance with sufficient commonality requires much time- and energy-consuming attention" (p. 150). Thus the notion of *community* can become hollow when a teacher education program fails to include opportunities for groups of education students to learn together in a supportive environment for a sustained time. In a learning community, education students can develop with their peers and faculty the personal, professional, and intellectual courage to pursue controversial and complex multicultural education issues.

Ethically, Murrell's (1998) research suggests that colleges and universities may be unwise when experimenting on public schools rather than practicing learning community concepts initially upon their own campuses. This is the case especially for public schools in low-income areas with culturally diverse student populations. Teacher educators and their students need to understand the dynamics of a learning community within their own institution's teacher education program before exporting a model of learning they have not implemented at home (Kahne & Westheimer, 2000). The same recommendation applies to K–12 staff development (Barnes, 2000). Schools must first create the conditions for a learning community (see Reyes et al., 1999). In a supportive schooling culture, a teacher is able to take her or his learning community experience from a school-wide staff development program and begin to apply learning community concepts in the classroom.

This argument for both pragmatic and ethical reflection on the merits of the location of a learning community is predicated on Dewey's emphasis on the importance of interpersonal relationships in building a sense of community in schools. Noddings (1992) further explains that only in a safe and caring learning community can dialogue flourish. Presentation of knowledge alone is insufficient for students and teachers to grasp the complexity and implications of such topics as multicultural education. "Dialogue is required here," Noddings states, "and dialogue ends in questions or in great sadness as often as it does in solution" (p. 120). Greene (1995) wonders, though, how classroom settings for "significant dialogue" could be constructed so that "there might emerge some consciousness of interdependence as well as recognition of diverse points of view" (p. 177). Significant dialogue requires a curricular format such as a learning community. Dialogue is not an easily learned disposition because creating a democratic learning community requires that group participants "learn the foundational social skills necessary so that authentic conversations can take place" (McDermott, Knapp, & Setoguchi, 1999, p. 72). Sustained dialogue in an academic learning community is an uncommon educational experience for most adults. Teacher educators, in-service teachers, and teacher candidates need direct experiences as participants in meaningful learning communities.

First, teacher education programs on college and university campuses need to implement learning communities for preservice teachers and staff development programs that create a climate conducive for learning communities within public schools. Next, it becomes more timely for teacher education programs and public schools to engage deeply and regularly in a professional development school model of a learning community. This is not meant to imply that a teacher education program should not continue to make attempts at collaborative partnerships for multicultural education such as the emergent examples of Alverno College, Bank Street College, California State University–San Marcos, Santa Clara University, University of Alaska–Fairbanks, University of California–Los Angeles, University of Texas–Pan American, University of Wisconsin–Madison, University of Nevada–Las Vegas, and Wheeling College (Darling-Hammond & Macdonald, 2000; Gallavan et al., 2001; Ladson-Billings, 1999b; Miller & Silvernail, 2000; Oakes, 1996; Rios et al., 1997; Zeichner, 2000). However, teacher educators should also turn to their own institutional ethos, structures, and curriculum to create on-campus conditions in order to realize learning communities for multicultural teacher education.

RESTRUCTURING TO DESIGN A LEARNING COMMUNITY

An effective learning community that serves the aims of multicultural education should be an intentional undertaking. "Community life does not organize itself in an enduring way purely spontaneously," Dewey (1938/1974) explained. "It requires thought and planning ahead" (p. 56). In Chapter 3 I argue for the importance of faculty planning and deliberation to create a philosophical coherence that can be articulated in a teacher education program's guiding conceptual framework. Coherence around a commitment to transformative multicultural education can give direction to the teacher education curriculum. Yet pouring new curriculum content into old academic structures can undermine coherence.

Based on their research on teacher education, Guillaume, Zuniga, and Yee (1998) concluded,

> The problem of bringing educational equity to life is complex and cannot be solved with simple solutions of isolated strategies, such as short-term workshops, a single university course observation, or participation experience in a classroom with a diverse student population. (p. 156)

The internal restructuring of the conceptualization and delivery of a program, especially with an interdisciplinary, liberal arts orientation, is a missing ingredient in much of teacher education curriculum planning (Wisniewski, 2001). The professional development school model is a positive example of restructuring. However, for reasons described earlier, the exposure of preservice teachers to a learning community with multicultural sensibilities should begin on the college campus with thoughtful planning. More time for teacher education faculty communication is an important beginning component for building community. Structuring time for faculty dialogue in a community atmosphere can lead to deliberations on curricular practices to support multicultural learning.

Various teacher education curricular avenues exist to incorporate a multicultural sensibility through learning communities. Table 8.1 provides an overview of the participants and purposes for thinking about strategies for multicultural, teacher education learning communities.

The range of learning community participants can include all teacher education faculty within an institution planning in collaborative dialogue, two faculty with shared multicultural values, a faculty member and students within a single course, two or more faculty with block scheduled courses and a cohort of students, and/or two or more faculty linking previously discrete courses and a cohort of students (E. Decker, personal correspondence, November 9, 2000). The purposes for these learning community participants include faculty deliberations upon multicultural curricular reform and articulation of the pedagogical practices for transformative multicultural teacher education. With teacher education students as participants with their faculty in a learning community, the aim becomes an opportunity to deepen affective and cognitive dimensions of multicultural knowledge. The strategies summarized here and outlined in Table 8.1 assume that restructuring is an empty gesture toward pedagogical processes unless multicultural content remains central to a teacher education curriculum.

Documented forms of higher education learning communities unrelated to teacher preparation exist on approximately 400 college and university campuses (B.L. Smith, 2001). The following is a common definition of a collegiate learning community:

Table 8.1. Strategies for Multicultural, Teacher Education Learning
Communities

Participants	*Purpose*
All teacher education faculty within an institution	Deliberate on curricular practices, content, and structures necessary to support multicultural learning by preservice and in-service teachers
Two faculty with shared multicultural values	Share multiculturally oriented perspectives and assignments between their teacher education courses
Faculty and students within a single course	Restructure content and time to deepen affective and cognitive dimensions of multicultural knowledge
Two or more faculty with *block* scheduled courses and a cohort of students	(a) Restructure time and content from interdisciplinary perspective to deepen affective and cognitive dimensions of multicultural knowledge (b) Share multiculturally oriented perspectives and assignments
Two or more faculty *linking* previously discrete courses and a cohort of students	Implement a thematic, interdisciplinary and holistic program with extended time for students to deepen affective and cognitive dimensions of multicultural knowledge

A learning community is any one of a variety of curricular structures that link together several existing courses—or actually restructure the curricular material entirely—so that students have opportunities for deeper understanding and integration of the material they are learning, and more interaction with one another and their teachers as fellow participants in the learning enterprise. (Gabelnick, MacGregor, Matthews, & Smith, 1990, p. 19)

Implied in this definition of a learning community is "purposeful restructuring" to provide students "a more coherent curriculum" in which they are actively engaged in meaningful, interdisciplinary learning with their peers and faculty (B.L. Smith, 2001, p. 118).

In addition to increased coherency, research reveals that campus-based learning communities contribute positively to college student learning (Gabelnick et al., 1990; Tinto, 1997). "Persistence" in learning complex material is enhanced in a learning environment where students "are placed in situations in which they have to share learnings in some positive, connected manner" (Tinto,

1997, p. 601). The learning community concept lends itself well to the interdisciplinary and challenging nature of multicultural education and the accompanying dialogue and persistence in learning that are required to grasp multicultural perspectives. Furthermore, when an institution attempts to develop and implement multicultural curriculum initiatives, faculty collaborative planning and teaching around multicultural topics can help disseminate learning community approaches and diversity concepts within a college's faculty (B.L. Smith, 2001).

An example of a learning community, as outlined in Table 8.1, is when at least two different courses are linked together to create an interdisciplinary, coherent curriculum between areas of study for teacher education students. Figure 8.1 illustrates the linking of a course in educational psychology and one in multicultural education to create an interdisciplinary, team-taught thematic program titled "The Social Psychology of Learning, Teaching, and Schooling in a Culturally Diverse Society."

This arrangement involves collaborative planning and teaching by faculty who have formerly taught separate education courses. The number of credit hours generated per faculty member in this example is the same as if each faculty member were teaching two separate courses. Students in cohorts in linked courses, as well as blocked scheduling, can have an increased time for dialogue and a deeper consideration of the complexity of subject matter material when presented in an interdisciplinary curriculum within a learning community context. Moving beyond two linked courses is the example provided in Chapter 7 of an entire teacher education curriculum that is organized as a coordinated studies learning community program with an absence of discrete courses.

The case for decreasing the fragmentation of a teacher education curriculum was introduced in Chapter 3. This condition exists despite the leadership of individual teacher educators who draw from interdisciplinary materials to provide multicultural content within the traditional curriculum (e.g., Larkin & Sleeter, 1995; Nieto, 1999). The teacher education curriculum as a whole, however, remains in its historically fragmented condition with little opportunity for extended consideration by teacher candidates of multicultural topics that affect teaching, learning, and schooling. Preparation models of the "reflective teacher" are reduced to a mere caricature if preservice teachers are not provided curricular structures to reflect with their peers and faculty upon meaningful multicultural content through inquiry, dialogue, and practice (see Zeichner, 1996).

Restructuring Considerations

To enact learning community strategies to support multicultural education requires the organizational attention of teacher education faculty and administrators. Once established, learning communities are not necessarily more time-consuming or expensive than traditional collegiate curriculum. A learning com-

Figure 8.1. Linking Two Courses Thematically Into a Learning Community Program

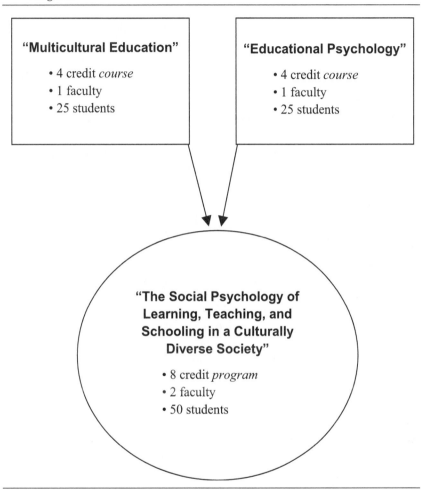

munity approach does, however, raise issues about a program's curricular focus and faculty multicultural competence.

Learning community advocacy for multicultural teacher education is built on an understanding that preservice and in-service teachers need strong multicultural education knowledge, skills, and dispositions. A teacher education program should have multicultural specialists familiar with this interdisciplinary field to teach a stand-alone foundational multicultural education course. Retaining an introductory course helps guarantee that a program provides a fundamental grounding in multicultural theories and practices. With a multicultural education background, teacher education students can then be better prepared to enter, learn, and participate in an integrated learning community facilitated by faculty holding varied degrees of multicultural expertise.

Program faculty deliberations on learning community curricular restructuring are crucial in addressing dynamics posed when transformative multicultural education encounters conventional teacher education models. The presence of transformative multicultural education in a learning community with a mainstream teacher education curriculum does not make traditional instructional methods, educational psychology, and field experiences "multicultural." Serious considerations should be given to political, social, and economic perspectives that multicultural education inherently raises in juxtaposition with conventional teacher education concepts and approaches. Chapter 5 describes the strong emotional responses that preservice and in-service teachers often have to multicultural education when long-held values supportive of dominant social arrangements are challenged. If faculty in a learning community are ambivalent about transformative commitments, teacher education students can be confused about the multicultural messages they receive. To meet multicultural education goals, a learning community faculty should prioritize transformative perspectives under the guidance of a faculty team member who is a multicultural specialist. To do otherwise can create a learning community in which the purposes and outcomes remain crossed and strained between transformative and mainstream perspectives. Rather than liberating teacher education students from culturally hidebound concepts and actions, socially dominant perspectives can simply be reproduced inside a learning community. Teacher education staff development may be necessary to create a learning community that is transformative in orientation (also see Banks, 1997, pp. 117–121).

Research university faculty also need time to investigate multicultural issues connected to teacher education. Such faculty can play an important role in advancing a knowledge base for transformative multicultural education. Hence research faculty in teacher education may only occasionally participate in a learning community that has high time demands. It is incumbent upon a teacher education program at all levels of higher education to have a cadre of faculty with multicultural education qualifications and commitments. When a program can hire more than one faculty with multicultural expertise, all multicultural responsibilities in a learning community do not consistently fall to one designated faculty member.

Learning Community Planning Domains

Any curriculum restructuring effort usually requires various kinds of support prior to full implementation. As a curriculum restructuring endeavor, the establishment of a learning community implies domains to which educators should attend: (a) the people—faculty, administrators, support staff—who will be involved in establishing a learning community; (b) the administrative location of the organization under restructuring; (c) adequate funding to work through the restructuring process; and (d) justification of a learning community (Elliott & Decker, 1999; also see Shapiro & Levine, 1999). The following discussion draws upon categories and analyses developed by Elliott and Decker (1999) and applies the information to teacher education programs.

Personnel. A learning community can be initiated by interested faculty or by the administrative unit head, such as the dean, director, or chair of an education college, school, or department. As outlined in Table 8.1, a learning community that is started by one faculty member with expertise in multicultural education within a single course or in collaboration with another faculty can provide the first instance of the model within a teacher education program. On the other hand, an academic administrator can take the leadership in convening an entire teacher education faculty to begin deliberations to restructure. A combination of the two approaches—grassroots faculty interest plus administrative support—offers a means to introduce an interdisciplinary learning community that incorporates transformative multicultural perspectives.

When moving toward blocked scheduling and a linking of courses, other personnel involved in restructuring should include those who are responsible for scheduling course times and locations, advising students, preparing transcripts, assembling catalog/program handbook descriptions, and determining full-time equivalencies (FTEs) for faculty and students. A learning community obligates academic support staff to reconsider traditional models of course scheduling and space assignment. A learning community with blocked or linked courses usually needs both a large area for whole-group instruction and smaller rooms suitable for student seminars where dialogue is the focus. Therefore, staff responsible for scheduling courses and making room assignments can facilitate locating appropriate campus space for a learning community. Academic advisors can help teacher education students understand how a learning community experience fits with other aspects of the curriculum. Staff who oversee catalog and program descriptions can underscore the role of a learning community as part of a systemic effort by a teacher education program to help teachers better understand the dynamics of their career choice in a diverse society. Staff and an administrative leader need to develop a plan to calculate FTEs in the context of a student–faculty ratio for a learning community.

As learning community concepts take hold within a teacher education program, hiring committees should look beyond traditional disciplines in making selections. Position descriptions ought to reflect the multicultural values of a program's conceptual framework. Faculty in a learning community should value the importance of multicultural education reform and hold an academic interest in diversity issues, interdisciplinary scholarship, and collaborative teaching and learning (see Holmes Partnership, 2000).

Organizational Structure. A learning community crosses disciplinary boundaries. An academic learning community infused with transformative multicultural education themes is inherently drawn to interdisciplinary collaboration. When higher education faculty collaborate across their subject fields, learning communities "have the greatest potential for contributing to educational reform within the institution" (Elliott & Decker, 1999, p. 22). K–12 staff development collaboration in a learning community environment can arouse curriculum planning "from being a frozen tundra to a warm, supportive haven for the generation of new, diverse ideas and practices" (Zapeda, 1999, p. 65). Organizational facilitation among faculty from various disciplines is a necessary factor to sustain and increase planning inclusive of multicultural education.

To restructure a teacher education program for multicultural education reform takes institutional commitment and cooperation. When an academic administrator designates, for example, an associate dean or a faculty member with partial release time as a learning community coordinator, faculty find relief from management tasks necessary to navigate and advocate for resource support. Composed of key personnel who are vital to the formation and implementation of a learning community, a coordinating committee can be convened to facilitate restructuring. For a learning community coordinating committee in a multicultural teacher education program to act constructively, the academic head of the teacher education unit ideally should be a visible advocate within the institution to marshal resources.

Funding and Justification. Any successful higher education curricular restructuring requires funding for faculty deliberations, development of action plans, implementation, and evaluation. The academic administrator for a teacher education program can help in the reallocation of campus faculty development funds to support faculty retreats and institutes devoted to investigating the pedagogical value and implications of a learning community for a particular teacher education program. Reallocation of faculty development funds should also include opportunities for faculty to plan and assess an emergent learning community.

Justification for subsequent funding reallocation necessary to support restructuring through the creation of a learning community of blocked and linked courses should be clearly connected to a program's conceptual framework that articulates the importance of a multicultural emphasis. Without a connection to a program's theme or mission, such as a commitment to multicultural education reform goals, the decision to restructure into a learning community "may appear to be an expensive experiment" (Elliott & Decker, 1999, p. 26). A program should be explicit about the importance for restructuring into learning communities to expose future and current teachers to a transformative multicultural knowledge base. The strong relationship between a learning community and the development of multicultural education knowledge, dispositions, and teaching skills should be kept in the forefront of a teacher education program's deliberations and actions.

TOWARD A TRANSFORMATIVE MULTICULTURAL EDUCATION PEDAGOGY

Teaching and learning in a learning community can create conditions for teacher education students to investigate challenging multicultural issues in collaboration with their peers and faculty. This can be accomplished by consciously adopting a transformative approach to both teaching and the teacher education curriculum. Traditional concepts of pedagogical processes and texts mirror a metanarrative informed by a dominant culture's interpretation of "truth" and reality. Alternatively, a transformative multicultural education pedagogy recognizes multiple possibilities and perspectives that can inform the design and substance of a teacher education curriculum. Transformative multicultural education can create a "curriculum without borders" (McCarthy, 1998b, p. 26) as characterized by interdisciplinary fluidity and contrasting voices and experiences beyond isolated pockets of a teacher education program.

Reconceptualizing Teaching–Learning Processes

Traditional hierarchical roles between teacher educators and preservice and inservice teachers are significantly reduced in a learning community. Faculty lessen their role as experts transmitting information. Instead, faculty shift their approach to that of facilitators for teacher education student learning while simultaneously becoming co-learners with their students in a democratic, caring community. The affective, dispositional nature of multicultural education comes into curricular balance with multicultural content. Multiple perspectives are encouraged through readings, research, case studies, integrated field experiences, films, simulations, reflection, and dialogue as education students construct their own understandings and knowledge about multicultural education. When moving toward a transformative multicultural education pedagogy through restructuring for learning communities, teacher education program participants will want to consider the opportunities provided by interdisciplinary curricular themes and expanded conceptions of texts.

Interdisciplinary Curricular Themes.   Teacher education students who historically have been drawn to teaching out of their interest in children and youth and in their disciplinary field of teaching too often expect to find from their faculty cookbook solutions to the challenges surrounding teaching, learning, and schooling (see, e.g., Ginsburg, 1988). Collaborative learning from a transformative, interdisciplinary approach can dispel the notion that a single blueprint exists to make schools culturally responsive for all.

An interdisciplinary curricular approach is central to a transformative multicultural education pedagogy. Jacobs (1989) defines *interdisciplinary* as "a knowledge view and curriculum approach that consciously applies methodology and language from more than one discipline to examine a central theme, problem, topic, or experience" (p. 8). Rather than depending on a particular discipline to define a curriculum, an interdisciplinary theme becomes an organizing principle. A learning community with an interdisciplinary curriculum can try to achieve what Greene (1995) calls conditions that "provide possibilities for thematizing very diverse human experiences" (p. 182). A transformative thematic perspective "dislodges fixities, resists one-dimensionality, and allows multiple personal voices to become articulate in a more and more vital dialogue" (p. 183). For multicultural education in a theme-based, interdisciplinary curriculum, problems and topics are presented for reflection, deliberation, and potential action.

No single, fixed, essentialist answers to problems emerge when multicultural education is organized around interdisciplinary curricular themes. Multicultural topics unfold in their interdisciplinary complexities. Reflection on public school teaching experiences within an interdisciplinary curriculum can counterbalance linear and decontextualized understandings of multicultural education. Complex topics previously ignored, objectified, or given cursory attention can be integrated into multicultural education for teachers (see Hollins et al., 1994; Smith, 1998a). Racism and globalization grounded in a critical race theory perspective, as introduced in Chapter 1 and further discussed in Chapters 5 and 6, can be interwoven thematically into an interdisciplinary curriculum. Inclusion of perspectives from the liberal arts and humanities can ultimately enrich professional education studies for multicultural teacher education. When courses are blocked or linked, multicultural education concepts can be embedded more substantially within the curriculum when faculty members who plan together across their disciplines support each other in this interdisciplinary endeavor. Finally, through an interdisciplinary learning community faculty can assist preservice and in-service teachers to break down one-dimensional ideas about schooling and turn the curricular gaze to actual lived experiences of K–12 students in their schools, classrooms, and local and national communities.

Texts in a Learning Community.   The notion of texts in a learning community is broadened to include not only books but the experiences within and connected to a learning community. These may include lectures, workshops, films, and teaching experiences. Seeing these experiences as texts opens possibilities for creating a richness of dialogue and exploration. Subjectivities associated with personal perspectives on multicultural education topics find a place as texts alongside other curricular activities. Diverse voices and experiences are received as texts to be expressed, not censored by omission. Democracy in a learning community demands inclusion of multiple perspectives and ways of learning and knowing expressed as texts.

Learning community pedagogy can problematize multicultural topics that are too often found in standard teacher education textbooks as reductionist synopses of complex issues. Counteracting this situation with a deep exploration of primary texts and topics is fundamental to a learning community. This use of texts is compatible with Soder's (1996) recognition that when teachers delve into provocative texts with interdisciplinary substance, the texts' academic value to teachers at various career stages is increased. Professional development deliberations around case studies, for example, can also help teachers grapple with the challenges of group work in diverse classrooms (Darling-Hammond, 1998). However, to successfully interrogate case studies designed to stress issues arising from diversity in K–12 classroom, preservice and in-service teachers need background readings to help frame cases as well as extended time in dialogue (Shulman, Lotan, & Whitcomb, 1998). A learning community can provide a structural condition for reflective inquiry and dialogue based on texts with a multicultural perspective.

Primarily through a dependence upon survey texts, teachers are generally socialized academically into their profession from a rather narrow introduction to the social sciences. Besides missing a broad-based interdisciplinary concept of the social sciences, also lost are the humanities and arts. One means to counteract this absent link and enrich a thematic curriculum is the use of contemporary postcolonial literature by writers in former colonies of Asia, Africa, and Latin America as well as by Native Americans, African Americans, and other U.S. fiction writers of color. "Emergent discourses of multicultural education could profit," McCarthy (1998b) observes, "from a closer look at the complex ways in which literature treats issues of culture, identity, and knowledge production" (p. 149). Engagement in postcolonial literature by teacher education students with their faculty presents an additional means for enlarging understandings of community, identity, and what is valued knowledge.

Postcolonial literature decenters the schemata of preservice teachers and practitioners who may have essentialized the experiences of individuals from diverse communities by reified categorization and stereotyping. A pedagogical strength of this genre comes from exposing "a metanarrative that too often seems to doom minorities to life on the outermost borders" (Greene, 1995, p. 164). Such literature provides curricular space for a vigorous dialogue over themes of authority, privilege, freedom, culture that override binary opposition of "the West versus the third world" [and] space for the exploration of differences, not simply as a problem, but as an opportunity for a conversation over curricular reform and the radically diverse communities we now serve in the university and in schools. (McCarthy, 1998b, p. 149)

Teacher education students and faculty can advance in their collective awareness about underlying currents driving multicultural education reform by accessing a language and perspective that is frequently beyond the realm of traditional social science scholarship. Postcolonial literature and its counterpart in the United States offer an imaginative format that can capture unique, transformative multicultural viewpoints.

CONCLUSION

A transformative orientation toward multicultural education reform for teacher education has been emphasized throughout this book. In an era when standardized testing in the name of "excellence" and "standards" is on the rise and concerns about teacher shortages abound, teacher education programs are increasingly under pressure to disregard attempts to help teachers acquire a knowledge base in the social foundations of education. Indeed, teacher education programs are being pushed toward more fast-track models of preparation that focus mainly on teaching techniques disconnected from cultural contexts. Dominant cultural and political forces perceive interrelated multicultural education topics such as democracy, racism, economic globalization, social justice, and equity as superfluous to the foundational knowledge of a teacher. The result can be an incomplete and culturally biased teacher education in which children of color and those from low-income communities are objectified as problems to solve while children approximating a White middle-class norm are seen as the children to teach (see Gomez, 1996).

A transformative approach demands at a minimum analyzing a teacher education program to determine the extent to which its curricular practices are simply replicating status quo notions of "diversity" that leave unchallenged the implicit assumptions undergirding power relationships. The aim should be movement toward a transformed curriculum that seeks to infuse multicultural education reform throughout the experiences of preservice and in-service teachers. Ultimately, a transformed teacher education curriculum engages teachers in aspects of social action that can pedagogically benefit all K–12 students (Banks, 1993a, 2000).

Learning communities for multicultural education created through teacher education restructuring offer a means for developing reflective and knowledge-based conditions for transformation. A learning community provides an alternative approach for teachers to seriously investigate and internalize multicultural concepts. Long-standing higher education curricular structures can undermine transformative multicultural education. Rather than "working around the system," teacher education reform necessitates fundamental institutional restructuring. Teacher educators can elect to start with a manageable pilot project guided by careful planning, pedagogical experimentation, and multiple assessments. Restructuring should seek a balance between deepening multicultural content knowledge and creating teacher candidate time for necessary attitudinal expression, exploration, and development. A learning community can be a curricular means for teachers to investigate their racial and global identity formation as it pertains to K–12 teaching and learning (see Chapters 5, 6).

Teacher educators can choose professionally and personally to make a long-term commitment to develop sustainable structures within a teacher education program for multicultural education practices to flower. To avoid the hard and sometimes difficult conversations that should ensue with teacher education colleagues may result in "casually perpetuating tired practices of yesterday" that Goodlad (1990, p. 67) encountered in his study of teacher education programs. "In the face of rampant carelessness and alienation and fragmentation," Greene (1995) encourages teacher educators to keep "visions of possibilities before our eyes" (p. 197). By holding a focus on long-range goals of multicultural education reform, a teacher education program for preservice and in-service teachers can invest itself in a moral enterprise in helping teachers be culturally responsive to the children they serve.

Notes

Chapter 2

1. See, for example, Grant and Secada's (1990) "Preparing Teachers for Diversity"; Grant's (1993) "The Multicultural Preparation of US Teachers: Some Hard Truths"; Gollnick and Chinn's (1994) *Multicultural Education in a Pluralistic Society*; Sleeter and Grant's (1999) *Making Choices for Multicultural Education*; Hollins, King, and Hayman's (1994) *Teaching Diverse Populations: Formulating a Knowledge Base*; Kanpol and McLaren's (1995) collection *Critical Multiculturalism: Uncommon Voices in a Common Struggle*; Larkin and Sleeter's (1995) *Developing Multicultural Teacher Education Curricula*; Sleeter and McLaren's (1995) *Multicultural Education, Critical Pedagogy, and the Politics of Difference*; Kincheloe and Steinberg's (1997) *Changing Multiculturalism*; Irvine's (1997) *Critical Knowledge for Diverse Teachers and Learners*; Dilworth's (1992) *Diversity in Teacher Education: New Expectations* and (1998) *Being Responsive to Cultural Differences: How Teachers Learn*; García's (1999) *Student Cultural Diversity: Understanding and Meeting the Challenge*; Smith's (1998a) *Common Sense about Uncommon Knowledge: Knowledge Bases for Diversity*; Banks's (1991) *Teaching Strategies for Ethnic Studies*, (1993a) "Approaches to Multicultural Curriculum Reform," (1993b) "The Canon Debate, Knowledge Construction, and Multicultural Education," (1993d) "Multicultural Education: Historical Development, Dimensions, and Practice," (1994) *An Introduction to Multicultural Education*, (1995) "The Historical Reconstruction of Knowledge about Race: Implications for Transformative Teaching," and (1998) "The Lives and Values of Researchers: Implications for Educating Citizens in a Multicultural World"; and Banks and Banks's (1995) *Handbook of Research on Multicultural Education* and (1997) *Multicultural Education: Issues and Perspectives*.

2. As related to "Levels of Integration of Multicultural Content" (Banks, 1993a), a common content analysis function was utilized by describing "the relative frequency and importance of certain topics" (Anderson, 1990, p. 121). Realizing that categories may overlap (Banks, 1993a), analysts sought to differentiate among the instructional approaches for inclusion of multicultural education concepts. Comments of student teachers and cooperating teachers were categorized on the basis of the commonality of their instructional purpose and activity to Banks's approaches. Similar strategies were used for all three of the studies (Vavrus, 1994; Vavrus & Ozcan, 1996; Vavrus & Ozcan, 1998).

Chapter 3

1. Valli and Rennert-Ariev (2000) compared recommendations of the National Commission on Teaching and America's Future to those from the Carnegie Forum on Education and the Economy, The Holmes Group, Center for Educational Renewal, Na-

tional Commission for Excellence in Teacher Education, National Council for the Accreditation of Teacher Education, Project 30 Alliance, Renaissance Group, The Teacher Education Initiative of the National Education Association, and the Teacher Education Accreditation Council (see pp. 7–9).

Chapter 5

1. Harris (1993) uses the phrase "white supremacy" while acknowledging that she does "not mean to allude only to the self-conscious racism of white supremacist groups" (p. 1714, fn. 10). However, the use of White *supremacy* can detract from analyses of racisms for Whites who consider themselves color-blind (Daniels, 1997). For that reason, my preference for clarity of meaning and intent is to use the term White *privilege* rather than White supremacy.

2. Although the focus here is on the concept of racialized positionalities underlying teacher identity formation, other markers of positionality such as ethnic groupings, gender, class, handicapping conditions, and sexual orientation also influence identity (Banks, 1993b; Grant & Ladson-Billings, 1997).

Chapter 6

1. According to a 2000 Pew Research Center for the People & the Press survey conducted by Princeton Survey Research Associates, only 28% of U.S. citizens believe that "promoting and defending human rights in other countries" should be a top U.S. trade priority, and 23% feel that way when it comes to "helping improve the living standards in developing nations" (PollingReport.com, 2001).

2. Prior to 1492, interregional economic systems were the primary systems of planetary relationships. The exponential expansion of European colonialism is evident by the 17th century (Arrighi, 1994; Dussel, 1995, 1998; Wallerstein, 1999).

3. The author served as a teacher education representative on the Iowa Education Strategic Planning Committee from 1991 to 1993, during which time these deliberations were undertaken.

References

Adams, D.W. (1995). *Education for extinction: American Indians and the boarding school experience, 1875–1928*. Lawrence: University Press of Kansas.

Adams, M., Bell, L.A., & Griffin, P. (Eds.). (1997). *Teaching for diversity and social justice: A sourcebook*. New York: Routledge.

Alfieri, A.V. (1997). Black and white. *California Law Review, 85*(5), 1647–1686.

Allport, G.W. (1954). *The nature of prejudice*. Reading, MA: Addison-Wesley.

Althusser, L. (1971). *Lenin and philosophy and other essays* (B. Brewster, Trans.). London: New Left Books.

Ambrosio, A.L. (2000, November). *Final report on the multicultural/diversity lesson plan requirement in teacher education*. Paper presented at Emporia State University's National Conference on Assessment of Multicultural/Diversity Outcomes, Kansas City, MO.

American Anthropological Association. (1998, May 17). American Anthropological Association statement on "race." [On-line]. Available: http://www.aaanet.org/stmts/racepp.htm

American Association of Physical Anthropology. (1996). AAPA statement on biological aspect of race. [On-line]. Available: http://www.physanth.org.positions/race.html

American Council on Education. (1999). *To touch the future: Transforming the way teachers are taught*. Washington, DC: Author.

Anderson, G. (1990). *Fundamentals of educational research*. New York: The Falmer Press.

Anderson, G.L. (1998). Toward authentic participation: Deconstructing the discourses of participatory reforms in education. *American Educational Research Journal, 35*(4), 571–603.

Angier, N. (2000, August 22). Do races differ? Not really, DNA shows. *New York Times*. [On-line]. Available: http://www.nytimes.com/library/national/science/082200sci-genetics-race.html

Anyon, J. (1994). The retreat of Marxism and socialist feminism: Postmodern and post-structural theories in education. *Curriculum Inquiry, 24*(2), 115–133.

Apple, M.W. (1993). *Official knowledge: Democratic education in a conservative age*. New York: Routledge.

Apple, M.W. (1996). Power, meaning, and identity: Critical sociology of education in the United States. *British Journal of Sociology of Education, 17*(2), 125–144.

Apple, M.W. (2001). Markets, standards, teaching, and teacher education. *Journal of Teacher Education, 52*(3), 182–196.

Archibald, O.Y. (1998). *Ideology and the essay*. Unpublished doctoral dissertation, University of Iowa, Iowa City.

Armaline, W.D. (1995). Reflecting on cultural diversity through early field experiences:

Pitfalls, hesitations, and promise. In R.J. Martin (Ed.), *Practicing what we teach: Confronting diversity in teacher education* (pp. 163–180). Albany: State University of New York Press.

Aronowitz, S., & DeFazio, W. (1997). The new knowledge of work. In P. Brown, A.H. Halsey, H. Lauder, & A.S. Wells (Eds.), *Education: Culture, economy, and society* (pp. 193–206). Oxford, UK: Oxford University Press.

Arrighi, G. (1994). *The long twentieth century: Money, power, and the origins of our times.* London: Verso.

Athanasiou, T. (1996). *Divided planet: The ecology of rich and poor.* Boston: Little, Brown.

Au, W. (1999, November). *A teacher's perspective on AACTE's "No One Model American" statement.* Paper presented at the annual meeting of the National Association for Multicultural Education, San Diego, CA.

Au, W. (2000). Thinking about the WTO. *Rethinking Schools, 14*(3), 4–5.

Bakari, R. (2001, April). *Preservice teacher attitudes toward teaching African American students: Contemporary research.* Paper presented at the annual meeting of the American Educational Research Association, Seattle, WA.

Bales, K. (1999). *Disposable people: New slavery in the global economy.* Berkeley: University of California Press.

Banks, C.A.M. (1996). Intellectual leadership and African American challenges to meta-narratives. In J.A. Banks (Ed.), *Multicultural education, transformative knowledge, and action: Historical and contemporary perspectives* (pp. 46–63). New York: Teachers College Press.

Banks, J.A. (1991). *Teaching strategies for ethnic studies* (5th ed.). Boston: Allyn and Bacon.

Banks, J.A. (1993a). Approaches to multicultural curriculum reform. In J.A. Banks & C.A.M. Banks (Eds.), *Multicultural education: Issues and perspectives* (2nd ed., pp. 195–214). Boston: Allyn and Bacon.

Banks, J.A. (1993b). The canon debate, knowledge construction, and multicultural education. *Educational Researcher, 22*(5), 4–14.

Banks, J.A. (1993c). Multicultural education: Characteristics and goals. In J.A. Banks & C.A.M. Banks (Eds.), *Multicultural education: Issues and perspectives* (2nd ed., pp. 3–28). Boston: Allyn and Bacon.

Banks, J.A. (1993d). Multicultural education: Historical development, dimensions, and practice. In L. Darling-Hammond (Ed.), *Review of research in education 19* (pp. 3–49). Washington, DC: American Educational Research Association.

Banks, J.A. (1994). *An introduction to multicultural education.* Boston: Allyn and Bacon.

Banks, J.A. (1995). The historical reconstruction of knowledge about race: Implications for transformative teaching. *Educational Researcher, 24*(2), 15–25.

Banks, J.A. (Ed.). (1996). *Multicultural education, transformative knowledge, and action: Historical and contemporary perspectives.* New York: Teachers College Press.

Banks, J.A. (1997). *Educating citizens in a multicultural society.* New York: Teachers College Press.

Banks, J.A. (1998). The lives and values of researchers: Implications for educating citizens in a multicultural world. *Educational Researcher, 27*(7), 4–17.

Banks, J.A. (2000). The social construction of difference and the quest for educational equality. In R.S. Brandt (Ed.), *Education in a new era* (Yearbook 2000, pp. 21–45). Alexandria, VA: Association for Supervision and Curriculum Development.

Banks, J.A. (2001a). Citizenship education and diversity: Implications for teacher education. *Journal of Teacher Education, 52*(1), 5–16.

Banks, J.A. (2001b). *Cultural diversity and education: Foundations, curriculum, and teaching* (4th ed.). Boston: Allyn and Bacon.

Banks, J.A. (2001c). Multicultural education: Goals, possibilities, and challenges. In C.F. Diaz (Ed.), *Multicultural education for the 21st century* (pp. 11–22). New York: Longman.

Banks, J.A., & Banks, C.A.M. (Eds.). (1995). *Handbook of research on multicultural education*. New York: Macmillan.

Banks, J.A., & Banks, C.A.M. (1997). Glossary. In J.A. Banks & C.A.M. Banks (Eds.), *Multicultural education: Issues and perspectives* (3rd ed., pp. 433–436). Boston: Allyn and Bacon.

Banks, J.A., & Banks, C.A.M. (Eds.). (1997). *Multicultural education: Issues and perspectives* (3rd ed.). Boston: Allyn and Bacon.

Banks, J.A., Cookson, P., Gay, G., Hawley, W.D., Irvine, J.J., Nieto, S., Schofield, J.W., & Stephan, W.G. (2001). *Diversity within unity: Essential principles for teaching and learning in a multicultural society*. Seattle: Center for Multicultural Education, University of Washington.

Baptiste, H.P., Jr., Baptiste, M., & Gollnick, D.M. (1980). *Multicultural teacher education: Preparing educators to provide educational equity*. Washington, DC: American Association of Colleges for Teacher Education.

Barnes, N. (2000, January 19). Teachers teaching teachers. *Education Week*, pp. 38, 42.

Barreto, R.M. (1997). Reform in teacher education through the CLAD/BCLAD policy: A critique. *Multicultural Education, 5*(2), 11–15.

Bassey, M.O. (1996). Teachers as cultural brokers in the midst of diversity. *Educational Foundations, 10*(2), 37–52.

Battistich, V., Solomon, D., Kim, D., Watson, M., & Schaps, E. (1995). Schools as communities, poverty levels of student populations, and student attitudes, motives, and performance: A multilevel analysis. *American Educational Research Journal, 32*(3), 627–658.

Bell, D.A., Jr. (1995a). *Brown vs. Board of Education* and the interest convergence dilemma. In K. Crenshaw, N. Gotanda, G. Peller, K. Thomas (Eds.), *Critical race theory: The key writings that formed the movement* (pp. 20–29). New York: The New Press.

Bell, D.A., Jr. (1995b). Racial realism. In K. Crenshaw, N. Gotanda, G. Peller, & K. Thomas (Eds.), *Critical race theory: The key writings that formed the movement* (pp. 302–312). New York: The New Press.

Bennett, C. (1989, March). *Preservice multicultural teacher education: Predictors of student readiness*. Paper presented at the annual meeting of the American Educational Research Association, San Francisco. (ERIC Document Reproduction Service No. ED 308 161)

Bennett, C.I. (1999). *Comprehensive multicultural education: Theory and practice* (4th ed.). Boston: Allyn and Bacon.

Bernstein, N. (2000, February 1). Study documents homelessness in America children each year. *New York Times*, p. A12.

Best, S., & Kellner, D. (1997). *The postmodern turn*. New York: The Guilford Press.

Beyer, L.E. (Ed.). (1996). *Creating democratic classrooms: The struggle to integrate theory and practice*. New York: Teachers College Press.

Beyer, L.E., & Zeichner, K. (1987). Teacher education in cultural context: Beyond reproduction. In T. Popkewitz (Ed.), *Critical studies in teacher education* (pp. 298–334). Philadelphia: Falmer Press.

Bhopal, R., & Rankin, J. (1999). Concepts and terminology in ethnicity, race, and health: Be aware of the ongoing debate. *British Dental Journal, 186*(10), 483–484.

Bigelow, B. (Ed.). (1997). *Rethinking Columbus: Teaching about the 500th anniversary of Columbus's arrival in America*. Milwaukee, WI: Rethinking Schools.

Bigelow, B. (1999, Summer). Standards and multiculturalism. *Rethinking Schools, 13*(4), 6–7.

Blackmon, D.A. (2001, July 16). Hard time: From Alabama's past, capitalism and racism in a cruel partnership. *The Wall Street Journal*, pp. A1, A10.

Blewett, L.L. (2000). *White antiracist identity: A communication case study*. Unpublished doctoral dissertation, University of Illinois, Urbana-Champaign.

Bliss, I. (1990). Intercultural education and the professional knowledge of teachers. *European Journal of Teacher Education, 13*(3), 141–151.

Blum, L. (1999). What is "racism" in antiracist education? *Teachers College Record, 100*(4), 860–880.

Bollin, G.G., & Finkel, J. (1995). White racial identity as a barrier to understanding diversity: A study of preservice teachers. *Equity & Excellence in Education, 28*(1), 25–30.

Bonnett, A. (2000). *Anti-racism*. New York: Routledge.

Bourdieu, P. (1998). A reasoned utopia and economic fatalism. *New Left Review* (227), 125–130.

Bowers, C.A. (1977). Emergent ideological characteristics of educational policy. *Teachers College Record, 79*(1), 33–54.

Bowles, S., & Gintis, H. (1976). *Schooling in capitalist America: Educational reform and the contradictions of economic life*. New York: Basic Books.

Bowman, D.H. (2000, September 20). Most states don't limit schools' business deals, GAO reports. *Education Week*, p. 7.

Boyer, J.B. (1990). Teacher education that enhances equity. In H.P. Baptitste, Jr., H.C. Waxman, J. Walker de Felix, & J.E. Anderson (Eds.), *Leadership, equity, and school effectiveness* (pp. 57–92). Hillsdale, NJ: Lawrence Erlbaum.

Bradley, A. (1995, January 25). Urban study faults teacher-development programs. *Education Week*, p. 3.

Brinkley, J. (2000, April 2). Vast trade in forced labor portrayed in C.I.A. report. *New York Times*, p. A18.

Britzman, D.P. (2000). Teacher education in the confusion of our times. *Journal of Teacher Education, 51*(3), 200–205.

Bronfenbrenner, K. (2000). *Uneasy terrain: The impact of capital mobility on workers, wages, and union organizing*. Ithaca, NY: Cornell University, New York School of Industrial and Labor Relations.

Brooks, R.L., & Newborn, M.J. (1994). Critical race theory and classical-liberal civil rights scholarship: A distinction without a difference? *California Law Review*, *82*(4), 787–845.

Brown, P., Halsey, A.H., Lauder, H., & Wells, A.S. (1997). The transformation of education and society: An introduction. In P. Brown, A.H. Halsey, H. Lauder, & A.S. Wells (Eds.), *Education: Culture, economy, and society* (pp. 1–44). Oxford, UK: Oxford University Press.

Brown, P., & Lauder, H. (1997). Education, globalization, and economic development. In P. Brown, A.H. Halsey, H. Lauder, & A.S. Wells (Eds.), *Education: Culture, economy, and society* (pp. 172–192). Oxford, UK: Oxford University Press.

Brown, P., & Lauder, H. (2001). *Capitalism and social progress: The future of society in the global economy.* New York: Palgrave.

Brown, S.C., & Kysilka, M.L. (1994). In search of multicultural and global education in real classrooms. *Journal of Curriculum and Supervision*, *9*(3), 313–316.

Bruner, J.S. (1971). *The relevance of education.* New York: W.W. Norton.

Buchmann, M., & Floden, R. (1992, December). Coherence, the rebel angel. *Educational Researcher*, *21*(9), 4–9.

Burbach, R., Núñez, O., & Kagarlitsky, B. (1997). *Globalization and its discontents: The rise of postmodern socialism.* Chicago: Pluto Press.

Calderwood, P. (2000). *Learning community: Finding common ground in difference.* New York: Teachers College Press.

Carlson, D. (1997). *Making progress: Education and culture in new times.* New York: Teachers College Press.

Carnoy, M. (1997). The great work dilemma: Education, employment, and wages in the new global economy. *Economics of Education Review*, *16*(3), 247–254.

Carter, R.T. (1997). Is white a race? Expressions of white racial identity. In M. Fine, L. Weis, L.C. Powell, & L.M. Wong (Eds.), *Off white: Readings on race, power, and society* (pp. 198–209). New York: Routledge.

Carter, R.T., & Goodwin, A.L. (1994). Racial identity and education. In L. Darling-Hammond (Ed.), *Review of research in education 20* (pp. 291–336). Washington, DC: American Educational Research Association.

Castenell, L.A., Jr., & Pinar, W.F. (1993). Introduction. In L.A. Castenell, Jr., & W.F. Pinar (Eds.), *Understanding curriculum as racial text: Representations of identity and difference in education* (pp. 1–30). Albany: State University of New York Press.

Causey, V.E., Thomas, C.D., & Armento, B.J. (2000). Cultural diversity is basically a foreign term to me: The challenge of diversity for preservice teacher education. *Teaching and Teacher Education*, *16*(1), 33–45.

Chan, S., & East, P. (1998). Teacher education and race equality: A focus on an induction course for primary BEd students. *Multicultural Teaching*, *16*(2), 43–46.

Chang, G. (2000). *Disposable domestics: Immigrant women workers in the global economy.* Cambridge, MA: South End Press.

Cherryholmes, C.H. (1988). *Power and criticism: Poststructural investigations in education.* New York: Teachers College Press.

Chomsky, N. (1998). Free trade and free market: Pretense and practice. In F. Jameson &

M. Miyoshi (Eds.), *The cultures of globalization* (pp. 356–370). Durham, NC: Duke University Press.

Chomsky, N. (1999). *Profit over people: Neoliberalism and global order.* New York: Seven Stories Press.

Chossudovsky, M. (1997). *The globalization of poverty: Impacts of IMP and World Bank reforms.* Penang, Malaysia: Third World Network.

Christensen, L. (1990). Teaching standard English: Whose standard? *English Journal, 79*(2), 36–40.

Clark, C., & Medina, C. (2000). How reading and writing literacy narratives affect pre-service teachers' understanding of literacy, pedagogy, and multiculturalism. *Journal of Teacher Education, 51*(1), 63–76.

Clark, C., & O'Donnell, J. (1999). Rearticulating a racial identity: Creating oppositional spaces to fight for equality and social justice. In C. Clark & J. O'Donnell (Eds.), *Becoming and unbecoming white: Owning and disowning a racial identity* (pp. 1–9). Westport, CT: Bergin & Garvey.

Clifford, G.J., & Guthrie, J.W. (1988). *Ed school: A brief for professional education.* Chicago: The University of Chicago Press.

Cochran-Smith, M. (1995a). Color blindness and basket making are not the answers: Confronting the dilemmas of race, culture, and language diversity in teacher education. *American Educational Research Journal, 32*(3), 493–522.

Cochran-Smith, M. (1995b). Uncertain allies: Understanding the boundaries of race and teaching. *Harvard Educational Review, 65*(4), 541–570.

Cochran-Smith, M. (1997). Knowledge, skills, and experiences for teaching culturally diverse learners: A perspective for practicing teachers. In J.J. Irvine (Ed.), *Critical knowledge for diverse teachers and learners* (pp. 27–87). Washington, DC: American Association of Colleges for Teacher Education.

Cochran-Smith, M. (2000). Blind vision: Unlearning racism in teacher education. *Harvard Educational Review, 72*(2), 157–190.

Cohen, E.G. (1994). *Designing group instruction: Strategies for the heterogeneous classroom* (2nd ed.). New York: Teachers College Press.

Collins, C., Leondar-Wright, B., & Sklar, H. (1999). *Shifting fortunes: The perils of the growing American wealth gap.* Boston: United for a Fair Economy.

Collins, R.L. (1993). Responding to cultural diversity in our schools. In L.A. Castenell, Jr., & W.F. Pinar (Eds.), *Understanding curriculum as racial text: Representations of identity and differences in education* (pp. 195–208). Albany: State University of New York.

Comer, J.P. (1980). *School power: Implications of an intervention project.* New York: Free Press.

Comer, J.P. (Ed.). (1996). *Rallying the whole village: The Comer process for reforming education.* New York: Teachers College Press.

Conoley, J.C. (1989). Professional communication and collaboration among educators. In M.C. Reynolds (Ed.), *Knowledge base for the beginning teacher* (pp. 245–54). Oxford, UK: Pergamon Press.

Cortéz, C.E. (2000). *The children are watching: How the media teach about diversity.* New York: Teachers College Press.

Council of Chief State School Officers. (1999, Fall). INTASC launches new teacher preparation project. *INTASC in Focus, 2*(1), 3.

Council of Chief State School Officers. (2002). Interstate New Teacher Assessment and Support Consortium. [On-line]. Available: http://www.ccsso.org/intasc.html

Council of Learned Societies in Education. (1996). *Standards for academic and professional instruction in foundations of education, educational studies, and educational policy studies* (2nd ed.). San Francisco: Caddo Gap Press.

Crenshaw, K.W. (1995). Race, reform, and retrenchment: Transformation and legitimation in antidiscrimination law. In K. Crenshaw, N. Gotanda, G. Peller, K. Thomas (Eds.), *Critical race theory: The key writings that formed the movement* (pp. 103–122). New York: The New Press.

Crenshaw, K.W. (1997). Color-blind dreams and racial nightmares: Reconfiguring racism in the post-civil rights era. In T. Morrison & C.B. Lacour (Eds.), *Birth of a nation'hood: Gaze, script, and spectacle in the O.J. Simpson case* (pp. 97–168). New York: Pantheon.

Crenshaw, K.W. (1998). Color blindness, history, and the law. In W. Lubiano (Ed.), *The house that race built* (pp. 280–288). New York: Vintage Books.

Crenshaw, K., Gotanda, N., Peller G., & Thomas K. (Eds.). (1995a). *Critical race theory: The key writings that formed the movement.* New York: The New Press.

Crenshaw, K., Gotanda, N., Peller G., & Thomas, K. (1995b). Introduction. In K. Crenshaw, N. Gotanda, G. Peller, K. Thomas (Eds.), *Critical race theory: The key writings that formed the movement* (pp.xii–xxxii). New York: The New Press.

Crossette, B. (2001, July 11). Rights leaders urge Powell to attend U.N. racism conference. *New York Times*, p. A8.

Cunat, M. (1996). Vision, vitality, and values: Advocating the democratic classroom. In L.E. Beyer (Ed.), *Creating democratic classrooms: The struggle to integrate theory and practice* (pp. 127–149). New York: Teachers College Press.

Cvetkovich, A., & Kellner, D. (Eds.). (1997a). *Articulating the global and the local: Globalization and cultural studies.* Boulder, CO: Westview Press.

Cvetkovich, A., & Kellner, D. (1997b). Introduction: Thinking global and local. In A. Cvetkovich & D. Kellner (Eds.), *Articulating the global and the local: Globalization and cultural studies* (pp. 1–30). Boulder, CO: Westview Press.

Daniels, J. (1997). *White lies, race, class, gender in white supremacist discourse.* New York: Routledge.

Danielson, C. (1996). *Enhancing professional practice: A framework for teaching.* Alexandria, VA: Association for Supervision and Curriculum Development.

Darling-Hammond, L. (1992, July). *Standards of practice for learner-centered schools.* New York: National Center for Restructuring Education, Schools, and Teaching, Columbia University.

Darling-Hammond, L. (1994). Who will speak for the children? How "Teach for America" hurts urban schools and students. *Phi Delta Kappan, 76*(1), 21–34.

Darling-Hammond, L. (1997a). *Doing what matters most: Investing in quality teaching.* New York: National Commission on Teaching and America's Future.

Darling-Hammond, L. (1997b). Restructuring schools for student success. In P. Brown, A.H. Halsey, H. Lauder, & A.S. Wells (Eds.), *Education: Culture, economy, and society* (pp. 332–337). Oxford, UK: Oxford University Press.

Darling-Hammond, L. (1998). Foreword. In J.H. Shulman, R.A. Lotan, & J.A. Whitcomb (Eds.), *Facilitators guide to groupwork in diverse classrooms: A casebook for educators* (pp. vii-viii). New York: Teachers College Press.

Darling-Hammond, L. (2000a). Foreword. *Studies of excellence in teacher education: Preparation in a five-year program* (pp. v–xi). Washington, DC: American Association of Colleges for Teacher Education.

Darling-Hammond, L. (2000b). Foreword. *Studies of excellence in teacher education: Preparation at the graduate level* (pp. v–xi). Washington, DC: American Association of Colleges for Teacher Education.

Darling-Hammond, L. (2000c). Foreword. *Studies of excellence in teacher education: Preparation in the undergraduate years* (pp. v–xi). Washington, DC: American Association of Colleges for Teacher Education.

Darling-Hammond, L., Ancess, J., & Falk, B. (1995). *Authentic assessment in action: Studies of schools and students at work*. New York: Teachers College Press.

Darling-Hammond, L., & Macdonald, M.B. (2000). Where there is learning there is hope: The preparation of teachers at the Bank Street College of Education. In L. Darling-Hammond (Ed.), *Studies in excellence in teacher education: Preparation at the graduate level* (pp. 1–95). Washington, DC: American Association of Colleges for Teacher Education.

Darling-Hammond, L., & McLaughlin, M.W. (1999). Investing in teaching as a learning profession: Policy problems and prospects. In L. Darling-Hammond & G. Sykes (Eds.), *Teaching as the learning profession: Handbook of policy and practice* (pp. 376–411). San Francisco: Jossey-Bass.

Delgado, R. (Ed.). (1995a). *Critical race theory: The cutting edge*. Philadelphia: Temple University Press.

Delgado, R. (1995b). Introduction. In R. Delgado (Ed.), *Critical race theory: The cutting edge* (pp. xiii–xvi). Philadelphia: Temple University Press.

Deloria, V., & Lytle, C.M. (1984). *The nations within: The past and future of American Indian sovereignty*. New York: Pantheon.

Delpit, L.D. (1995). *Other people's children: Cultural conflict in the classroom*. New York: W.W. Norton.

deMarrais, K.B., & LeCompte, M.D. (1995). *The way schools work: A sociological analysis of education* (2nd ed.). White Plains, NY: Longman.

Derman-Sparks, L. (1998). Educating for equality: Forging a shared vision. In E. Lee, D. Menkart, & M. Okazawa-Rey (Eds.), *Beyond heroes and holidays: A practical guide to K–12 anti-racist, multicultural education and staff development* (pp. 2–6). Washington, DC: Network of Educators of Americas.

Derman-Sparks, L., & Phillips, C.B. (1997). *Teaching/learning anti-racism: A developmental approach*. New York: Teachers College Press.

Dewey, J. (1916). *Democracy and education: An introduction to the philosophy of education*. New York: Macmillan.

Dewey, J. (1974). *Experience and education*. New York: Collier Books. (Original work published 1938)

Deyle, D., & Swisher, K. (1997). Research in American and Alaska native education: From assimilation to self-determination. In M.W. Apple (Ed.), *Review of research in education 22* (pp. 113–194). Washington, DC: American Educational Research Association.

Diaz, C., Massialas, B.G., & Xanthopoulos, J.A. (1999). *Global perspectives for educators*. Boston: Allyn and Bacon.

Dilworth, M.E. (Ed.). (1992). *Diversity in teacher education: New expectations*. San Francisco: Jossey-Bass.

Dilworth, M.E. (Ed.). (1998). *Being responsive to cultural differences: How teachers learn*. Thousand Oaks, CA: Corwin Press.

Dorman, P. (1997). The publicly controlled economy: Crisis and renewal. *The Legal Studies Forum, 21*(1), 87–128.

Dorman, P. (2000). Actually existing globalization. In P.S. Aulakh & M.G. Schechter (Eds.), *Rethinking globalization(s): From corporate transnationalism to local interventions* (pp. 32–55). New York: St. Martin's Press.

Duesterberg, L.M. (1999). Theorizing race in the context of learning to teach. *Teachers College Record, 100*(4), 751–775.

Dussel, E. (1995). *The invention of the Americas: Eclipse of "the other" and the myth of modernity* (M.D. Barber, Trans.). New York: Continuum.

Dussel, E. (1998). Beyond Eurocentrism: The world-system and the limits of modernity (E. Mendieta, Trans.). In F. Jameson & M. Miyoshi (Eds.), *The cultures of globalization* (pp. 3–31). Durham, NC: Duke University Press.

Dyson, M.E. (1994). Essentialism and the complexities of racial identity. In D.T. Goldberg (Ed.), *Multiculturalism: A critical reader* (pp. 218–229). Cambridge, MA: Blackwell.

Edler, J., & Irons, B. (1998). Distancing behaviors often used by white people. In E. Lee, D. Menkart, & M. Okazawa-Rey (Eds.), *Beyond heroes and holidays: A practical guide to K-12 anti-racist, multicultural education and staff development* (p. 114). Washington, DC: Network of Educators of Americas.

Elliott, J.L., & Decker, E. (1999). Garnering the fundamental resources for learning communities. In J.H. Levine (Ed.), *Learning communities: New structures, new partnerships for learning* (Monograph No. 26, pp. 19–28). Columbia: University of South Carolina, National Resource Center for The First-Year Experience and Students in Transition.

Ellsworth, E. (1997). Double binds of whiteness. In M. Fine, L. Weis, L.C. Powell, & L.M. Wong (Eds.), *Off white: Readings on race, power, and society* (pp. 259–269). New York: Routledge.

Engel, M. (2000). *The struggle for control of public education*. Philadelphia: Temple University Press.

Epstein, T. (2000). Adolescents' perceptions of racial diversity in U.S. history: Case studies from an urban classroom. *American Educational Research Journal, 37*(1), 185–214.

Erickson, F. (1997). Culture in society and educational practices. In J.A. Banks & C.A.M. Banks (Eds.), *Multicultural education: Issues and perspectives* (3rd ed., pp. 32–60). Boston: Allyn and Bacon.

Esposito, L., & Murphy, J.W. (2000). Another step in the study of race relations. *The Sociological Quarterly, 41*(2), 171–187.

Estrada, K., & McLaren, P. (1993). A dialogue on multiculturalism and democratic culture. *Educational Researcher, 22*(3), 27–33.

Evans, E.D., Torrey, C.C., & Newton, S.D. (1997). Multicultural education requirements in teacher certification: A national survey. *Multicultural Education, 4*(3), 9–11.

The Evergreen State College. (1998). *Response to state of Washington 1997 program approval standards*. Olympia, WA: Author.

The Evergreen State College. (2000). *Student teaching handbook*. Olympia, WA: Author.

The Evergreen State College. (2001). *Master in teaching program* (catalog). Olympia, WA: Author.

Fendler, L. (1999). Making trouble: Prediction, agency, and critical intellectuals. In T.S. Popkewitz & L. Fendler (Eds.), *Critical theories in education: Changing terrains of knowledge and politics* (pp. 169–188). New York: Routledge.

Fennimore, B.S. (2001). Historical white resistance to equity in public education: A challenge to white teacher educators. In S.H. King & L.A. Castenell (Eds.), *Racism and racial inequality: Implications for teacher education* (pp. 43–49). Washington, DC: American Association of Colleges for Teacher Education.

Finney, S., & Orr, J. (1995). "I've really learned a lot, but . . . ": Cross-cultural understanding and teacher education in a racist society. *Journal of Teacher Education, 46*(5), 327–33.

Flagg, B.J. (1998). *Was blind, but now I see: White race consciousness and the law*. New York: New York University Press.

Floden, R. (1997). Communication: Reflection and implications. In D.M. Byrd & D.J. McIntyre (Eds.), *Research on the education of our nation's teachers: Teacher education yearbook V* (pp. 277–284). Thousand Oaks, CA: Corwin Press.

Floden, R.E., & Buchmann, M. (1993). Between routines and anarchy: Preparing teachers for uncertainty. In M. Buchmann & R.E. Floden (Eds.), *Detachment and concern: Conversations in the philosophy of teaching and teacher education* (Advances in Contemporary Thought, Vol. 11, pp. 211–221). New York: Teachers College Press.

Ford, T. (1999). *Becoming multicultural: Personal and social construction through critical teaching*. New York: Falmer Press.

Fox, H. (1999). Residential college social science program 360: Unteaching racism. *Composition Studies, 27*(1), 31–59.

Frank, T. (2000, October 30). The rise of market populism: America's new secular religion. *The Nation, 271*(13), 13–19.

Freire, P. (1970). *Pedagogy of the oppressed* (M.B. Ramos, Trans.). New York: Seabury Press.

Freire, P. (1998). *Teachers as cultural workers: Letters to those who dare teach* (D. Macedo, D. Koike, & A. Oliveira, Trans.). Boulder, CO: Westview Press.

Fullan, M.G. (1990). Staff development, innovation, and institutional development. In B. Joyce (Ed.), *Changing school culture through staff development* (pp. 3–25). Alexandria, VA: Association for Supervision and Curriculum Development.

Fullan, M., Galluzzo, G., Morris, P., & Watson, N. (1998). *The rise and stall of teacher education reform*. Washington, DC: American Association of Colleges for Teacher Education.

Gabelnick, F., MacGregor, J., Matthews, R.S., & Smith, B.L. (1990). *Learning communities: Creating connections among students, faculty, and disciplines.* San Francisco: Jossey-Bass.

Gallavan, N.P., Troutman, P.L, & Jones, W.P. (2001). Cultural diversity and the NCATE standards: A story in process. *Multicultural Perspectives, 3*(2), 13–18.

García, E. (1996). Preparing instructional professionals for linguistically and culturally diverse students. In J. Skula, T.J. Buttery, & E. Guyton (Eds.), *Handbook of research on teacher education* (2nd ed., pp. 802–813). New York: Simon & Schuster Macmillan.

García, E. (1999). *Student cultural diversity: Understanding and meeting the challenge* (2nd ed.). Boston: Houghton Mifflin.

García, J., & Pugh, S. L. (1992). Multicultural education in teacher preparation programs: A political or an educational concept? *Phi Delta Kappan, 74*(3), 214–219.

Garcia, R.L. (2001). Educating for human rights. In C.F. Diaz (Ed.), *Multicultural education for the 21st century* (pp. 208–216). New York: Longman.

García Canclini, N. (1995). *Hybrid cultures: Strategies for entering and leaving modernity* (C.L. Chiappari & S.L. López, Trans.). Minneapolis: University of Minnesota Press.

Gardner, H. (1993). *Frames of mind: The theory of multiple intelligences* (2nd ed.). New York: Basic Books.

Gastil, J. (1993). *Democracy in small groups: Participation, decision-making, and communications.* Gabriola Island, BC, Canada: New Society.

Gates, H.L., Jr., & West, C. (1996). *The future of the race.* New York: Vintage Books.

Gay, G. (1995). Mirror images on common issue: Parallels between multicultural education and critical pedagogy. In C.E. Sleeter & P.L. McLaren (Eds.), *Multicultural education, critical pedagogy, and the politics of difference* (pp. 155–189). Albany: State University of New York Press.

Gay, G. (1997). Multicultural infusion in teacher education. Foundations and applications. *Peabody Journal of Education, 72*(1), 150–177.

Gay, G. (1999). Ethnic identity development and multicultural education. In R.H. Sheets & E.R. Hollins (Eds.), *Racial and ethnic identity in school practices: Aspects of human development* (pp. 195–211). Mahwah, NJ: Lawrence Erlbaum.

Gay, G. (2000). *Culturally responsive teaching: Theory, research, and practice.* New York: Teachers College Press.

Gellner, E. (1999). The coming of nationalism, and its interpretation: The myths of nations and class. In S. Bowles, M. Franzini, & U. Pagano (Eds.), *The politics and economics of power* (pp. 179–224). New York: Routledge.

Gewirtz, S. (2001). Rethinking social justice: A conceptual analysis. In J. Demaine (Ed.), *Sociology of education today* (pp. 49–64). New York: Palgrave.

Gideonse, H.D. (1989). *Relating knowledge to teacher education: Responding to NCATE's knowledge base and related standards.* Washington, DC: American Association of Colleges for Teacher Education.

Gideonse, H.D. (1993). The governance of teacher education and systemic reform. *Educational Policy, 7*(4), 395–426.

Gillborn, D. (1995). *Racism and antiracism in real schools.* Philadelphia: Open University Press.

Gillborn, D., Youdell, D., & Kirton, A. (1999). Government policy and school effects: Racism and social justice in policy and practice. *Multicultural Teaching, 17*(3), 11–17.

Gillette, M., & Boyle-Baise, M. (1996). Multicultural education at the graduate level: Assisting teachers in gaining multicultural understandings. *Theory and Research in Social Education, 24*(3), 273–293.

Gilliom, M.E. (1993). Mobilizing teacher educators to support global education in preservice programs. *Theory Into Practice, 32*(1), 40–46.

Ginsburg, M.B. (1988). *Contradictions in teacher education and society.* Philadelphia: Falmer Press.

Giroux, H.A. (1988). *Schooling and the struggle for public life: Critical pedagogy in the modern age.* Minneapolis: University of Minnesota Press.

Giroux, H.A. (1999). Rewriting the discourse of racial identity: Toward a pedagogy and politics of whiteness. In C. Clark & J. O'Donnell (Eds.), *Becoming and unbecoming white: Owning and disowning a racial identity* (pp. 224–252). Westport, CT: Bergin & Garvey.

Global Source Education. (2000). Welcome to the global source network. [On-line]. Available: http://www.globalsourcenetwork.org

Goldberg, D.T. (1993). *Racist culture: Philosophy and the politics of meaning.* Cambridge, MA: Blackwell.

Goldberg, D.T. (1994). Introduction: Multicultural conditions. In D.T. Goldberg (Ed.), *Multiculturalism: A critical reader* (pp. 1–41). Cambridge, MA: Blackwell.

Gollnick, D.M. (1992a). Multicultural education: Policies and practices in teacher education. In C.A. Grant (Ed.), *Research and multicultural education: From the margins to the mainstream* (pp. 218–239). London: Falmer.

Gollnick, D.M. (1992b). Understanding the dynamics of race, class, and gender. In M.E. Dilworth (Ed.), *Diversity in teacher education: New expectations* (pp. 63–78). San Francisco: Jossey-Bass.

Gollnick, D.M. (1995). National and state initiatives for multicultural education. In J.A. Banks & C.A.M. Banks (Eds.), *Handbook of research on multicultural education* (pp. 44–64). New York: Macmillan.

Gollnick, D.M., & Chinn, P.C. (1994). *Multicultural education in a pluralistic society* (3rd ed.). Columbus, OH: Charles E. Merrill.

Gollnick, D.M., Osayande, K.I.M., & Levy, J. (1980). *Multicultural teacher education: Case studies of thirteen programs.* Washington, DC: American Association of Colleges for Teacher Education.

Gomez, M.L. (1996). Prospective teachers' perspective on teaching "other people's children." In K. Zeichner, S. Melnick, & M.L. Gomez (Eds.), *Currents of reform in preservice teacher education* (pp. 109–132). New York: Teachers College Press.

González, F.E. (1999). Formations of *Mexican*aness: *Trenza de identidades múltiples* [Growing up Mexicana: Braids of multiple identities]. In L. Parker, D. Deyhel, & S. Villenas (Eds.), *Race is . . . race isn't: Critical race theory and qualitative studies in education* (pp. 125–154). Boulder, CO: Westview Press.

Goodlad, J.I. (1990). *Teachers for our nation's schools.* San Francisco: Jossey-Bass.

Goodlad, J.I. (1996). Democracy, education, and community. In R. Soder (Ed.), *Democracy, education, and the schools* (pp. 87–124). San Francisco: Jossey-Bass.

Goodlad, J.I. (1999). Whither schools of education? *Journal of Teacher Education, 50*(5), 325–338.

Goodwin, A.L. (1997). Multicultural stories: Preservice teachers conceptions of and responses to issues of diversity. *Urban Education, 32*(1), 117–145.

Goodwin, A.L. (2001). Seeing with different eyes: Reexamining teachers' expectations through racial lenses. In S.H. King & L.A. Castenell (Eds.), *Racism and racial inequality: Implications for teacher education* (pp. 69–76). Washington, DC: American Association of Colleges for Teacher Education.

Gormley, K. (1995, April). *Expert and novice teachers' beliefs about culturally responsive pedagogy.* Paper presented at the Annual Meeting of the American Educational Research Association, San Francisco. (ERIC Document Reproduction Service No. ED 384 599)

Gotanda, N. (1995). A critique of "Our Constitution is color-blind." In K. Crenshaw, N. Gotanda, G. Peller, & K. Thomas (Eds.), *Critical race theory: The key writings that formed the movement* (pp. 257–275). New York: The New Press.

Gould, S.J. (1996). *The mismeasure of man* (Rev. ed.). New York: W.W. Norton.

Governor's Target Alliance. (1990). *Iowa workforce agenda: Options for business, education, labor, and government.* Des Moines, IA: Governor's Office.

Grant, C.A. (1993). The multicultural preparation of U.S. teachers: Some hard truths. In G.K. Verma (Ed.), *Inequality and teacher education: An international perspective* (pp. 41–57). Washington, DC: The Falmer Press.

Grant, C.A. (1997). Critical knowledge, skills, and experiences for the instruction of culturally diverse students: A perspective for the preparation of preservice teachers. In J.J. Irvine (Ed.), *Critical knowledge for diverse teachers and learners* (pp. 1–26). Washington, DC: American Association of Colleges for Teacher Education.

Grant, C.A., & Ladson-Billings, G. (Eds.). (1997). *Dictionary of multicultural education.* Phoenix, AZ: Oryx Press.

Grant, C.A., & Secada, W.G. (1990). Preparing teachers for diversity. In W.R. Houston (Ed.), *Handbook of research on teacher education* (pp. 403–422). New York: Macmillan.

Grant, C.A., & Sleeter, C.E. (1993). Race, class, gender, and disability in the classroom. In J.A. Banks & C.A. M. Banks (Eds.), *Multicultural education: Issues and perspectives* (2nd ed., pp. 48–67). Boston: Allyn and Bacon.

Grant, C.A., & Zozakiewicz, C.A. (1995). Student teachers, cooperating teachers, and supervisors: Interrupting the multicultural silences of student teaching. In J.M. Larkin & C.E. Sleeter (Eds.), *Developing multicultural teacher education curricula* (pp. 259–278). Albany: State University of New York Press.

Green, P.E. (1999). Separate and still unequal: Legal challenges to school tracking and ability grouping in America's public schools. In L. Parker, D. Deyhel, & S. Villenas (Eds.), *Race is . . . race isn't: Critical race theory and qualitative studies in education* (pp. 231–250). Boulder, CO: Westview Press.

Greene, M. (1978). *Landscapes of learning.* New York: Teachers College Press.

Greene, M. (1995). *Releasing the imagination: Essays on education, the arts, and social change.* San Francisco: Jossey-Bass.

Greenhouse, S. (2001a, May 16). Labor abuses in El Salvador are detailed in document. *New York Times*, p. A8.

Greenhouse, S. (2001b, June 14). Report outlines the abuses of foreign domestic workers. *New York Times*, p. A16.

Greenman, N.P., & Kimmel, E.B. (1995). The road to multicultural education: Potholes of resistance. *Journal of Teacher Education, 46*(5), 360–368.

Guillaume, A., Zuniga, C., & Yee, I. (1998). What difference does preparation make? Educating preservice teachers for learner diversity. In M.E. Dilworth (Ed.), *Being responsive to cultural differences: How teachers learn* (pp. 143–159). Thousand Oaks, CA: Corwin Press.

Gutmann, A. (1999). *Democratic education* (Rev. ed.). Princeton, NJ: Princeton University Press.

Haberman, M. (1996). Selecting and preparing culturally competent teachers for urban schools. In J. Skula, T.J. Buttery, & E. Guyton (Eds.), *Handbook of research on teacher education* (2nd ed., pp. 747–760). New York: Simon & Schuster Macmillan.

Haberman, M., & Post, L. (1990). Cooperating teachers' perceptions of the goals of multicultural education. *Action in Teacher Education, 12*(3), 31–35.

Haberman, M., & Post, L. (1998). Teachers for multicultural schools: The power of selection. *Theory Into Practice, 37*(2), 96–104.

Hamelink, C.J. (1993). Globalization and national sovereignty. In K. Nordenstreng & H.I. Schiller (Eds.), *Beyond national sovereignty: International communications in the 1990s* (pp. 371–393). Norwood, NJ: Ablex.

Hammond, J.L. (1998). *Fighting to learn: Popular education and guerrilla war in El Salvador*. New Brunswick, NJ: Rutgers University Press.

Harris, A.P. (1994). Foreword: The jurisprudence of reconstruction. *California Law Review, 82*(4), 741–786.

Harris, C.I. (1993, June). Whiteness as property. *Harvard Law Review, 106*(8), 1709–1791.

Hartman, C. (2001). Facts and figures: Wealth patterns/income patterns/health patterns. [On-line]. Available: http://www.inequality.org/factsfr.html

Haymes, S.N. (1995). White culture and the politics of racial difference: Implications for multiculturalism. In C.E. Sleeter & P.L. McLaren (Eds.), *Multicultural education, critical pedagogy, and the politics of difference* (pp. 105–127). Albany: State University of New York Press.

Held, D. (1995). *Democracy and the global order: From the modern state to cosmopolitan governance*. Stanford, CA: Stanford University Press.

Held, D., McGrew, A., Goldblatt, D., & Perraton, J. (1999). *Global transformations: Politics, economics and culture*. Stanford, CA: Stanford University Press.

Helms, J.E. (1990a). An overview of black racial identity theory. In J.E. Helms (Ed.), *Black and white racial identity: Theory, research, and practice* (Contributions in Afro-American and African Studies, No. 129, pp. 9–32). New York: Greenwood Press.

Helms, J.E. (1990b). Introduction: Review of racial identity terminology. In J.E. Helms (Ed.), *Black and white racial identity: Theory, research, and practice* (Contributions in Afro-American and African Studies, No. 129, pp. 3–8). New York: Greenwood Press.

Helms, J.E. (1990c). Toward a model of white racial identity development. In J.E. Helms (Ed.), *Black and white racial identity: Theory, research, and practice* (Contributions in Afro-American and African Studies, No. 129, pp. 49–66). New York: Greenwood Press.

Helms, J.E. (1994). The conceptualization of racial identity and other "racial" constructs. In E.J. Trickett, R.J. Watts, & D. Birman (Eds.), *Human diversity: Perspectives on people in context* (pp. 285–311). San Francisco: Jossey-Bass.

Helms, J.E. (1999). Another meta-analysis of the white racial identity attitude scale's Cronbach Alphas: Implications for validity. *Measurement and Evaluation in Counseling and Development, 32*(3), 122–137.

Helms, J.E., & Cook, D.A. (1999). *Using race and culture in counseling and psychotherapy: Theory and process.* Boston: Allyn and Bacon.

Hidalgo, F., Chávez-Chávez, R., & Ramage, J.C. (1996). Multicultural education: Landscape for reform in the twenty-first century. In J. Skula, T.J. Buttery, & E. Guyton (Eds.), *Handbook of research on teacher education* (2nd ed., pp. 761–778). New York: Simon & Schuster Macmillan.

Hirsch, E., Koppich, J.E., & Knapp, M.S. (1998, December). *What states are doing to improve the quality of teaching: A brief review of current patterns and trends.* Center for the Study of Teaching and Policy working paper. Seattle: University of Washington.

Hoff, D.J. (2000, September 13). A world apart: Educators hope to change history. *Education Week*, pp. 1, 17.

Hoffman, D.M. (1996). Culture and self in multicultural education: Reflection on discourse, text, and practice. *American Educational Research Journal, 33*(3), 545–569.

Hoge, W. (2001, May 29). Rioting in Britain give voice to silent minorities. *New York Times*, p. A3.

Hollins, E.R., King, J.E., & Hayman, W.C. (Eds.). (1994). *Teaching diverse populations: Formulating a knowledge base.* Albany: State University of New York Press.

Holmes Group. (1990). *Tomorrow's schools: Principles for the design of professional development schools.* East Lansing: College of Education, Michigan State University.

Holmes Group. (1995). *Tomorrow's schools of education.* East Lansing: Michigan State University.

Holmes Partnership. (2000). The Holmes Partnership goals. [On-line]. Available: http://www.holmespartnership.org/goals.html

hooks, b. (1994). *Teaching to transgress: Education as the practice of freedom.* New York: Routledge.

Horton, J., Garcia, G., Scott, D., & Chavez, R.C. (1999, November). *Constructing a community ethnography: Undergraduate multicultural education students practicing praxis.* Paper presented at the annual conference of the National Association of Multicultural Education, San Diego, CA.

Horton, M. (1990). *The long haul: An autobiography.* New York: Doubleday.

Howard, G. (1999). *We can't teach what we don't know: White teachers, multiracial schools.* New York: Teachers College Press.

Hudak, G.N. (2000). Reaping the harvest of shame: Racism and teaching in a time of radical economic insecurity (lessons from a high school mass media course). In R. Mahalingham & C. McCarthy (Eds.), *Multicultural curriculum: New directions for social theory, practice, and policy* (pp. 286–301). New York: Routledge.

Ignatiev, N., & Garvey, J. (1996). *Race traitor*. New York: Routledge.

Igoa, C. (1995). *The inner world of the immigrant child*. Mahwah, NJ: Lawrence Erlbaum.

Imig, D.G., & Switzer, T.J. (1996). Changing teacher education programs: Restructuring collegiate-based teacher education programs. In J. Skula, T.J. Buttery, & E. Guyton (Eds.), *Handbook of research on teacher education* (2nd ed., pp. 213–226). New York: Simon & Schuster Macmillan.

International Labour Organization. (1964). Declaration concerning the aims and purposes of the International Labour Organization. [On-line]. Available: http://www.ilo.org/public/english/about/iloconst.htm#annex

Interstate New Teacher Assessment and Support Consortium. (1992, September). *Model standards for beginning teacher licensure and development: A resource for state dialogue*. Washington, DC: Council of Chief State School Officers.

Interstate New Teacher Assessment and Support Consortium. (1995). *Next steps: Moving toward performance-based licensing in teaching*. Washington, DC: Council of Chief State School Officers.

Iowa Department of Education. (1989, May). *A guide for integrating global education across the curriculum*. Des Moines, IA: Author.

Iowa Department of Education. (1994, March). *Education is Iowa's future: The state plan for educational excellence in the 21st century*. Des Moines, IA: Grimes State Office Building.

Irvine, J.J. (1992). Making teacher education culturally responsive. In M.E. Dilworth (Ed.), *Diversity in teacher education: New expectations* (pp. 79–92). San Francisco: Jossey-Bass.

Irvine, J.J. (Ed.). (1997). *Critical knowledge for diverse teachers and learners*. Washington, DC: American Association of Colleges for Teacher Education.

Irvine, J.J. (2001). The critical elements of culturally responsive pedagogy: A synthesis of the research. In J.J. Irvine, B.J. Armento, V.E. Causey, J.C. Jones, R.S. Frasher, & M.H. Weinburgh (Eds.), *Culturally responsive teaching: Lesson planning for elementary and middle grades* (pp. 3–17). Boston: McGraw-Hill.

Irvine, J.J., Armento, B.J., Causey, V.E., Jones, J.C., Frasher, R.S., & Weinburgh, M.H. (Eds.). (2001). *Culturally responsive teaching: Lesson planning for elementary and middle grades*. Boston: McGraw-Hill.

Irvine, J.J., & York, D.E. (1995). Learning styles and culturally diverse students: A literature review. In J.A. Banks & C.A.M. Banks (Eds.), *Handbook of research on multicultural education* (pp. 486–497). New York: Macmillan.

Jacobs, H.H. (1989). The growing need for interdisciplinary curriculum content. In H.H. Jacobs (Ed.), *Interdisciplinary curriculum: Design and implementation* (pp. 1–11). Alexandria, VA: Association for Supervision and Curriculum Development.

Jameson, F. (1998a). Notes on globalization as a philosophical issue. In F. Jameson & M. Miyoshi (Eds.), *The cultures of globalization* (pp. 54–77). Durham, NC: Duke University Press.

Jameson, F. (1998b). Preface. In F. Jameson & M. Miyoshi (Eds.), *The cultures of globalization* (pp. xi–xvii). Durham, NC: Duke University Press.

Jeevanantham, L.S. (2001). A new focus for multicultural education. *Multicultural Perspectives, 3*(2), 8–12.

Johnson, M., & Ochoa, A. (1993). Teacher education for global perspectives: A research agenda. *Theory Into Practice, 32*(1), 64–68.

Johnston, J.S., Jr., Spalding, J.R., Paden, R., & Zifren, A. (1989). *Those who can: Undergraduate programs to prepare arts and science majors for teaching.* Washington, DC: Association of American Colleges.

Jones, V. (1996). Classroom management. In J. Sikula, T.J. Buttery, & E. Guyton (Eds.), *Handbook of research on teacher education* (2nd ed., pp. 503–521). New York: Macmillan.

Joyce, B. (1990). Prologue. In B. Joyce (Ed.), *Changing school culture through staff development* (pp. xv–xviii). Alexandria, VA: Association for Supervision and Curriculum Development.

Jung, B. (1997). Multicultural education and monocultural students: Curriculum struggles in teacher education. In D.M. Byrd & D.J. McIntyre (Eds.), *Research on the education of our nation's teachers: Teacher education yearbook V* (pp. 189–206). Thousand Oaks, CA: Corwin Press.

Kahn, J. (2000a, October 21). I.M.F.'s hand often heavy, a study says. *New York Times,* pp. B1, B14.

Kahn, J. (2000b, January 29). Swiss forum has its focus on memories from Seattle. *New York Times,* pp. B1–B2.

Kahne, J., & Westheimer, J. (2000). A pedagogy of collective action and reflection: Preparing teachers for school leadership. *Journal of Teacher Education, 51*(5), 372–383.

Kailin, J. (1999). How white teachers perceive the problem of racism in their schools: A case study in "liberal" Lakeview. *Teachers College Record, 100*(4), 724–750.

Kanpol, B., & McLaren, P. (Eds.). (1995). *Critical multiculturalism: Uncommon voices in a common struggle.* Westport, CT: Bergin & Garvey.

Katz, J. (1978). *White awareness handbook for anti-racism training.* Norman: University of Oklahoma Press.

Katz, S.B. (1999). Teaching in tensions: Latino immigrant youth, their teachers, and the structure of schooling. *Teachers College Record, 100*(4), 809–840.

Kennedy, M.M. (1999). The role of preservice teacher education. In L. Darling-Hammond & G. Sykes (Eds.), *Teaching as the learning profession: Handbook of policy and practice* (pp. 54–85). San Francisco: Jossey-Bass.

Khan, S.R. (1999). Teaching an undergraduate course on the psychology of racism. *Teaching of Psychology, 26*(1), 28–33.

Kincheloe, J.L., & Steinberg, S.R. (1997). *Changing multiculturalism.* Philadelphia: Open University Press.

Kincheloe, J., & Steinberg, S. (1998). Addressing the crisis of whiteness: Reconfiguring white identity in a pedagogy of whiteness. In J. Kincheloe, S. Steinberg, N.M. Rodriguez, & R.E Chennault (Eds.), *White reign: Deploying whiteness in America* (pp. 3–30). New York: St. Martin's Press.

Kincheloe, J., Steinberg, S., Rodriguez, N.M., & Chennault, R.E (Eds.). (1998). *White reign: Deploying whiteness in America.* New York: St. Martin's Press.

King, S.H., & Castenell, L.A. (2001a). Introduction. In S.H. King & L.A. Castenell (Eds.), *Racism and racial inequality: Implications for teacher education* (pp. 9–13). Washington, DC: American Association of Colleges for Teacher Education.

King, S.H., & Castenell, L.A. (2001b). Tenets to guide antiracist teacher education practice. In S.H. King & L.A. Castenell (Eds.), *Racism and racial inequality: Implications for teacher education* (pp. 77–81). Washington, DC: American Association of Colleges for Teacher Education.

Kite, A. (2001, May 2). Free trade? Someone always has to pay. *Business Week.* [Online]. Available: http://www.businessweek.com/bwdaily/dnflash/may2001/nf2001 052_941.htm?mainwindow

Kivel, P. (1996). *Uprooting racism: How white people can work for racial justice.* Gabriola Island, BC, Canada: New Society Publishers.

Kliebard, H.M. (1992). *Forging the American curriculum: Essays in curriculum history and theory.* New York: Routledge.

Kolb, D. (1985). *The learning style inventory.* Boston: McBer.

Koppich, J.E. (2000). Trinity University: Preparing teachers for tomorrow's schools. In L. Darling-Hammond (Ed.), *Studies in excellence in teacher education: Preparation in a five-year program* (pp. 1–48). Washington, DC: American Association of Colleges for Teacher Education.

Koster, B., & Korthagen, F.A.J. (2001). Training teacher educators for the realistic approach. In F.A.J. Korthagen (Ed.), *Linking practice and theory: The pedagogy of realistic teacher education* (pp. 239–253). Mahwah, N.J.: Lawrence Erlbaum.

Kousser, J.M. (1999). *Colorblind injustice: Minority voting rights and the undoing of the second reconstruction.* Chapel Hill: The University of North Carolina Press.

Kozol, J. (1991). *Savage inequalities: Children in American schools.* New York: Crown.

Ladson-Billings, G. (1995a). Multicultural teacher education: Research, practice, and policy. In J.A. Banks & C.A.M. Banks (Eds.), *Handbook of research on multicultural education* (pp. 747–759). New York: Macmillan.

Ladson-Billings, G. (1995b). Toward a theory of culturally relevant pedagogy. *American Educational Research Journal, 32*(3): 465–491.

Ladson-Billings, G. (1999a). Just what is critical race theory and what's it doing in a *nice* field like education? In L. Parker, D. Deyhel, & S. Villenas (Eds.), *Race is . . . race isn't: Critical race theory and qualitative studies in education* (pp. 7–30). Boulder, CO: Westview Press.

Ladson-Billings, G. (1999b). Preparing teachers for diverse student populations: A critical race theory perspective. In A. Iran-Nejad & P.D. Pearson (Eds.), *Review of research in education 24* (pp. 211–247). Washington, DC: American Educational Research Association.

Ladson-Billings, G. (2000). Fighting for our lives: Preparing teachers to teach African American students. *Journal of Teacher Education, 51*(3), 206–214.

Ladson-Billings, G., & Tate, W.F., IV. (1995). Toward a critical race theory of education. *Teachers College Record, 97*(1), 47–68.

Ladwig, J.G. (2000). World institutions, world dispositions: Curriculum in the world-cultural institution of schooling. In R. Mahalingam & C. McCarthy (Eds.), *Multicultural curriculum: New directions for social theory, practice, and policy* (pp. 56–69). New York: Routledge.

Larkin, J.M. (1995). Curriculum themes and issues in multicultural teacher education programs. In J.M. Larkin & C.E. Sleeter (Eds.), *Developing multicultural teacher education curricula* (pp. 1–16). Albany: State University of New York Press.

Larkin, J.M., & Sleeter, C.E. (Eds.). (1995). *Developing multicultural teacher education curricula.* Albany: State University of New York Press.

Lawrence, S.M. (1997). Beyond race awareness: White racial identity and multicultural teaching. *Journal of Teacher Education, 48*(2), 108–117.

Lawrence, S.M., & Krause, H.E. (1996). Multicultural teaching in a monocultural school: One cooperating teacher's personal and political challenges. *Equity & Excellence in Education, 29*(2), 30–36.

Lawrence, S.M., & Tatum, B.D. (1997a). Teachers in transition: The impact of antiracist professional development on classroom practice. *Teachers College Record, 99*(1), 162–178.

Lawrence, S.M., & Tatum, B.D. (1997b). White educators as allies: Moving from awareness to action. In M. Fine, L. Weis, L.C. Powell, & L.M. Wong (Eds.), *Off white: Readings on race, power, and society* (pp. 333–342). New York: Routledge.

Leahy, D. (1998, November). *Effects of neo-liberal policies on U.S. public education: Regulation, sales and purchase.* Paper presented at the Hemispheric Conference on Public Education, Mexico City.

Lee, E. (1998a). Anti-racist education: Pulling together to close the gaps. In E. Lee, D. Menkart, & M. Okazawa-Rey (Eds.), *Beyond heroes and holidays: A practical guide to K-12 anti-racist, multicultural education and staff development* (pp. 26–34). Washington, DC: Network of Educators of Americas.

Lee, E. (1998b). Looking through an anti-racist lens. In E. Lee, D. Menkart, & M. Okazawa-Rey (Eds.), *Beyond heroes and holidays: A practical guide to K-12 anti-racist, multicultural education and staff development* (pp. 402–404). Washington, DC: Network of Educators of Americas.

Lehman Brothers. (1998). *Investment opportunities in the education industry.* New York: Author.

Leys, C. (1974). *Underdevelopment in Kenya: The political economy of neo-colonialism.* Berkeley: University of California Press.

Lieberman, A. (1996, November). Creating intentional learning communities. *Educational Leadership, 54*(3), 51–55.

Liston, D.P. (1988). *Capitalist schools: Explanation and ethics in radical studies of schooling.* New York: Routledge.

Liston, D.P., & Zeichner, K.M. (1991). *Teacher education and the social condition of schooling.* New York: Routledge.

Loewen, J.W. (1995). *Lies my teacher told me: Everything your American history textbook got wrong.* New York: Touchstone.

López, G.R. (2001). Re-visiting white racism in education research: Critical race theory and the problem of method. *Educational Researcher, 30*(1), 29–33.

Lubiano, W. (1998). Introduction. In W. Lubiano (Ed.), *The house that race built* (pp. vii–ix). New York: Vintage Books.

Luft, J.A. (1997, October). *Border crossings: The student teaching experience of a multicultural science education enthusiast.* Paper presented at the Arizona K–16 Teaching Reforms Conference, Phoenix. (ERIC Document Reproduction Service No. ED 417 144)

Lyall, S. (2001, May 31). In ravaged English city, racial mix was volatile. *New York Times*, p. A4.

Lynch, J. (1986). An initial typology of perspectives on staff development for multicultural teacher education. In S. Modgil, G.K. Verma, K. Mallick, & C. Modgil (Eds.), *Multicultural education: The interminable debate* (pp. 149–166). London: The Falmer Press.

Lynn, M. (1999). Toward a critical race pedagogy. *Urban Education, 33*(5), 606–626.

Mac an Ghaill, M. (1999). *Contemporary racisms and ethnicities: Social and cultural transformations.* Buckingham, UK: Open University Press.

Macedo, D. (2000). The colonialism of the English only movement. *Educational Researcher, 29*(3), 15–24.

Macedo, D., & Bartolomé, L.I. (1999). *Dancing with bigotry: Beyond the politics of tolerance.* New York: St. Martin's Press.

MacGregor, J. (2000, July). *Organizing for learning in learning communities.* Paper presented at the American Association of Higher Education Summer Academy "Organizing for Learning," Snowbird, UT.

MacLeod, H.A. (2001, April). *Mixed feelings: Three white teachers' emotions about race and racism.* Paper presented at the annual meeting of American Educational Research Association, Seattle, WA.

MacLeod, J. (1995). *Ain't no making it: Aspirations and attainment in a low-income neighborhood.* Boulder, CO: Westview Press.

Mahalingam, R., & McCarthy, C. (2000). Introduction. In R. Mahalingham & C. McCarthy (Eds.), *Multicultural curriculum: New directions for social theory, practice, and policy* (pp. 1–11). New York: Routledge.

Martin, R.E. (1991). The power to empower: Multicultural education for student-teachers. In C.E. Sleeter (Ed.), *Empowerment through multicultural education* (pp. 287–297). Albany: State University of New York.

Marx, A.W. (1996). Race-making and the nation-state. *World Politics, 48*(2), 180–208.

Mason, R. (1987). Helping student teachers broaden their conception of art curricula. *Art Education, 39*(4), 46–51.

May, S. (1999). Critical multiculturalism and cultural difference: Avoiding essentialism. In S. May (Ed.), *Critical multiculturalism: Rethinking multicultural and antiracist education* (pp. 11–41). Philadelphia: Falmer Press.

McAllister, G., & Irvine, J.J. (2000). Cross cultural competency and multicultural teacher education. *Review of Educational Research, 70*(1), 3–24.

McCain-Reid, E. (1995). A pilot study of senior preservice teachers' responses to issues of human diversity in one university course. In R.J. Martin (Ed.), *Practicing what we teach: Confronting diversity in teacher education* (pp. 235–254). Albany: State University of New York Press.

McCarthy, C. (1994). Multicultural discourse and curriculum reform: A critical perspective. *Educational Theory, 44*(1), 81–98.

McCarthy, C. (1998a). Living with anxiety: Race and the renarration of public life. In J.L. Kincheloe, S.R. Steinberg, N.M. Rodriguez, & R.E. Chennault (Eds.), *White reign: Deploying whiteness in America* (pp. 329–341). New York: St. Martin's Press.

McCarthy, C. (1998b). *The uses of culture: Education and the limits of ethnic affiliation.* New York: Routledge.

McCarthy, C., & Willis, A.I. (1995). The politics of culture: Multicultural education after the content debate. In S. Jackson & J. Solís (Eds.), *Beyond comfort zones in multiculturalism: Confronting the politics of privilege* (pp. 67–87). Westport, CT: Bergin & Garvey.

McDermott, J.C., Knapp, C., & Setoguchi, S. (1999). How to create a community. In J.C. McDermott (Ed.), *Beyond the silence: Listening for democracy* (pp. 71–75). Portsmouth, NH: Heinemann.

McDiarmid, G.W., & Price, J. (1990). *Prospective teachers' views of diverse learners: A study of the participants in the ABCD project.* E. Lansing: National Center for Research on Teacher Education, Michigan State University. (ERIC Document Reproduction Service No. ED 324 308)

McIntosh, P. (1995). White privilege and male privilege: A personal account of coming to see correspondence through work in women's studies. In M.L. Anderson & P.H. Collins (Eds.), *Race, class, and gender: An anthology* (2nd ed., pp. 76–87). Belmont, CA: Wadsworth Publishing. (Original work published 1988)

McIntyre, A. (1997). *Making meaning of whiteness: Exploring racial identity with white teachers.* Albany: State University of New York.

McIntyre, A. (2000). A response to Rosa Hernández Sheets. *Educational Researcher, 29*(9), 26–27.

McLaren, P. (1989). *Life in schools: An introduction to critical pedagogy in the foundations of education.* New York: Longman.

McLaren, P. (1994). White terror and oppositional agency: Towards a critical multiculturalism. In D.T. Goldberg (Ed.), *Multiculturalism: A critical reader* (pp. 45–74). Cambridge, MA: Blackwell.

McLaren, P. (1995). *Critical pedagogy and predatory culture: Oppositional politics in a postmodern era.* New York: Routledge.

McLaren, P. (1997). Multiculturalism and the postmodern critique: Toward a pedagogy of resistance and transformation. In P. Brown, A.H. Halsey, H. Lauder, & A.S. Wells (Eds.), *Education: Culture, economy, and society* (pp. 520–540). Oxford, UK: Oxford University Press.

McLaren, P. (1998). Whiteness is . . . The struggle for postcolonial hybridity. In J. Kincheloe, S. Steinberg, N.M. Rodriguez, & R.E Chennault (Eds.), *White reign: Deploying whiteness in America* (pp. 63–75). New York: St. Martin's Press.

McLaren, P., & Farahmandpur, R. (2001a). Class, cultism, multiculturalism: A notebook on forging a revolutionary politics. *Multicultural Education, 8*(3), 2–14.

McLaren, P., & Farahmandpur, R. (2001b). Teaching against globalization and the new imperialism: Toward a revolutionary pedagogy. *Journal of Teacher Education, 52*(2), 136–150.

McLaren, P., & Torres, R. (1999). Racism and multicultural education: Rethinking "race" and "whiteness" in late capitalism. In S. May (Ed.), *Critical multicultur-alism: Rethinking multicultural and antiracist education* (pp. 42–76). Philadelphia: Falmer Press.

Melnick, S.L., & Zeichner, K.M. (1997). Enhancing the capacity of teacher education institutions to address diversity issues. In J.E. King, E.R. Hollins, & W.C. Hayman (Eds.), *Preparing teachers for cultural diversity* (pp. 23–39). New York: Teachers College Press.

Memmi, A. (2000). *Racism* (S. Martinot, Trans.). Minneapolis: University of Minnesota Press.

Merryfield, M.M. (1996). Learning from current practice: Looking across profiles of teacher educators and teacher education programs. In M.M. Merryfield (Ed.), *Making connections between multicultural and global education: Teacher educators and teacher education programs* (1–12). Washington, DC: American Association of Colleges for Teacher Education.

Merryfield, M.M. (1997). A framework for teacher education in global perspectives. In M.M. Merryfield, E. Jarchow, & S. Pickert (Eds.), *Preparing teachers to teach global perspectives: A handbook for teacher educators* (pp. 1–24). Thousand Oaks, CA: Corwin Press.

Merryfield, M.M., Jarchow, E., & Pickert, S. (Eds.). (1997). *Preparing teachers to teach global perspectives: A handbook for teacher educators.* Thousand Oaks, CA: Corwin Press.

Merz, C., & Furman, G. (1997). *Community and schools: Promise and paradox.* New York: Teachers College Press.

Miedema, S., & Wardekker, W.L. (1999). Emergent identity versus consistent identity: Possibilities for a postmodern repoliticization of critical pedagogy. In T.S. Popkewitz & L. Fendler (Eds.), *Critical theories in education: Changing terrains of knowledge and politics* (pp. 67–83). New York: Routledge.

Mignolo, W.D. (1998). Globalization, civilization processes, and the relocation of languages and cultures. In F. Jameson & M. Miyoshi (Eds.), *The cultures of globalization* (pp. 32–53). Durham, NC: Duke University Press.

Miller, L., & Silvernail, D. (2000). Learning to become a teacher: The Wheelock way. In L. Darling-Hammond (Ed.), *Studies in excellence in teacher education: Preparation in a fifth year program* (pp. 67–107). Washington, DC: American Association of Colleges for Teacher Education.

Moll, L.C. (Ed.). (1990). *Vygotsky and education: Instructional implications and applications of sociohistorical psychology.* Cambridge, UK: Cambridge University Press.

Montecinos, C. (1995). Culture as an ongoing dialog: Implications for multicultural teacher education. In C.E. Sleeter & P.L. McLaren (Eds.), *Multicultural education, critical pedagogy, and the politics of difference* (pp. 291–308). Albany: State University of New York.

Moody, K. (1997). *Workers in a lean world: Unions in the international economy.* New York: Verso.

Moore, J.A. (1996, February). *Empowering student teachers to teach from a multicultural perspective.* Paper presented at the annual conference of the American Association of Colleges for Teacher Education, Chicago (ERIC Document Reproduction Service No. ED 394 979)

Morrison, T. (1998). Home. In W. Lubiano (Ed.), *The house that race built* (pp. 3–12). New York: Vintage Books.

Murphy, J.W., & Choi, J.M. (1997). *Postmodernism, unraveling racism, and democratic institutions*. Westport, CT: Prager.

Murray, F.B. (2001). The overreliance of accreditors on consensus standards. *Journal of Teacher Education, 52*(3), 211–222.

Murrell, P.C., Jr. (1998). *Like stone soup: The role of the professional development school in the renewal of urban schools*. Washington, DC: American Association of Colleges for Teacher Education.

Murrell, P.C., Jr. (1999). Responsive teaching for African American male adolescents. In V.C. Polite & J.E. Davis (Eds.), *African American males in school and society: Practices and policies for effective education* (pp. 82–96). New York: Teachers College Press.

National Archives and Records Administration. (2001). Constitution of the United States of America, article 1, section 2, clause 3. [On-line]. Available: http://www.nara. gov/exhall/charters/constitution/constitution.html

National Commission on Teaching and America's Future. (1996, September). *What matters most: Teaching for America's Future*. New York: Author.

National Council for the Accreditation of Teacher Education. (2001a). About NCATE. [On-line]. Available: http://www.ncate.org/ncate/m_ncate.htm

National Council for the Accreditation of Teacher Education. (2001b). *Professional standards for the accreditation of schools, colleges and departments of education*. Washington, DC: Author.

National Council for the Accreditation of Teacher Education (2001c). *Standards for professional development schools*. Washington, DC: Author.

National Council for the Accreditation of Teacher Education. (2001d). State partners. [On-line]. Available: http://www.ncate.org/partners/m_partners.htm

National Education Association. (2001). Code of ethics of the education profession. [On-line]. Available: http://www.nea.org/aboutnea/code.html (Original work published 1975)

Nel, J. (1992). Pre-service teacher resistance to diversity: Need to reconsider instructional methodologies. *Journal of Instructional Psychology, 19*(1), 23–27.

Ngũgĩ wa Thiong'o. (1993). *Moving the centre: The struggle for cultural freedoms*. Portsmouth, NH: Heinemann.

Nieto, S. (1995). From brown heroes and holidays to assimilationist agendas: Reconsidering the critiques of multicultural education. In C.E. Sleeter & P.L. McLaren (Eds.), *Multicultural education, critical pedagogy, and the politics of difference* (pp. 191–220). Albany: State University of New York.

Nieto, S. (1997). School reform and student achievement: A multicultural perspective. In J.A. Banks & C.A.M. Banks (Eds.), *Multicultural education: Issues and perspectives* (3rd ed., pp. 387–407). Boston: Allyn and Bacon.

Nieto, S. (1998). Affirmation, solidarity and critique. Moving beyond tolerance in education. In E. Lee, D. Menkart, & M. Okazawa-Rey (Eds.), *Beyond heroes and holi-*

days: A practical guide to K–12 anti-racist, multicultural education and staff development (pp. 7–18). Washington, DC: Network of Educators of Americas.

Nieto, S. (1999). *The light in their eyes: Creating multicultural learning communities.* New York: Teachers College Press.

Nieto, S., & Rolón, C. (1997). Preparation and professional development of teachers: A perspective from two Latinas. In J.J. Irvine (Ed.), *Critical knowledge for diverse teachers and learners* (pp. 89–123). Washington, DC: American Association of Colleges for Teacher Education.

Noddings, N. (1992). *The challenge to care in schools: An alternative approach to education.* New York: Teachers College Press.

Nussbaum, M. (2000, September 8). Globalization debate ignores the education of women. *The Chronicle of Higher Education*, pp. B16–B17.

Oakes, J. (1996). Making the rhetoric real. *Multicultural Education, 4*(2), 4–10.

Oakes, J., Gamoran, A., & Page, R.N. (1992). Curriculum differentiation: Opportunities, outcomes, and meanings. In P.W. Jackson (Ed.), *Handbook of research on curriculum* (pp. 570–608). New York: Macmillan.

Ogbu, J.U. (1995). Understanding cultural diversity and learning. In J.A. Banks & C.A.M. Banks (Eds.), *Handbook of research on multicultural education* (pp. 582–593). New York: Macmillan.

Ogbu, J.U. (1997). Racial stratification and education in the United States: Why inequality persists. In P. Brown, A.H. Halsey, H. Lauder, & A.S. Wells (Eds.), *Education: Culture, economy, and society* (pp. 765–778). Oxford, UK: Oxford University Press.

Olneck, M. (2000). Can multicultural education change what counts as cultural capital? *American Educational Research Journal, 37*(2), 317–348.

O'Loughlin, M. (1992). Engaging teachers in emancipatory knowledge construction. *Journal of Teacher Education, 43*, 336–346.

O'Loughlin, M. (2001). Seven principles underlying socially just and ethnically inclusive teacher preparation. In S.H. King & L.A. Castenell (Eds.), *Racism and racial inequality: Implications for teacher education* (pp. 59–67). Washington, DC: American Association of Colleges for Teacher Education.

Olsen, R.A. (1998). White privilege in schools. In E. Lee, D. Menkart, & M. Okazawa-Rey (Eds.), *Beyond heroes and holidays: A practical guide to K–12 anti-racist, multicultural education and staff development* (pp. 83–4). Washington, DC: Network of Educators of Americas.

Orenstein, P. (1994). *Schoolgirls: Young women, self-esteem, and the confidence gap.* New York: Anchor Books.

Organisation for Economic Co-operation and Development & UNESCO Institute for Statistics. (2001). *Teachers for tomorrow's schools: Analyses of the world education indicators: Executive summary* (2001 edition). Paris: Authors.

Organisation for Economic Co-operation and Development. (1998). *Education policy analysis 1998.* Paris: Author.

Oshinsky, D. (2000, August 26). The humpty dumpty of scholarship: American history has broken pieces. *New York Times*, pp. A17, A19.

Oxford English Dictionary (Vol. XII, 2nd ed.). (1989a). Oxford, UK: Clarendon Press.

Oxford English Dictionary (Vol. XIII, 2nd ed.). (1989b). Oxford, UK: Clarendon Press.

Pagano, U. (1999). Is power an economic good? Notes on social scarcity and the economics of positional goods. In S. Bowles, M. Franzini, & U. Pagano (Eds.), *The politics and economics of power* (pp. 63–84). New York: Routledge.

Parenti, M. (1995). *Against empire*. San Francisco: City Lights Books.

Peller, G. (1995). Race consciousness. In K. Crenshaw, N. Gotanda, G. Peller, & K. Thomas (Eds.), *Critical race theory: The key writings that formed the movement* (pp. 127–158). New York: The New Press.

Persell, C.H. (1977). *Education and inequality: A theoretical and empirical synthesis.* New York: Free Press.

Persell, C.H. (1997). Social class and educational equality. In J.A. Banks & C.A.M. Banks (Eds.), *Multicultural education: Issues and perspectives* (3rd ed., pp. 87–107). Boston: Allyn and Bacon.

Piaget, J. (1968). *Six psychological studies*. London: University of London Press.

Pickert, S. (1997). Appendix: Global education infoguide. In M.M. Merryfield, E. Jarchow, & S. Pickert (Eds.), *Preparing teachers to teach global perspectives: A handbook for teacher educators* (pp. 226–248). Thousand Oaks, CA: Corwin Press.

Pinar, W.F., Reynolds, W.M., Slattery, P., & Taubman, P.M. (1995). *Understanding curriculum: An introduction to the study of historical and contemporary curriculum discourses*. New York: Peter Lang.

Pitsch, M. (1994, June 22). "Human capital" touted in Clinton economic agenda. *Education Week*, pp. 1, 24–25.

PollingReport.com. (2001). International trade. [On-line]. Available: http://www.pollingreport.com/trade.htm

Popkewitz, T.S. (1994). Professionalization in teaching and teacher education: Some notes on its history, ideology, and potential. *Teaching and Teacher Education, 10*(1), 1–14.

Popkewitz, T.S. (1998). *Struggle for the soul: The politics of schooling and the construction of the teacher.* New York: Teachers College Press.

Popkewitz, T.S. (1999). Introduction: Critical traditions, modernisms, and the "posts." In T.S. Popkewitz & L. Fendler (Eds.), *Critical theories in education: Changing terrains of knowledge and politics* (pp. 1–13). New York: Routledge.

Powell, R. (1996). Confronting white hegemony. *Multicultural Education, 4*(2), 12–15.

Powell, R. (1997). Then the beauty emerges: A longitudinal case study of culturally relevant teaching. *Teaching and Teacher Education, 13*(5), 467–484.

Quality Counts 2000. (2000, January). A special edition of *Education Week.*

Qureshi, M., & von Weizsäcker, R. (1995). *Report of the independent working group on the future of the United Nations*. New York: Ford Foundation. [On-line]. Available: http://www.library.yale.edu/un/UN_Report.txt

Raines, F.V. (1998). Is the benign really harmless? Deconstructing some "benign" manifestations of operationalized white privilege. In J.L. Kincheloe & S.R. Steinberg (Eds.), *White reign: Deploying whiteness in America* (pp. 77–101). New York: St. Martin's Press.

Ramsey, P.G., Vold, E.B., & Williams, L.R. (1989). *Multicultural education: A source book.* New York: Garland.

Reid, G. (1995). The other side of the road: An autobiographical approach to thinking about race in the teacher education classroom. *Journal for a Just and Caring Education, 1*(2), 238–244.

Reyes, P., Scribner, J.D., & Scribner, A.P. (Eds.). (1999). *Lessons from high-performing Hispanic schools: Creating learning communities.* New York: Teachers College Press.

Rios, F.A. (1991). *Teachers' implicit theories of multicultural classrooms.* Unpublished doctoral dissertation, University of Wisconsin, Madison.

Rios, F.A., Stowell, L.P., Christopher, P.A., & McDaniel, J.E. (1997). Looking over the edge: Preparing teachers for cultural and linguistic diversity in middle schools. *Teacher Education Quarterly, 24*(4), 67–83.

Robertson, S.L. (2000). *A class act: Changing teachers' work, the state, and globalization.* New York: Falmer Press.

Rodriguez, A.J. (1999). Making ethnicity invisible in the name of equity: Standard contradictions in *National Science Education Standards. Multicultural Perspectives, 1*(2), 3–7.

Roediger, D.R. (1999). Is there a healthy white personality? *The Counseling Psychologist, 27*(2), 239–244.

Rohter, J., & Rich, J.L. (2001, December 19). Brazil takes a trade stance and offers a warning to U.S. *New York Times.* [On-line]. Available: http://www.nytimes.com/2001/12/19/business/worldbusiness/19BRAZ.html

Roithmayr, D. (1999). Introduction to critical race theory in educational research and praxis. In L. Parker, D. Deyhel, & S. Villenas (Eds.), *Race is . . . race isn't: Critical race theory and qualitative studies in education* (pp. 1–6). Boulder, CO: Westview Press.

Roman, L.G. (1997). Denying (white) racial privilege: Redemptive discourses and the uses of fantasy. In M. Fine, L. Weis, L.C. Powell, & L.M. Wong (Eds.), *Off white: Readings on race, power, and society* (pp. 270–82). New York: Routledge.

Rosenberg, P.M. (1998). The presence of an absence: Issues of race in teacher education at a predominately white college campus. In M.E. Dilworth (Ed.), *Diversity in teacher education: New expectations* (pp. 3–20). San Francisco: Jossey-Bass.

Ross, D.D., & Yeager, E. (1999). What does democracy mean to prospective elementary teachers? *Journal of Teacher Education, 50*(4), 255–266.

Ruigrok, W., & van Tulder, R. (1995). *The logic of international restructuring.* New York: Routledge.

Rushton, S.P. (2001). Cultural assimilation: A narrative case study of a student-teacher in an inner-city school. *Teaching and Teacher Education, 17*(2), 147–160.

Sanger, D.E. (2000, November 18). Huge crowds in Hanoi for Clinton who speaks of "shared suffering." *New York Times,* pp. A1, A8.

Santos Rego, M.A., & Nieto, S. (2000). Multicultural/intercultural teacher education in two contexts: Lessons from the United States and Spain. *Teaching and Teacher Education, 16*(4), 413–427.

Schoem, D. (1993). Teaching about ethnic identity and intergroup relations. In D. Schoem, L. Frankel, X. Zúñiga, & E.A. Lewis (Eds.), *Multicultural teaching in the university* (pp. 15–25). Westport, CT: Praeger.

Schofield, J.W. (1995). Improving intergroup relations among students. In J.A. Banks & C.A.M. Banks (Eds.), *Handbook of research on multicultural education* (pp. 635–646). New York: Macmillan.

Scribner, J.D., & Reyes, P. (1999). Creating learning communities for high-performing Hispanic students: A conceptual framework. In P. Reyes, J.D. Scribner, & A.P. Scribner (Eds.), *Lessons from high-performing Hispanic schools: Creating learning communities* (pp. 188–210). New York: Teachers College Press.

Segura-Mora, A. (1998/1999, Winter). What color is beautiful? *Rethinking Schools, 13*(2), 7–8.

Seldon, S. (1999). *Inheriting shame: The story of eugenics and racism in America.* New York: Teachers College Press.

Sengupta, S. (2001, July 8). How many poor children is too many? *New York Times,* p. WK3.

Shapiro, N.S., & Levine, J.H. (1999). *Creating learning communities: A practical guide to winning support, organizing for change, and implementing programs.* San Francisco: Jossey-Bass.

Shapiro, S. (1990). *Between capitalism and democracy: Educational policy and the crisis of the welfare state.* New York: Bergin & Garvey.

Shea, C. (1989). Pentagon vs. multinational capitalism: The political economy of the 1980s school reform movement. In C. Shea, E. Kahane, & P. Sola (Eds.), *The new servants of power: A critique of the 1980s school reform movement* (pp. 3–36). New York: Greenwood.

Shohat, E., & Stam, R. (1994). *Unthinking Eurocentrism: Multiculturalism and the media.* New York: Routledge.

Shor, I., & Freire, P. (1987). *A pedagogy for liberation: Dialogues on transforming education.* South Hadley, MA: Bergin & Garvey.

Shulman, J.H., Lotan, R.A., & Whitcomb, J.A. (1998). *Facilitators guide to groupwork in diverse classrooms: A casebook for educators.* New York: Teachers College Press.

Simon, L. (1997). *Fear and learning at Hoover Elementary* (P.O.V. series). Washington, DC: Public Broadcasting System.

Simpson, E.L. (1972). An end to ethnocentrism: A bilateral model for training in intercultural studies. *Notre Dame Journal of Education, 3,* 219–234.

Sklair, L. (1998). Social movements and global capitalism. In F. Jameson & M. Miyoshi (Eds.), *The cultures of globalization* (pp. 291–311). Durham, NC: Duke University Press.

Skrobanek, S., Boonpakdi, N., & Janthakeero, C. (1997). *The traffic in women: The human realities of the international sex trade.* New York: Zed Books.

Sleeter, C.E. (1991). Introduction: Multicultural education and empowerment. In C.E. Sleeter (Ed.), *Empowerment through multicultural education* (pp. 1–23). Albany: State University of New York Press.

Sleeter, C.E. (1992). *Keepers of the American dream: A study of staff development and multicultural education.* London: The Falmer Press.

Sleeter, C.E. (1994). White racism. *Multicultural Education, 1*(4), 5–8, 39.

Sleeter, C.E. (1995a). Reflections on my use of multicultural and critical pedagogy when students are white. In C. Sleeter & P.L. McLaren (Eds.), *Multicultural education, critical pedagogy, and the politics of difference* (pp. 415–437). Albany: State University of New York Press.

Sleeter, C.E. (1995b). White preservice students and multicultural education coursework. In J.M. Larkin & C.E. Sleeter (Eds.), *Developing multicultural teacher education curricula* (pp. 17–30). Albany: State University of New York Press.

Sleeter, C.E. (2001). Preparing teachers for culturally diverse schools: Research and the overwhelming presence of whiteness. *Journal of Teacher Education, 52*(2), 94–106.

Sleeter, C.E., & Grant, C.A. (1999). *Making choices for multicultural education: Five approaches to race, class, and gender* (3rd ed.). New York: Macmillan.

Sleeter, C.E., & McLaren, P.L. (Eds.). (1995). *Multicultural education, critical pedagogy, and the politics of difference*. Albany: State University of New York Press.

Smith, B.L. (2001). Learning communities: A convergence zone for statewide education reform. In B.L. Smith & J. McCann (Eds.), *Reinventing ourselves: Interdisciplinary education, collaborative learning, and experimentation in higher education* (pp. 118–134). Bolton, MA: Anker.

Smith, G.P. (1998a). *Common sense about uncommon knowledge: The knowledge bases for diversity*. Washington, DC: American Association of Colleges for Teacher Education.

Smith, G.P. (1998b). Who shall have the moral courage to heal racism in America? *Multicultural Education, 5*(3), 4–10.

Smith, G.P. (2000, November). *Achieving educational justice: Assessment of multicultural competencies*. Keynote address at Emporia State University's National Conference on Assessment of Multicultural/Diversity Outcomes, Kansas City, MO.

Snyder, J. (2000). Knowing children—understanding teaching: The developmental teacher education program at the University of California-Berkeley. In L. Darling-Hammond (Ed.), *Studies in excellence in teacher education: Preparation at the graduate level* (pp. 97–172). Washington, DC: American Association of Colleges for Teacher Education.

Soder, R. (1996). Teaching the teachers of the people. In R. Soder (Ed.), *Democracy, education, and the schools* (pp. 244–274). San Francisco: Jossey-Bass.

Solórzano, D.G. (1997). Images and words that wound: Critical race theory, racial stereotyping, and teacher education. *Teacher Education Quarterly, 24*(3), 5–19.

Solórzano, D.G., & Villapano, O. (1998). Critical race theory: Marginality and the experience of students of color in higher education. In C.A. Torres & T.R. Mitchell (Eds.), *Sociology of education: Emerging perspectives* (pp. 211–224). Albany: State University of New York Press.

Soltis, J.F. (Ed.) (1987). *Reforming teacher education: The impact of the Holmes Group report*. New York: Teachers College Press.

Sorenson, E. (2001, February 11). Race gene does not exist, say scientists. *Seattle Times*. [On-line]. Available: http://archives.seattletimes.nwsource.com/cgi-bin/texis/web/vortex/display?slug=race11m&date=20010211&query=race+gene

Spears, J.D., Oliver, J.P., & Maes, S.C. (1990). *Accommodating change and diversity: Multicultural practices in rural schools*. Manhattan: Kansas State University, Rural Clearinghouse for Lifelong Education and Development.

Spring, J. (1976). *The sorting machine: National educational policy since 1945*. New York: McKay.

Spring, J. (1998). *Education and the rise of the global economy*. Mahwah, NJ: Lawrence Erlbaum.

Spring, J. (2001). *The American school, 1642–2000* (5th ed.). Boston: McGraw-Hill.

Stephan, W. (1999). *Reducing prejudice and stereotyping in schools*. New York: Teachers College Press.

Stevens, E., Jr., & Wood, G.H. (1995). *Justice, ideology, and education: An introduction to the social foundations of education* (3rd ed.). New York: McGraw-Hill.

Stotsky, S. (1999). *Losing our language: How multicultural classroom instruction is undermining our children's ability to read, write, and reason*. New York: Free Press.

Striedieck, I.M. (1997). The representation of multiple cultures and perspectives in one preservice elementary teacher education class: A case study from a postmodern feminist perspective. In D.M. Byrd & D.J. McIntyre (Eds.), *Research on the education of our nation's teachers: Teacher education yearbook V* (pp. 7–25). Thousand Oaks, CA: Corwin Press.

Students of Middle College High School. (2000). *Stand back! A report on the World Trade Organization*. Seattle, WA: Author c/o W. Au, A. Ybarra, & A. Woldu.

Suárez-Orozco, C., & Suárez-Orozco, M.M. (2001). *Children of immigration*. Cambridge, MA: Harvard University Press.

Subrahmanyan, L., Hornstein, S., & Heine, D. (2000). Multicultural discourse in teacher education: The case of one integrated teaching methods block. In R. Mahalingam & C. McCarthy (Eds.), *Multicultural curriculum: New directions for social theory, practice, and policy* (pp. 168–188). New York: Routledge.

Takaki, R. (1993). *A different mirror: A history of multicultural America*. Boston: Little, Brown.

Talbert-Johnson, C., & Tillman, B. (1999). Perspectives on color in teacher education programs: Prominent issues. *Journal of Teacher Education, 50*(3), 200–208.

Talbot, M. (2001, November 18). Other woes. *New York Times Magazine* (sec. 6), pp. 23–24.

Tate, W.F., IV. (1997). Critical race theory and education: History, theory, and implications. In M.W. Apple (Ed.), *Review of research in education 22* (pp. 195–247). Washington, DC: American Educational Research Association.

Tatum, B.D (1999a). Lighting candles in the dark: One black woman's response to white antiracist narratives. In C. Clark & J. O'Donnell (Eds.), *Becoming and unbecoming white: Owning and disowning a racial identity* (pp. 56–63). Westport, CT: Bergin & Garvey.

Tatum, B.D. (1999b). *"Why are all the black kids sitting together in the cafeteria?" and other conversations about race* (Rev. ed.). New York: Basic Books.

Taylor, D.R. (2000, October 23). Developing powerful learning communities using technology. *AACTE Briefs, 21*(14), 3–4.

Taylor, E. (1999a). Critical race theory and interest convergence in the desegregation of higher education. In L. Parker, D. Deyhel, & S. Villenas (Eds.), *Race is . . . race isn't: Critical race theory and qualitative studies in education* (pp. 181–204). Boulder, CO: Westview Press.

Taylor, E. (1999b). Lessons for leaders: Using critical inquiry to promote identity development. In R.H. Sheets & E.R. Hollins (Eds.), *Racial and ethnic identity in school practices: Aspects of human development* (pp. 231–244). Mahwah, NJ: Lawrence Erlbaum.

Taylor, E. (2000). Critical race theory and interest convergence in the backlash against affirmative action: Washington state and Initiative 200. *Teachers College Record, 102*(3), 539–560.

Teacher Preparation Accountability and Evaluation Commission. (2000). *An opportunity to teach: Meeting Title II teacher education reporting requirements.* Washington, DC: American Association of Colleges for Teacher Education.

Terry, D. (2000, August 10). U.S. child poverty rate fell as economy grew, but is above 1979 level. *Los Angeles Times.* [On-line]. Available: http://www.childrennow.org/newsroom/news-00/ra-8-10-00.htm

Thandeka. (1999). *Learning to be white: Money, race, and god in America.* New York: Continuum.

Thompson, B., & Tyagi S. (Eds.). (1996). *Names we call home: Autobiography on racial identity.* New York: Routledge.

Thompson, G. (2001, July 22). Farm unrest roils Mexico, challenges new chief. *New York Times*, pp. A1, A4.

Thompson, J.B. (1990). *Ideology and modern culture: Critical social theory in the era of mass communications.* Stanford, CA: Stanford University Press.

Thurow, L. (1999). Foreword. In C. Collins, B. Leondar-Wright, & H. Sklar, *Shifting fortunes: The perils of the growing American wealth gap* (pp. 1–3). Boston: United for a Fair Economy.

Tinto, V. (1997). Classrooms as communities: Exploring the educational character of student persistence. *Journal of Higher Education, 68*(6), 599–623.

Tocqueville, A. de. (1984). *Democracy in America.* New York: Penguin Books. (Original work published in 1840)

Tom, A.R. (1996). External influences on teacher education programs: National accreditation standards and state certification. In K. Zeichner, S. Melnick, & L. Gomez (Eds.), *Currents of reform in preservice teacher education* (pp. 11–29). New York: Teachers College Press.

Torres, C.A. (1995). State and education revisited: Why educational researchers should think politically about education. In M.W. Apple (Ed.), *Review of research in education 21* (pp. 255–331). Washington, DC: American Educational Research Association.

Torres, C.A. (1998). *Democracy, education, and multiculturalism: Dilemmas of citizenship in a global world.* Lanham, MD: Rowman & Littlefield.

Tran, M.T., Young, R.L., & DiLella, J.D. (1994). Multicultural education courses and the student teacher: Eliminating stereotypical attitudes in our ethnically diverse classrooms. *Journal of Teacher Education, 45*(3), 183–189.

Troyna, B., & Carrington, B. (1990). *Education, racism and reform.* New York: Routledge.

Troyna, B., & Rizvi, F. (1997). Racialization of differences and the cultural politics of teaching. In B.J. Biddle, T.L. Good, & I.F. Goodson (Eds.), *International handbook of teachers and teaching* (pp. 237–266). Boston: Kluwer Academic.

Trueba, E.T., & Bartolomé, L.I. (Eds.). (2000). *Immigrant voices: In search of educational equity.* Lanham, MD: Rowman & Littlefield.

Tye, K.A., & Tye, B.B. (1993). The realities of schooling: Overcoming teacher resistance to global education. *Theory Into Practice, 32*(1), 58–63.

Tyson, H. (1994). *Who will teach the children: Progress and resistance in teacher education.* San Francisco: Jossey-Bass.

United Nations. (1948). Universal declaration of human rights. [On-line]. Available: http://www.un.org/Overview/rights.html

United Nations Educational, Scientific, and Cultural Organization. (2001). Education and poverty eradication. [On-line]. Available: http://unesco.org/education/educprog/poverty/index.html

U.S. Bureau of the Census. (1998). World population profile: 1998. [On-line]. Available: http://www.census.gov/ipc/www/wp98001.html

U.S. Department of State. (2000, September). *The conventions on the elimination of all forms of racial discrimination: Initial report of the United States of America to the United Nations committee on the elimination of racial discrimination.* [On-line]. Available: http://www.state.gov/www/global/human_rights/cerd_report/cerd_report.pdf

U.S. National Commission on Excellence in Education. (1984). *A nation at risk: The full account.* Cambridge, MA: USA Research.

Valdés, G. (1996). *Con respeto: Bridging the distances between culturally diverse families and schools: An ethnographic portrait.* New York: Teachers College Press.

Valli, L. (1992). *Reflective teacher education: Cases and critiques.* Albany: State University of New York Press.

Valli, L. (1995). The dilemma of race: Learning to be color blind and color conscious. *Journal of Teacher Education, 46*(2), 120–129.

Valli, L., & Rennert-Ariev, P.L. (2000). Identifying consensus in teacher education reform documents: A proposed framework and action implications. *Journal Teacher Education, 51*(1): 5–17.

Vavrus, M. (1994). A critical analysis of multicultural education infusion during student teaching. *Action in Teacher Education, 16*(3), 47–58.

Vavrus, M. (1998, May 4). Whose side are you on? Multicultural education at the close of the 20th century. *AACTE Briefs* (pp. 4–5). Washington, DC: American Association of Colleges for Teacher Education.

Vavrus, M. (2001a). Deconstructing the multicultural animus held by monoculturalists. *Journal of Teacher Education, 52*(1), 70–77.

Vavrus, M. (2001b). Successful teacher education programs in an era of reform. *Teaching and Teacher Education, 17*, 645–651.

Vavrus, M., & Archibald, O. (1998, August). *Teacher education practices supporting social justice: Approaching an individual self-study inquiry into institutional self-study processes.* Paper presented at the Second International Conference on Self-Study of Teacher Education Practices, a special interest group of the American Educational Research Association, East Sussex, England. [On-line]. Available: http://educ.queensu.ca/~ar/sstep2/vavrarch.htm

Vavrus, M., & Determan, T. (1996). *An analysis of a school district's multicultural/nonsexist policy.* Des Moines, IA: FINE Foundation.

Vavrus, M., & Ozcan, M. (1996, February). *Preservice teacher acquisition of a critical multicultural and global perspective: A reform path with ideological tensions.* Paper presented at the annual meeting of the American Association of Colleges for Teacher Education, Chicago. (ERIC Document Reproduction Service No. ED 393 826)

Vavrus, M., & Ozcan, M. (1998). Multicultural content infusion by student teachers: Perceptions and beliefs of cooperating teachers. In M.E. Dilworth (Ed.), *Being responsive to cultural differences: How teachers learn* (pp. 94–109). Thousand Oaks, CA: Corwin Press.

Vavrus, M., Ozcan, M., Determan, T., & Steele, C. (1996, November). *An analysis of a school district's multicultural/non-sexist policy: Implications for classroom practices and pedagogy.* Paper presented at the annual meeting of the National Association of Multicultural Education, St. Paul, MN. (ERIC Document Reproduction Service No. ED 402 291)

Villenas, S., Deyhle, D., & Parker, L. (1999). Critical race theory and praxis: Chicano(a)/ Latino(a) and Navajo struggles for dignity, education equity, and social justice. In L. Parker, D. Deyhel, & S. Villenas (Eds.), *Race is . . . race isn't: Critical race theory and qualitative studies in education* (pp. 31–52). Boulder, CO: Westview Press.

Vizenor, G. (1994). *Manifest manners: Postindian warriors of survivance.* Hanover, NH: University Press of New England.

von Glasersfeld, E. (1991). Constructivism in education. In A. Lewy (Ed.), *The international encyclopedia of curriculum* (pp. 31–32). Oxford, UK: Pergamon.

Vukelich, D. (1999). The devastation of debt. *NACLA [North American Congress on Latin America] Report of the Americas, 33*(2), 24–27, 42.

Vygotsky, L.S. (1978). *Mind in society: The development of higher psychological processes.* Cambridge, MA: Harvard University Press.

Walker, D. (1990). *Fundamentals of curriculum.* San Diego, CA: Harcourt Brace Jovanovich.

Wallerstein, I. (1984). *The politics of the world economy: The states, the movements, and the civilizations.* Cambridge, UK: Cambridge University Press.

Wallerstein, I. (1999). *The end of the world as we know it: Social science for the twenty-first century.* Minneapolis: University of Minnesota Press.

Walton, P.H., & Carlson, R.E. (1997). Responding to social change: California's new standards for teacher credentialing. In J.E. King, E.R. Hollins, & W.C. Hayman (Eds.), *Preparing teachers for cultural diversity* (pp. 222–239). New York: Teachers College Press.

Waters, W.F. (2001). Globalization, socioeconomic restructuring, and community health. *Journal of Community Health, 26*(2), 79–92.

Watkins, W.H. (1991). Social reconstructionist approach. In A. Lewy (Ed.), *The international encyclopedia of curriculum* (pp. 32–35). Oxford, UK: Pergamon.

Watkins, W.H. (1994). Multicultural education: Toward a historical and political inquiry. *Educational Theory, 44*(1), 99–117.

Weisman, J. (1991, March 6). Report cautiously optimistic on school-business ties. *Education Week*, p. 19.

Weissert, W. (2001, April 30). With some doubts, Guatemala moves toward adopting U.S. dollar. *Associated Press.* [On-line]. Available: http://ap.tbo.com/ap/breaking/ MGAG1V927MC.html

Welner, K., & Oakes, J. (1997, October). *The importance of judicial values.* Working Paper, The Civil Rights Project, Harvard University. [On-line]. Available: http://www.law.harvard.edu/civilrights/publications/workingpapers/welner.html

West, C. (1995). Foreword. In K. Crenshaw, N. Gotanda, G. Peller, K. Thomas (Eds.), *Critical race theory: The key writings that formed the movement* (pp. xi–xii). New York: The New Press.

Whang, P.A., & Waters, G.A. (2001). Transformational spaces in teacher education: MAP(ing) a pedagogy linked to a practice of freedom. *Journal of Teacher Education, 52*(3), 197–210.

Wieczorek, C., & Grant, C. (2000). Teacher education and knowledge in "the knowledge society": The need for social mooring in our multicultural schools. *Teachers College Record, 102*(5), 913–935.

Wiest, L.R. (1998). Using immersion experiences to shake up preservice teachers' views about cultural differences. *Journal of Teacher Education, 49*(5): 358–365.

Wildman, T.M., & Niles, J.A. (1987). Reflective teachers: Tensions between abstractions and realities. *Journal of Teacher Education, 38*(4), 25–31.

Wilford, J.N. (2001, December 2). African artifacts suggest an earlier modern human. *New York Times,* pp. A1, A16.

Wilgoren, J. (2001, June 13). Education study finds U.S. falling short: Teachers are found not benefiting in era of economic expansion. *New York Times,* p. A28.

Winant, H. (1994). *Racial conditions: Politics, theory, comparisons.* Minneapolis: University of Minnesota Press.

Winant, H. (1997). Behind blue eyes: Whiteness and contemporary U.S. racial politics. In M. Fine, L. Weis, L.C. Powell, & L.M. Wong (Eds.), *Off white: Readings on race, power, and society* (pp. 40–53). New York: Routledge.

Winant, H. (1998). Racial dualism at century's end. In W. Lubiano (Ed.), *The house that race built* (pp. 87–115). New York: Vintage Books.

Wise, A.E., & Leibbrand, J.A. (2001). Standards in the new millennium: Where we are, where we're headed. *Journal of Teacher Education, 52*(3), 244–255.

Wisniewski, R. (1999, March). *NCATE standards and teacher education reform.* National Partnership for Excellence and Accountability in Teaching Project 1.4.7 prepared for the National Commission on Teaching and America's Future, Teachers College, Columbia University, New York.

Wisniewski, R. (2001). *Recreating colleges of teacher education.* Atlanta, GA: BellSouth Foundation.

Woodhall, M. (1997). Human capital concepts. In P. Brown, A.H. Halsey, H. Lauder, & A.S. Wells (Eds.), *Education: Culture, economy, and society* (pp. 219–223). Oxford, UK: Oxford University Press.

Woodward, C.V. (1974). Blacks and poor whites in the south. In T.R. Frazier (Ed.), *The underside of American history: Vol. II. Since 1865* (2nd ed., pp. 53–77). New York: Harcourt Brace Jovanovich.

Wyatt, E. (1999, November 4). Investors see room for profit in demand for education. *New York Times*: A1, A21.

Yamato, G. (1995). Something about the subject makes it hard to name. In M.L. Anderson & P.H. Collins (Eds.), *Race, class and gender* (2nd ed., pp. 70–75). Belmont, CA: Wadsworth.

Yon, D.A. (2000). *Elusive culture: Schooling, race, and identity in global times*. Albany: State University of New York Press.

Yost, D.S., Senter, S.M., & Forlenza-Bailey, A. (2000). An examination of the construct of critical reflection: Implications for teacher education programs in the 21st century. *Journal of Teacher Education, 51*(1), 39–49.

Young, J., & Buchanan, N. (1996). Anti-racist/multicultural teacher education: A focus on student teachers. *The Alberta Journal of Educational Research, 42*(1), 60–64.

Zapeda, S.J. (1999). *Staff development: Practices that promote leadership in learning communities*. Larchmont, NY: Eye on Education.

Zeichner, K.M. (1991). Contradictions and tensions in the professionalization of teaching and the democratization of schools. *Teachers College Record, 92*(3), 363–379.

Zeichner, K.M. (1992). Conceptions of reflective teaching in contemporary U. S. teacher education programs. In L. Valli (Ed.), *Reflective teacher education: Cases and critiques* (pp. 161–173). Albany: State University of New York Press.

Zeichner, K.M. (1993). Connecting genuine teacher development to the struggle for social justice. *Journal of Education for Teaching, 19*(1), 5–20.

Zeichner, K.M. (1996). Educating teachers for cultural diversity. In K. Zeichner, S. Melnick, & M.L. Gomez (Eds.), *Currents of reform in preservice teacher education* (pp. 133–175). New York: Teachers College Press.

Zeichner, K.M. (1999). The new scholarship in teacher education. *Educational Researcher, 28*(9), 4–15.

Zeichner, K.M. (2000). Ability-based teacher education: Elementary teacher education at Alverno College. In L. Darling-Hammond (Ed.), *Studies in excellence in teacher education: Preparation in the undergraduate years* (pp. 1–66). Washington, DC: American Association of Colleges for Teacher Education.

Zeichner, K.M., Grant, C., Gay, G., Gillette, M., Valli, L., & Villegas, A.M. (1998). A research informed vision of good practice in multicultural teacher education: Design principles. *Theory Into Practice, 37*(2), 163–171.

Zeichner, K.M. & Hoeft, K. (1996). Teacher socialization for cultural diversity. In J. Skula, T.J. Buttery, & E. Guyton (Eds.), *Handbook of research on teacher education* (2nd ed., pp. 525–547). New York: Simon & Schuster Macmillan.

Zeichner, K.M., & Liston, D. (1987). Teaching student teachers to reflect. In M. Okazawa-Rey, J. Anderson, & R. Traver (Eds.), *Teaching, teachers, & teacher education* (pp. 284–309). Cambridge, MA: Harvard Educational Review.

Zeichner, K.M., Melnick, S., & Gomez, M.L. (Eds.). (1996). *Currents of reform in preservice teacher education*. New York: Teachers College Press.

Zernike (2000, August 24). Less training, more teachers: New math for staffing classes. *New York Times*, pp. A1, A8.

Zimpher, N.L., & Ashburn, E.A. (1992). Countering parochialism in teacher candidates. In M.E. Dilworth (Ed.), *Diversity in teacher education: New expectations* (pp. 40–62). San Francisco: Jossey-Bass.

Zinn, H. (1995). *A people's history of the United States–1492–present* (Rev. ed.). New York: HarperPerennial.

Zúñiga, X., & Nagda, B.A. (1993). Dialogue groups: An innovative approach to multicultural learning. In D. Schoem, L. Frankel, X. Zúñiga, & E.A. Lewis (Eds.), *Multicultural teaching in the university* (pp. 233–248). Westport, CT: Praeger.

Index

About the Author

Michael Vavrus is a past president of the Association of Independent Liberal Arts Colleges for Teacher Education, a constituent group of the American Association of Colleges for Teacher Education (AACTE), and a past president of the Washington State chapter of AACTE. He served as an appointed member on AACTE's Committee on Multicultural Education. He recently completed 16 years as faculty-administrator of higher education teacher education programs and is now teaching full-time as a tenured Member of the Faculty at The Evergreen State College in Olympia, Washington.

Dr. Vavrus has taught in Ethiopia in a junior secondary public school, and in rural Appalachia working with K–12 students. Prior to teaching and attending graduate school, he directed a university-based urban community service program. His scholarly interests include issues pertaining to teacher labor, the education of teachers, the politics of education, and multicultural education. He received his B.A. from Drake University and holds a M.A. and Ph.D. from Michigan State University.